CW01395342

INTER-ORGANIZATIONAL RELATIONS AND WORLD ORDER

Re-Pluralizing the Debate

Edited by
Ulrich Franke and Martin Koch

First published in Great Britain in 2023 by

Bristol University Press
University of Bristol
1-9 Old Park Hill
Bristol
BS2 8BB
UK
t: +44 (0)117 374 6645
e: bup-info@bristol.ac.uk

Details of international sales and distribution partners are available at bristoluniversitypress.co.uk

British Library Cataloguing in Publication Data
A catalogue record for this book is available from the British Library

ISBN 978-1-5292-3308-7 hardcover
ISBN 978-1-5292-3309-4 ePub
ISBN 978-1-5292-3310-0 ePdf

Cover design: Hayes Design and Advertising
Front cover image: Getty Images / Universal History Archive
Bristol University Press use environmentally responsible print partners.
Printed and bound in Great Britain by CPI Group (UK) Ltd, Croydon, CR0 4YY

FSC
www.fsc.org
MIX
Paper | Supporting responsible forestry
FSC® C013604

Contents

List of Figures and Tables

Figures

Tables

List of Abbreviations

ACDA	Arms Control and Disarmament Agency
AFISMA	African-led International Support Mission
AMISOM	African Union Mission in Somalia
APSA	African Peace and Security Architecture
AU	African Union
CAF	Confederation of African Football
CAN	Climate Action Network
CAR	Central African Republic
CEICCE	Comisión de Expertos Internacionales de lucha Contra la corrupción en Ecuador
CICC	Coalition for the International Criminal Court
CICIES	Comisión Internacional Contra la Impunidad de El Salvador
CICIG	Comisión Internacional Contra la Impunidad en Guatemala
CSR	corporate social responsibility
DoS	United States Department of State
DRC	Democratic Republic of Congo
ECHO	European Civil Protection and Humanitarian Aid Operations
ECJ	European Court of Justice
ECOWAS	Economic Community of West African States
EISF	European Interagency Security Forum
ESDP	European Security and Defence Policy
EULEX	European Union Rule of Law Mission in Kosovo
EUTM	European Union Training Mission
FAMA	Malian Armed Forces (Forces Armées Maliennes)
FAO	Food and Agriculture Organization of the United Nations
FAZ	Frankfurter Allgemeine Zeitung
FC-G5S	Joint Force of the Group of Five for the Sahel
FDI	foreign direct investment
FECI	Fiscalía Especial Contra la Impunidad

FIFA	Fédération Internationale de Football Association
GDP	gross domestic product
GISF	Global Interagency Security Forum
IASC	Inter-Agency Standing Committee
IGO	intergovernmental organization
IISS	International Institute for Strategic Studies
IMF	International Monetary Fund
IO	international organization
IOC	International Olympic Committee
IOR	inter-organizational relations
IR	international relations
ISIL	Islamic State in Iraq and the Levant
MACCIH	Misión de Apoyo Contra la Corrupción y la Impunidad en Honduras
MER	market exchange rate
MINUSMA	United Nations Multidimensional Integrated Stabilization Mission in Mali
MNE	multinational enterprise
MP	Ministerio Público (in Guatemala)
MSI	multi-stakeholder initiative
NATO	North Atlantic Treaty Organization
NGO	non-governmental organization
NOC	National Olympic Committee
OAS	Organization of American States
OCHA	United Nations Office for the Coordination of Humanitarian Affairs
ODI	Overseas Development Institute
OSCE	Organization for Security and Co-operation in Europe
PoC	protection of civilians
PPP	purchasing power parity
R2P	responsibility to protect
SDGT	specially designated global terrorist
SIPRI	Stockholm International Peace Research Institute
UEFA	Union of European Football Associations
UNCTAD	United Nations Conference on Trade and Development
UNCTC	United Nations Centre on Transnational Corporations
UNDPO	United Nations Department of Peace Operations
UNGC	United Nations Global Compact
UNHCR	United Nations High Commissioner for Refugees
UNODC	United Nations Office on Drugs and Crime
UNSC	United Nations Security Council
WADA	World Anti-Doping Agency

Notes on Contributors

Ulrich Franke is Senior Lecturer in the Faculty of Economics, Law and Social Sciences at the University of Erfurt. Inspired by the philosophy and social theory of classical pragmatism his research and teaching centre on the rules for action that shape world politics.

Anna Geis is Professor for International Security and Conflict Studies at Helmut Schmidt University/University of the Federal Armed Forces in Hamburg. Her research interests include the study of military interventions, democratic peace, citizen participation in German foreign policy, recognition in international politics and transitional justice.

Eva Herschinger is Senior Researcher at the Center for Intelligence and Security Studies (CISS) at University of the Bundeswehr, München. In her research she focuses on terrorism, counterterrorism, radicalization and gender.

Matthias Hofferberth is Associate Professor in the Department of Political Science and Geography at the University of Texas, San Antonio. His research and teaching focuses on global governance and the emergence of agency and world order(ing) beyond the nation state. He analyses new actors specifically in the context of the United Nations and in public-private partnerships.

Jutta Joachim is Associate Professor of Global Security Governance in the Department of Political Science at Radboud University, Nijmegen. Her research interests evolve around global security governance, international (non-)governmental organizations, gender, and private actors in international relations.

Martin Koch is Senior Lecturer in the Faculty of Sociology at Bielefeld University. His research interests include international organizations and groups, world society studies and global migration politics.

Louise Wiuff Moe is Associate Professor in the Department of Social Sciences and Business at Roskilde University. Her work centres on empirically grounded theoretization of how security, peace and war are practised, how these practices transform, and what effects they have across local, regional and international scales.

Thomas Müller is Post-Doctoral Researcher in the Faculty of Sociology and at the Collaborative Research Centre 1288 'Practices of Comparing' at Bielefeld University. He studies great-power politics, hierarchies and the quantification of world politics.

Theresa Reinold is Junior Professor of Global and Transnational Cooperation Research at the University of Duisburg-Essen. Her work lies at the intersection of international relations theory and international law.

Andrea Schneiker is Professor of Global Governance at Zeppelin University, Friedrichshafen. Her research focuses on transnational governance, peace and conflict studies and political communication.

Acknowledgements

The journey from the idea for an edited volume to its publication passes through several stations. At each of these, there are people without whose appreciated assistance the project would not have been successful. We would like to express our sincere thanks to them, in chronological order. First, we are grateful for the workshop grant from the Institute for World Society Studies, Faculty of Sociology, at Bielefeld University. For their support in preparing and running the workshop in October 2021, we thank Iris Bartelt, Natia Tsaritova and Catharina Wessing. Moreover, we thank the authors for their valuable contributions, productive discussions at the workshop, and openness to our suggestions. We also thank Zoe Forbes, Stephen Wenham and their colleagues from Bristol University Press for their encouraging support and professional assistance in the creation of the manuscript. Finally, we are grateful to Leah Bersch, Simon Hense and Vivien Sczesny for their thorough support in reviewing the chapter drafts.

Ulrich Franke and Martin Koch
June 2023

1

Introduction: Examining Inter-Organizational Relations

Ulrich Franke and Martin Koch

Inter-organizational relations as an emerging subfield

As an academic discipline, international relations (IR) is state-centric by definition. It is about relations between nations organized in or as states. Consequently, it has always been good advice for those interested in studying IR to focus on states and their relations. In the early 1990s, however, a common understanding gained acceptance in IR that the political world is no longer just a world of states but of societies – a *gesellschaftswelt* (Rosenau, 1992). For more than 30 years, the study of non-state entities has become quite prominent in IR, be it of intergovernmental organizations (IGOs) and non-governmental organizations (NGOs), multinational enterprises (MNEs) or other organized forms of representation. The focus of this research is often on relations between states and non-state entities and their impact on each other. It has been only in the past 15 years that IR scholars have started to analyse relations among non-state entities. With a strong focus on IGOs, this subfield was labelled *inter-organizational relations*. While inter-organizational relations (IOR) may not have joined the discipline's mainstream yet, there is a visible and growing group of scholars researching this topic and translating its importance into multiple research questions.

As a consequence, the subfield of IOR has developed and matured since its creation. This came at a price, though. In the early days, scholars experimented with various theoretical and methodological approaches to study specific cases of IOR. In the recent past, this experimental period was replaced by a tendency to conformity and canonization. This tendency is not only expressed in a concentration on certain theories, methods, organization types and policy fields, but also in a binary understanding of the nature of relations. In theoretical terms, those interested in enquiring into IOR prefer rationalist approaches such as resource dependence and regime complexity (both to be discussed later). Methodological issues are hardly reflected upon explicitly, so most studies can be described, at best, as based on content analysis. There is also an inclination towards studying relations among IGOs or between IGOs and NGOs, mostly those dealing with security or economic policies. Moreover, inter-organizational relations are usually conceptualized in a binary way as being either cooperative or conflictive/competitive.[1]

This volume aims at contributing to IOR research from a different vantage point. Bringing together empirical studies that use different theoretical angles, it seeks to overcome canonization, to expand the narrow confines of the field and to re-pluralize the debate. A shared premise of the contributions to this volume is to make it possible for non-rationalist approaches to have their say and to (re)instigate a much broader understanding of IOR as a subfield of IR. This implies that NGOs as well as policy fields other than security and economy should also be examined and that the binary differentiation of cooperation versus conflict should be left behind. In addition, the methodological approach to inter-organizational relations and their contributions to world order should become more reflective, more refined, and thus also more open to criticism.

This introduction briefly reflects on the disciplinary conditions that set the stage for IR scholarship on IOR. After a presentation of the purpose of this volume and the overall research interest along with underlying questions, the focus is on central contours of IOR research and its core concepts. The subsequent outline of the main theoretical approaches to IOR and their empirical application serves as a theoretical basis for the following contributions in this volume. It comprises a section on rationalist approaches and another one on their challengers. The introduction closes with the structure of the volume as a whole and summaries of the individual chapters.

Preconditions for the study of inter-organizational relations in international relations

While scholars in sociology, psychology, administration studies and economics have been addressing IOR since the 1960s and 1970s, when an understanding of organizations as open systems arose (see among others Aldrich, 1971), the topic – with two important exceptions (Jönsson and Söderholm, 1996; Mingst, 1987) – entered IR only in the mid-2000s (Raustiala and Victor, 2004; Biermann, 2008; Gehring and Oberthür, 2009). The reason for the long-standing neglect of IOR results from specific research traditions in IR as a discipline that primarily focuses on relations between states. IGOs have been considered only as intervening variables that might have an impact on these relations. With the emergence of social constructivism and global governance research, the state-centric perspective softened in the 1990s.

After the end of the Cold War, IR scholars were paying more attention to different sorts of entities besides states. They began to conceptualize IGOs and NGOs as actors in their own rights (Barnett and Finnemore, 1999) and significant 'pieces of global governance' (Karns et al, 2015; Avant et al, 2010). Even though many of these organizations were founded quite soon after the end of the Second World War, they have been accredited as meaningful actors only since the 1990s. Accordingly, IR scholars emphasized the relevance of non-state organizations and shifted the focus from governments to the process of governing 'without sovereign authority' (Finkelstein, 1995: 369). Referring to the 'sum of the many ways individuals and institutions, public and private, manage their common affairs' (Commission for Global Governance, 1995: Chapter 1), governance includes formal institutions and regimes as well as informal arrangements. While global governance studies concentrate on the very process of decision-making in which various actors are interconnected, they rarely investigate global governors and their agency (Avant et al, 2010).

Social constructivism, on the other hand, highlights the relevance of non-state organizations as actors in their own rights, with their own agendas and goals. Constructivist studies pay attention to non-state entities, in particular IGOs, and the way in which they can influence world politics due to the norms, values and ideas they represent. Social constructivists differentiate two key roles of IGOs, as *arenas* and *actors*. As arenas, IGOs establish a venue with an institutional setting for both states and other non-state organizations. By entering the arena, organizations such as NGOs, advocacy networks or epistemic communities get the opportunity to challenge member states and to pressure them to adhere to international norms and rules that they formally accepted (Katzenstein, 1996; see also Keck and Sikkink, 1998; Joachim, 2007; Park, 2005; Schemeil, 2004). Regarding IGOs as actors, the focus is on their roles and functions, among them norm entrepreneurs, rules supervisors or mediators (Finnemore and Sikkink, 1998; Fukuda-Parr and Hulme, 2011; Orchard, 2010; Karns et al, 2015). IGOs are also credited with the ability to maintain and enforce norms, to contribute to norm diffusion (Finnemore 1993; Park, 2006) and to monitor states in the process of implementing norms (Joachim et al, 2008; Dai, 2015). In addition to these functions, scholars regard IGOs as orchestrators (Abbott et al, 2015a; Hale and Roger, 2014) that assign certain tasks to other organizations, governmental or non-governmental, and as intermediaries to reach a target or to address target actors (Abbott et al, 2015b). Hence, IGOs can either carry out certain functions themselves or delegate and put other organizations in charge to accomplish certain goals.

Global governance research and social constructivism conceptually conditioned the study of IOR within IR. Both theoretical strands regard a variety of entities, particularly IGOs, and their interplay on the stage of world politics. Even though ideas from social constructivism are sometimes used in global governance accounts, the latter focus on the process of governance, whereas work inspired by social constructivism pays more attention to how the various units of action contribute to the establishment, diffusion and monitoring of global norms and values. Beyond developments on the theoretical level, some empirical developments foster the study of IOR too. In this regard, Brosig (2020) concludes that not just the number of non-state actors increased but also the number of tasks delegated to them. Some authors even claim that IGOs show a certain tendency towards self-empowerment as they reach out for additional tasks that have not been previously assigned to them but can be linked to the delegated issue (Hawkins et al, 2006). Therefore, issue-linkages provide another trigger for IOR, as organizations in similar issue-areas face the need to clarify their relations (Biermann and Koops, 2017).

The conditions mentioned have provided the disciplinary context of the rise of IOR research in IR. Both in theoretical and empirical terms this field has flourished and matured since the mid-2000s. An appreciable increase in studies on IOR made some scholars even observe 'an "inter-organizational turn" in world politics and the discipline of International Relations' (Biermann and Koops, 2017: 1). Even though this conclusion might be a bit premature, the increasing number of publications in the field can hardly be ignored. Today, there are studies on IOR in many policy fields, be it environment (Park, 2010; Zelli et al, 2013; Smith et al, 2021), migration (Moretti, 2021; Pécoud, 2018), development (Atouba and Shumate, 2010), health (Eckl and Hanrieder, 2023; Holzscheiter, 2015; Jönsson and Söderholm, 1996) or patent rights (Faude, 2015). However, a particular accumulation of studies concerns the fields of security (Aris et al, 2018; Biermann, 2008, 2015; Hofmann, 2009) and economy (Margulis, 2018; Gehring and Faude, 2014). At the same time, various types of organization are involved, despite a certain concentration on IGOs (to be discussed later).

Purpose of this volume

The aforementioned research achievements notwithstanding, some shortcomings in the study of IOR remain. Still underestimated are the various forms of organizations and relations involved, the variety of theoretical approaches and methodologies usable, and the impact of IOR on world politics. Accordingly, the purpose of this volume is to expand the narrow confines of the field and to re-pluralize the debate by means of innovative contributions that examine both the many forms and characteristics of IOR in various ways and the effects of IOR on world order.

Forms and characteristics of inter-organizational relations

Studies dealing with IOR often focus on either their competitive or cooperative character. In doing so, relations are depicted as either bad and undesired or as good, productive and efficient (Brosig, 2020). The contributions to this volume aim at unveiling various forms of IOR that might not fit into the narrow distinctions of competitive-versus-cooperative relations. Since inter-organizational relations are often limited to dyads of IGOs, it is neglected that organizations interact with a myriad of entities in their environment – not just IGOs or states but also NGOs, enterprises or expert groups.

Taking this wider environment into account, contributions to the volume use a variety of non-rationalist theoretical approaches or a combination of approaches to exhaust the complexity of IOR beyond the rather narrow explanation of getting access to resources or realizing a division of labour due to overlapping competencies on certain policy issues. Various approaches are covered, among them global governance (Chapters 2 and 7) and sociological neo-institutionalism (Chapters 3 and 5), post-structuralist discourse theory (Chapter 3), regime complexity and constructivist norms research (Chapter 4), public administration and organization studies (Chapter 6), relational sociology (Chapter 7), and classical pragmatism (Chapter 8).

Contributions to world order

Studies on IOR usually neglect to explicitly address the aspect of world order. World order is taken as a complex set of beliefs, concepts or ideas about how life is organized in (world) society. These ideas are realized by human actors as parts of various collectives also taken as realized ideas and thus as historical and changeable. Hence, the state is such an idea (which has historically trumped the idea of empires or city states) as is state sovereignty or supranationality, military or civil conflict-solving, multilateral or unilateral strategies of action, global distributive justice or exploitation. Like states and governments, enterprises and business associations, religious communities, or all other organizations from the spheres of politics, economy or culture (next to sets of relations between these organizations), are involved in the realization of those ideas that make up world order.

For at least two reasons, world order needs to be understood as highly dynamic and in a permanent process of reproduction and transformation. One is that, as the collectives mentioned here support, work against or ignore each other, the relative position of the ideas that rule and order the world is permanently strengthened or weakened. If, for instance, one country invades another without the international community, and in particular the United Nations Security Council (UNSC), effectively responding, this would weaken the idea of state sovereignty or formal equality among nations and strengthen the idea of international anarchy.

A closely connected second reason for the dynamics of world order and its potentially permanent modification is that the 'loyalty' of international actors to relevant ideas may decrease or increase over time (Roos, 2015: 187–9). This implies that the contribution of the idea of state sovereignty or formal equality of nations is also weakened if decision-makers of great powers attribute less importance to it. If, to give another example, a growing number of citizens and organizations in several countries turn away from the states they live in, this weakens the idea of the state as an effective way to organize public matters in political communities. Such changes on the level of ideas and concepts to which a (relative) majority of humans is loyal reveal whether the status of certain ideas as (potential) contributions to world order is strengthened or weakened within organizations or inter-organizational relationships in which they are involved.

The sum of all world-order contributions forms the empirically observable, permanently reproduced or transformed world order at a given point in time.[2] In terms of a research agenda, questions of primary concern are: What are the beliefs, concepts or ideas that decision-makers in organizations and their inter-organizational relationships are loyal to? How do these ideas remain stable or vary in specific organizations or inter-organizational relations, and under what circumstances? What similarities and differences can be found among the contributions to world order by various IGOs and their respective inter-organizational relations? How do configurations of world order develop over time? In IOR research, questions like these have not yet been made explicit and fertilized and thus will figure more prominently in this volume.

Mapping the field of research on inter-organizational relations

Although the study of IOR has emerged in the recent past only, it is not a niche research field any more. An ever-growing number of studies on various inter-organizational relations illustrate the diversity of the field, while at the same time a tendency to canonize the field is limiting scholars' room for development. There are predominant schools of thought, in particular resource dependence and regime complexity as major theoretical strands (Brosig, 2020), but also predominant types of organization under study, mainly IGOs (Biermann and Koops, 2017; Koops, 2013), and predominant policy fields looked at, particularly security and economy (Koops, 2017b). Furthermore, there is an inclination to describe inter-organizational relations in a binary fashion as either cooperative or competitive (Brosig, 2020; Lipson, 2017). Since we cannot map the entire field of inter-organizational relations nor portray all lines of its enquiry, this section aims to give an overview of the state of research on IOR. To do so, we start by approaching the very notion of inter-organizational relations and introduce our conceptual understanding before we identify recent developments in the study of it.

In our terminology, the term *inter-organizational relations* refers to relations between international organizations (IOs). The notion of *international organizations*, however, is not confined to IGOs even if there is a strong tendency to do so in inter-organizational relations research (Biermann and Koops, 2017; Koops, 2013). We use the term *international organization* inclusively and consider various forms of organization beyond the nation-state provided that these forms can be identified as an entity vis-à-vis its environment. Thus, we even account for entities such as the G7 or G20, which cannot count as organizations in a strict sense since they lack a formal agreement and formal membership. IOs and their relations cannot be confined to one country and can encompass a multitude of organizations, from IGOs, NGOs and MNEs to civil society organizations or informal groups, just to name a few. Since we perceive IOs as embedded in larger social environments that consist of entities and events surrounding IOs (Daft and Weick, 1984), relations between IGOs only make up a small amount of IOR.

In this context, the term *relations* denotes any sort of reference between at least two IOs. These references can range from established, formally structured and institutionalized relations, such as regular meetings between the International Monetary Fund (IMF) and the World Bank or the United Nations High Commissioner for Refugees (UNHCR) and the International Organization of Migration, to more informal meetings that could take place on an ad-hoc basis between bureaucracies or representatives of IOs (Biermann and Siebenhüner, 2009; Bauer et al, 2009; Reinalda and Kille, 2017; Kille and Hendrickson, 2010). In a broad sense, relations do not even require a meeting or an interaction between IOs to take place. Relations are references to the external environment; in particular to other IOs in the environment of a given IO. They have effects whenever IOs mutually observe each other and reflect these observations in their decision-making. The IMF and central banks, for instance, are constantly observing one another on changes in their interest rate policies and so coordinate their decisions without carrying out meetings.

Relations among IOs can be of various kinds. Most studies distinguish between cooperation and competition or similar descriptions, such as partnership or alliance and rivalry or conflict, as dominant characterizations of IOR (Aris and Snetkov, 2018; Brosig, 2020; Biermann and Koops, 2017). The importance of these general forms notwithstanding, we assume that there is a wider, more differentiated and more nuanced way to characterize IOR. Often, relations cannot be defined as either cooperative or competitive but rather figure as something in between or even beyond that dichotomy. More refined, more context-sensitive and less steady characterizations of IOR are needed.

As a process of environmental references and interactions, inter-organizational relations are continuously updated. They potentially change with every single interaction between IOs, be it exchange, contact or observation. Consequently, we assume not only that relations between two IOs can swiftly change but also that they can display different manifestations all at once depending on the issue at hand and the organizational units or staff involved. The World Bank and the International Labour Organization, for example, work together in a cooperative fashion concerning a universal child grant programme since both organizations share the same idea of how to design and finance it (Shriwise et al, 2020). At the same time, however, both organizations may have a dispute about political measures on old-age security since they view the issue differently (Wodsak and Koch, 2010). So, distinguishing IOR as either cooperative or competitive/conflictive oversimplifies the magnitude of characterizations, as every interaction at any given point in time has the potential to change the state of these relations.

In addition to characterizing forms of IOR, there is a growing amount of literature distinguishing certain dimensions of interaction according to the organizational entities involved, be it whole organizations, member states, organizational units or individuals (Brosig, 2020; Koops, 2017a). A four-part distinction includes meta, macro, mid-range and micro dimensions of IOR (Brosig, 2020). The meta dimension refers to meta-organizations[3], regime complexes or organizational overlap. Here, IOs are members of a meta-organization or embedded in a regime (Gulati et al, 2012; Raustiala and Victor, 2004). The macro dimension points to characteristics of interaction such as nestedness and intra-regional, multi-scalar or vertical and horizontal relations. According to this dimension, IOs interact since there is either a hierarchy (vertical interaction in nested relations) or horizontal interaction between IOs of a similar kind in different regions (Aris and Snetkov, 2018). The mid-range dimension comprises different kinds of interactions that link characteristics of IOs to their impact on IOR, among them social issues, degrees of institutionalization, organizational operations, and politics of actors within IOs (Brosig, 2020; Dijkstra, 2012; Kranke, 2020). The fourth dimension describes IOR on the micro level. Even though most research concentrates on relations between organizations or organizational units, some studies also take a closer look at relations between individuals or small bureaucratic units of various IOs (Kille and Hendrickson, 2010).

In line with this terminology, inter-organizational relations take place on various dimensions of IOs (meta, macro, mid-range and micro) with various factors (norms, standards and institutionalization) that can have an impact on different entities involved (organization, organizational units, senior officials and administrative members). However, the distinction between these dimensions, factors and entities might give the impression that inter-organizational relations are separate kinds of relations taking place in isolation. We thus emphasize the interconnectedness of these dimensions, factors and entities. Relations on the meta or macro dimension, for instance, can bring about relations on the mid-range or micro level, and vice versa.

Rationalist approaches to inter-organizational relations

The study of IOR is dominated by two rationalist accounts: resource dependence and regime complexity. Adherents to these accounts managed to frame what they do as the usual way of doing research in the field. The focus of resource dependence is on IOs, the material and immaterial resources used, and capabilities to interact with other organizations. This body of literature explains relations with other organizations by dealing with the exchange, usage or access of resources. Regime complexity pays more attention to regimes incorporating IOs. This approach is thus more interested in the overall structure that can have an impact on IOR. Studies drawing on regime complexity engage in the question of how IOs act when they realize that they must deal with colliding normative expectations or when they are facing competition from other organizations in a given regime. In what follows, resource dependence and regime complexity will be introduced by explicating key concepts, conceptualizations of IOR and empirical application.[4]

Resource dependence

The resource dependence approach rests on the assumption that organizations are interested in maintaining their autonomy and accomplishing their tasks. This requires resources. Organizations, however, do not entirely possess or control the resources needed. They must acquire and exchange resources with others, but endanger their autonomy when doing so. The concept of *resources* used is very broad, encompassing material as well as immaterial values – 'monetary or physical resources, information, or social legitimacy' (Pfeffer and Salancik, 1978: 43). Among the factors determining the control over a resource are possession of resources, access to resources and control of the use of resources, as well as effective regulation of the possession, allocation and use of resources (Pfeffer and Salancik, 1978: 48–9).

In response to their need for scarce resources, organizations engage in exchange relations with their environment. In so doing, however, they run the risk of losing their autonomy and becoming dependent on others due to external commitments (van de Ven, 1976). An organization's *dependence* on its environment varies with both the salience attributed to specific resources and the level of control others have over these resources (Pfeffer and Salancik, 1978). When no organization fully controls 'the conditions necessary for the achievement of an action or for obtaining the outcome desired from the action', organizations coexist in *interdependence* (Pfeffer and Salancik, 1978: 40). Under this condition of mutual dependence, organizations face 'problems of uncertainty or unpredictability' and they try to escape through relationships with others (Pfeffer and Salancik, 1978: 42).

From this angle, resource dependence is an approach about organizations managing dependence under conditions of asymmetric interdependence. Organizations begin and maintain relations with others mostly to procure resources because they seldom produce, control or have available all the resources they need to accomplish their tasks. Since this puts their autonomy at risk, organizations must engage with their environment without becoming hooked on it. Consequently, they strive for balanced exchange ratios and maintaining interdependence (Pfeffer and Salancik, 1978). Some organizations succeed better, others worse according to their *power*, that is, their ability to decrease dependence based on the resources already available (Cook, 1977).

Operating in the rationalist style of economic logic and adhering to a strategic notion of action, the resource dependence approach conceptualizes IOR as a strategy of coping with the scarcity of resources. As 'negotiated environments' to reduce environmental uncertainty (Cook, 1977: 65) inter-organizational relations based on the exchange of resources provide 'an action system to solve complex problems or attain joint goals' that organizations cannot accomplish alone (van de Ven, 1976: 24–5).

Applications of the resource dependence approach centre on security issues and aspects of economic development. NATO (North Atlantic Treaty Organization) and the UN, for instance, exchange military capabilities with civilian expertise and legitimacy in Bosnia, Kosovo and Afghanistan. Winning coalitions of member states within the two organizations perceived the respective partner's resources essential to realize one's aims (Harsch, 2015). In general, the Atlantic alliance gives its 'tangible hard security resources' such as the capacity to plan and execute long-distance operations, and it receives legitimacy as well as access to other 'intangible soft security resources' (Biermann, 2014: 229, 223) owned by the UN or the Organization for Security and Co-operation in Europe (OSCE).

Simultaneously, NATO shies away from cooperation with the Shanghai Cooperation Organization and other organizations that allied representatives consider illegitimate. For the same reasons, organizations favouring civilian instruments keep the alliance at distance (Biermann, 2014). One of these powers, the European Union (EU), is regarded as (interested in) pooling resources with the UN and OSCE concerning peacekeeping and peacebuilding in and beyond Europe (Brosig, 2014; Petrov et al, 2019). To avoid competition and overlaps, the EU not only engages in specific action (grasped as demarcated zones or functional niches) but also is expected to offer support 'tailored on the basis of UN needs' in the future (Brosig, 2014: 87).

Furthermore, the resource dependence approach has been applied to economic, financial and technological issues. The Food and Agriculture Organization of the UN (FAO) opens to transnational actors since it needs their resources. Afraid of losing autonomy, however, a risk-averse organizational culture restrains FAO's strive for money and expertise – and thus its collaboration with transnational actors (Liese, 2010). In a similar way, IGOs working together against corruption share strong concerns about autonomy, too (Gest and Grigorescu, 2010). In the field of nuclear safety, however, cooperation between the International Atomic Energy Agency and the UN Scientific Committee on the Effects of Atomic Radiation, based on the exchange of information, high levels of trust, and other resources, resulted in a clear separation of tasks and responsibilities (Kjøndal, 2021).

Regime complexity

The regime complexity approach draws on the concept of *regime*. This denotes a set of responses to problems of coordination and collaboration in world politics (Stein, 1982) and to detrimental effects of the unilateral pursuit of interests (Young, 1982). Regimes govern the activity of their members in stipulated regulatory areas beyond their members' jurisdiction (Young, 1982). Further key concepts refer to central aspects of the inter-organizational process. This process starts from *functional overlap*, the involvement in a particular policy field of two or more organizations that share many members. Functional overlap brings about *regulative competition* among the organizations as each of them wants to be the one to make the central rules of the field. Competition results in *adaptation* and a *differentiation* of rules. Organizations adapt to the interests of their members either by specializing or by adopting rules from others. This way, organizations create varieties of rules and a *division of labour* (Faude, 2015).

Regime complexity theorists portray organizations as substantive rules and institutional apparatuses, as structures and actors. Organizations (as structures) influence and are influenced by (individual) actors. In line with a sharper distinction between institutions such as regimes and their organizational components, organizations as (strategic) actors strive for substantial and organizational goals but adapt to the interests of their member states to maintain their function (Faude, 2015).

According to the regime complexity approach, inter-organizational relations are equivalent to institutional or regime complexes – 'systems of functionally overlapping international institutions that continuously affect each other's operations' (Gehring and Faude, 2013: 120; also Young, 1996: 6). As non-hierarchical networks that govern 'a particular issue-area' (Raustiala and Victor, 2004: 279) or 'relate to a common subject matter' (Orsini et al, 2013: 29), regime complexes generate undesired regulatory competition among organizations (Gehring and Faude, 2014; Alter and Meunier, 2009). Since their presence allows states to pick those organizations that fit their interests best, regime complexes bring about new opportunities for strategic state action (Gehring and Faude, 2013; Raustiala and Victor, 2004).

Among the terms for state strategies under the condition of functionally overlapping regime complexes are forum-shopping, regime-shifting and strategic inconsistency (Alter and Meunier, 2009; Hafner-Burton, 2009; Helfer, 2009; Margulis, 2013), but also à-la-carte behaviour (Hafner-Burton, 2009) and chessboard politics (Alter and Meunier, 2009). In particular, those states that are members of only one IO in a specific policy field and have distributional instead of communal preferences gain new veto opportunities. Since they can take the inter-organizational relationship hostage, functional overlap disproportionally empowers them (Hofmann, 2019). Sceptics also emphasize the inhibitive consequences of functional overlaps such as 'turf battles' over the functional and geographic scope of institutions (Hofmann, 2009: 49), lacks of hierarchy, and increasing costs of changing strategies over time (Struett et al, 2013).

More optimistic scholars claim that intentional and unintentional effects of strategic state action lead regime complexes to contribute significantly to global order. This order is constituted by organizations (grasped as substantial rules and institutional apparatuses) and procedural rules (Faude, 2015). Although regime complexes and the order they bring about are considered a mostly non-intentional, functional consequence of overlapping rules among organizations, some expect them to replace conflict (Gehring and Faude, 2013). From this perspective, functional overlaps alleviate cooperation on the global scale by contributing to an inter-organizational division of labour. Organizations unilaterally give in to the pressure to adapt to their members' interests when they are confronted with intensifying inter-organizational competition about regulative competencies. They do so either by specializing or by integrating rules from other organizations into their own sets of rules. Such an adaptation process is considered to result in both a differentiation of organizational rule-making and an inter-organizational division of labour that facilitates state gains from cooperation (Faude, 2015).

Applications of regime complexity encompasses environmental issues (Young, 2010; Keohane and Victor, 2011; Zelli et al, 2013), consumer protection and trade (Raustiala and Victor, 2004; Hafner-Burton, 2009; Helfer, 2009; Gehring and Faude, 2014; Faude, 2015), security and human rights (Betts, 2013; Hofmann, 2009; Margulis, 2013; Struett et al, 2013), as well as security and economic policies (Haftel and Hofmann, 2019). Most scholars drawing on regime complexity either emphasize the potential of IOR that can lead to a division of labour among organizations and the evolution of social order (Gehring and Faude, 2014; Faude, 2015) or point to the detrimental effects of inter-organizational competition and the specific interests of organizations and their representatives (Haftel and Hofmann, 2019). A more ambivalent third position stresses the simultaneity of cooperation and inefficiency through competition (Hofmann, 2009).

Challengers to the rationalist mainstream

Resource dependence and regime complexity may be at the centre of IOR research and have been frequently used to analyse IOR. However, the approaches and respective studies tend to overestimate the explicit exchange of resources or the immediate necessity to interact due to overlapping competencies in a given policy field. Like rationalist IR theories, they implicitly conceive of IOs as rational actors that assess the costs and benefits of their actions. The contributions in this edited volume start from a different point and regard IOs as embedded in a wider social environment. Due to this embeddedness, IOs maintain a variety of relations with various organizations in their environment.

From the margins of the field, approaches of a non-rationalist, constructivist and pragmatist leaning make valuable contributions, too. Three of them will be portrayed in the following chapters: network accounts, sociological neo-institutionalism and classical pragmatism. For the sake of a concise presentation and better comparability to each other and the two rationalist approaches sketched above, each account will be introduced as before, by means of key concepts, conceptualizations of IOR and empirical application.

Network accounts

Network accounts draw on concepts that describe the constituents of specific social bonds and the impacts and determinants of their relations (Ebers and Maurer, 2014). The cornerstones of these relations are termed *nodes*. Nodes are the actors. They are knotting themselves to each other. In a network of organizations, a node can be an organization, a unit of an organization or an individual. The formal term for relations among these nodes is *edge*. Whether an edge is strong or weak depends on the frequency, intensity and quality of interactions. Networks also vary in *size* and *density*. The size of a network increases with the number of organizations or nodes involved;

the density depends on the number of linkages and their strength (Ebers and Maurer, 2014).

Of particular importance is whether an organization, a unit or an individual is located in the centre or at the margins of a network and whether it connects with many other nodes. The concept used to refer to these aspects is *(structural) position*. Many connections to others make for a central position. Bridge-building positions link nodes otherwise not connected or only weakly (Ebers and Maurer, 2014). In a similar vein, actors with a *linking-pin* function serve as brokers between the constituents of a network (Jönsson, 1986). Concepts like these make it possible to examine dynamic properties of inter-organizational networks such as 'an increase or decrease in dominance, shifts in alliances or coalitions, the formation of mergers, the rise and fall of competitive activity, and the instigation of regulatory practices' (Cook, 1977: 79).

Combinations of network accounts with other approaches are common, be it role theory (Rese et al, 2013; Jönsson, 1986), sociological neo-institutionalism (Ebers and Maurer, 2014) or resource dependence (Gulati and Gargiulo, 1999; Biermann, 2008). A particular conceptual closeness to the latter is because network accounts often have the exchange of goods and information as a topic. In this case, organizations form, join and maintain networks due to their mutual dependence on these goods and information. Especially when it comes to explaining network creation, the concept of *boundary roles* comes in. Boundary roles enable their occupants to form networks by transforming organizations into linking-pins for integration (Jönsson, 1986).

As *key persons* with distinct roles, some individual occupants of boundary roles get special attention (Rese et al, 2013). Key persons provide points of contact for other organizations in the network. They also filter and transmit external information to their organization. Following Merton's concept of role-set, the totality of these roles is termed organization-set (Evan, 1965). Regarding the motivation of organizational actors, network theorists refer to various goals, among them the acquisition of money and authority (Benson, 1975). Several cooperative and non-cooperative strategies are available to achieve these goals (Cook, 1977; Benson, 1975; Brosig, 2011). Accordingly, the network structure, the positions within and the internal dynamics unfolded by individuals in boundary roles have an impact on organizations in networks.

Network accounts conceptualize inter-organizational relations as loose, non-hierarchical linkages that differ in size, density and other structural features. As 'exchange opportunity structures' (Cook, 1977: 69), inter-organizational networks enable action such as the exchange of goods and information. Among their constituents are individuals, organizational units and organizations but also industrial sectors and regions (Ebers and

Maurer, 2014). Combinations of network accounts with sociological neo-institutionalism or resource dependence bring in the factor of environmental embeddedness as an additional impact on network relations (Benson, 1975).

Applications of network accounts centre on security and economic issues. Comprising NATO, the EU, the OSCE, the Council of Europe and the UN, a Euro-Atlantic security network emerged from the Balkan crisis in the mid-1990s. Although considered 'one of the most mature networks among international governmental organizations' (Biermann, 2008: 154), cooperation within was mainly restricted to information sharing and was impeded by situational and structural factors such as conflicting political views or member concerns about preserving their autonomy (Biermann, 2008).

Regarding economic issues, the Financial Action Task Force against money laundering is portrayed as a problem-oriented and flexible, influential and effective, complex and legitimate network that successfully internationalizes US legislation (Jakobi, 2012). Organizations specializing in infrastructure development tend to work together in a network when, among other factors, their ties are reciprocal and they are related to a common other (Atouba and Shumate, 2010). In international aviation, for example, the Secretariat of the International Air Transport Association used its linking-pin position to mobilize a network of governments and airlines against US attempts to liberalize pricing (Jönsson, 1986).

Sociological neo-institutionalism

Sociological neo-institutionalism rests on the differentiation between two concepts: *organization* and *environment*. Organizations are embedded in and depend on an environment providing resources and legitimacy. Since organizations aim to survive in their environment, they avoid any action or decision that threatens their existence and adjust to external demands on them. Contrary to rationalist accounts, sociological neo-institutionalists argue that organizations are no pure rational actors. Their actions and decisions are also shaped by the social environment in the form of socially accepted ideas, norms and values subsumed under the term 'institutions' (Meyer and Rowan, 1977: 352). Not norms and values but 'taken for granted scripts, rules and classification are the stuff of which institutions are made' (DiMaggio and Powell, 1991: 15).

This is where the concept of *institutionalization* comes in. It refers to the process by which social practices and procedures become largely uncontested social facts and, thus, the basis for organizational actions and decisions. An organization's surroundings are seen as an institutionalized environment composed of those expectations and demands that, coupled with legitimacy, are directed to it. Since, empirically, such an environment primarily consists of other organizations, any organization embedded like this interacts with these organizations and, in so doing, is oriented to societally accepted and institutionalized environmental elements such as their formal or material characteristics. By adopting these institutionalized elements, an organization becomes accepted and can 'secure its survival' (Meyer and Rowan, 1977: 349).

Sociological neo-institutionalists refer to organizational environments that consist of similar kind of organizations as *organizational fields* and to structural similarities among organizations in such a field as *isomorphism* (DiMaggio and Powell, 1983). In the homogenizing process that brings these structural similarities about, organizations respond to and integrate environmental specifics. Conceptually rather than empirically, three mechanisms of institutional isomorphic change are distinguished from each other: *coercive isomorphism*, giving in to external pressures 'felt as force, as persuasion, or as invitations to join in collusion' (DiMaggio and Powell, 1983: 150); *mimetic isomorphism*, emulating the model of successful or legitimate organizations; and *normative isomorphism*, the diffusion of organizational patterns by professionals with a shared background.

From the perspective of sociological neo-institutionalism, inter-organizational relations are adaptive interactions among homogenizing kinds. An organization adapts to its institutional environment and conforms to external expectations 'since violating them may call into question the legitimacy of the organisation and thus affect its ability to obtain resources and social support' (Tolbert, 1985: 2). Regular adaption, however, is difficult to realize because it jeopardizes established routines and standardized procedures needed to stabilize decision-making processes. Organizations therefore form a dual structure; a formal and a working level (Thomson, 1967). While conformity with expectations is ensured at the formal level, the working level refers to day-to-day working activities. Since both levels are decoupled, adaptation on the formal level to increase legitimacy does not imply changes on the working level. The flexible mechanism of *decoupling* thus enables organizational autonomy from external demands.

Sociological neo-institutionalism has been applied to various policy fields, among them security, health, sustainability, economy and finance. Regarding non-military external intervention, state agencies and IOs decoupled rhetoric from day-to-day activity in the context of 'rebuilding' Albania in the 1990s and 2000s, for example. They supported the principle of coordination for legitimacy reasons but pursued their own agendas (Hensell, 2015). UN peacekeepers managed irreconcilable environmental demands in a similar way. Their pretention to comply with the traditional principles of peacekeeping, consent, impartiality and use of force only in self-defence, was accompanied by robust peacekeeping with less restricted use of force on the ground (Lipson, 2007).

In the field of health policy, neo-institutionalist research deals with the fight against infectious diseases. Led by the UN Programme on HIV/AIDS, the World Bank, the Global Fund to Fight AIDS, Tuberculosis and Malaria, as well as the World Health Organization, this fight is rhetorically leaning towards a meta-governance norm of harmonization. This norm was stipulated in 2005 when ministers and heads of development institutions adopted the Paris Declaration on Aid Effectiveness. Its interpretation, however, is contested in the organizational field of health governance and part of a discursive struggle about defining a good order (Holzscheiter, 2015). Formal similarities among organizations that govern transnational social and environmental sustainability are explained with the concept of organizational fields, too. It is the assumed effectiveness of a legitimized standard model of a transnational rule-making organization that accounts for convergence here (Dingwerth and Pattberg, 2009). Regarding economy and finance, food security at the country level is to some extent decoupled from the global level (Heucher, 2019), while policy change in the IMF varies in speed and scope depending on its position in the field and its openness towards inputs from the organizational field (Vetterlein and Moschella, 2014).

Classical pragmatism: structures of corporate practice

The classical pragmatist approach on IOR centres on the concept of *structures of corporate practice* (Roos, 2010; Franke and Roos, 2010; Dewey, 1991 [1927]). The concept of structures of corporate practice denotes collective attempts to cope with social problems and is not restricted to a particular kind of collective. States and governments as well as (inter)national and (non)governmental organizations are considered structures of corporate practice, as are enterprises and associations, their various units, families, social movements, formal and informal groups and, not least, relations among two or more of these or other entities.

Another concept that figures prominently in the pragmatist approach to IOR is *belief* as 'a rule for action' (Peirce, 1992 [1878]: 129). Consciously or unconsciously, beliefs guide human action as routines until they are challenged (James, 1975 [1907]). In a crisis, routines no longer work. Actors then have to find new ways to cope with their problems of action by dint of their socially constituted potential for creative action (Joas, 1996). When these new beliefs turn out to be helpful, they become new routines. Seeing competence to act as product of corporeality, reflexivity and creativity, the pragmatist approach portrays human beings as the only actors (Franke and Roos, 2010). At the same time, 'a system of common or social meanings' (Mead, 1967 [1934]: Section 12) connects human beings. This universe of meaning determines the scope of possible beliefs and enables creative action transforming it. Consequently, pragmatists consistently present beliefs as social creations per se, since for them individual action is an abstraction of social co-operation (Oevermann, 1991).

The concept of *structural position* (Franke and Roos, 2010) links structures of corporate practice to beliefs. Structural positions configure structures of corporate practice. Different structural positions offer the human beings who occupy them different possibilities for action (denoted as *structural potential*). The UN Secretary-General, for example, has different responsibilities from those of the President of the UNSC, the Pope, or the treasurer of Greenpeace. Moreover, different human beings realize these possibilities differently because they follow different beliefs as rules for action.

The pragmatist conceptualization of inter-organizational relations follows the conceptualization of their constituents. As structures of corporate practice, these relations refer to problems of action that individual organizations cannot solve alone and are considered as materialized ideas of how to cope with these problems in a collective endeavour (Franke and Koch, 2013; Franke, 2015). One-time meetings and institutionalized cooperation among representatives of different entities present inter-organizational structures of corporate practice. They refer to rules for action and, whenever they prove their worth, become routines.

Rules for action that guide inter-organizational relations potentially contribute to global order. The pragmatist examination of global order rests on the assumption that actors, to varying degrees, are loyal to the structures of corporate practice they are operating in as well as to their action and its products. These loyalties shift along with the strengthening or weakening of the underlying beliefs an actor holds (Roos, 2015). Whenever loyalties to relevant beliefs – such as 'Support the (idea of the) UN' or 'Strengthen the (idea of the) sovereignty of nation states' – shift, global order slightly changes. Whenever the sets of loyalties of relevant actors shift in a similar way at the same time, the changes to global order are greater.

Applications of the pragmatist approach focus on security, humanitarian and socio-economic issues. The rules for action that guided the German government towards the relationship between NATO and the (pre-Lisbon) European Security and Defence Policy (ESDP), for example, were to emancipate ESDP from US hegemony; to set up autonomous European security instruments beyond NATO; and to strengthen EU influence on NATO's design and operations (Roos, 2010). Regarding UN relations with regional Western (security) organizations, pragmatist studies point to a considerable degree of ambivalence (Franke, 2018). Since its formation, NATO, for instance, has stuck to its belief of being more effective in realizing the principles and purposes of the UN Charter than the UN itself (Franke, 2010).

Another application of the pragmatist approach deals with the Inter-Agency Standing Committee (IASC) for the coordination of humanitarian assistance.

Created by the UN General Assembly in 1992, the IASC connects several intergovernmental organizations of the UN system with representatives from coalitions of NGOs. Accordingly, participants' self-understanding expresses the belief to strengthen coordination in the humanitarian field (Franke, 2015). The belief to strengthen coordination efforts has also led the UN Secretary-General to join meetings of the G20 and to assign the head of the UN Department for Social and Economic Affairs the role of the UN's G20 chief negotiator (Franke and Koch, 2013: 98–9).

Structure of this book and its contributions

Committed to the idea of re-pluralizing the discussion of IOR in IR, only one of the contributions to this volume is based on a rationalist approach – regime complexity – blended with constructivist considerations from norms research (Chapter 4). Two pairs of contributions borrow from sociological neo-institutionalism (Chapters 3 and 5) and the global governance paradigm (Chapters 2 and 7). One combines the first with post-structuralist discourse theory (Chapter 3), another one escapes the latter's socio-theoretical void with the help of relational sociology (Chapter 7). Two further contributions combine knowledge from public administration and organization studies (Chapter 6) or blend an open-systems perspective on organizations with classical pragmatism (Chapter 8).

Five of the seven contributions address the sphere of politics (Chapters 2–6). The first two deal with the rule of law regarding anti-impunity (Chapter 2) and counterterrorism (Chapter 3), the following two focus on military issues, military interventions (Chapter 4) and military statistics (Chapter 5). Humanitarianism is the topic of the fifth contribution on politics (Chapter 6). The two remaining contributions address the economic sphere (Chapter 7) and, in the form of global sports, culture (Chapter 8). Chapters 2–8 are all organized in the same way. The introduction is followed by sections on the respective state of research, theory and methodology. After the main section, consisting of the analyses, the chapters end with an answer to the research question (results) and some conclusions.

Theresa Reinold (Chapter 2), interested in judicial cooperation, studies a hybrid anti-impunity commission and the lasting impact of this novel form of governance and its entanglement in a web of manifold inter-organizational relations on the culture of lawfulness in its host state. Her focus is on CICIG, the Comisión Internacional Contra la Impunidad en Guatemala, which was created through an agreement between the UN and the government of Guatemala in 2006, became the country's most trusted institution, and then was brought down by a 'pact of the corrupt' in 2019 when the commission expanded its investigation to include the then-president. Reinold examines CICIG's relations to the UN as its sending organization, institutions of the

Guatemalan state, Guatemalan societal actors, and donor states, mostly the US. She identifies three conditions for the studied hybrid anti-impunity commission to carry out its mandate effectively: an alliance with powerful donor states, significant support from civil society organizations, and a cooperative Attorney General's office. Certainly, unconditional support from a global organization or the host government had been helpful too, but the UN only offered qualified forms of support, while the Guatemalan government rejected CICIG in the later stages of its existence. Hence, CICIG could not foster an internalization of the norm of anti-immunity and the 'pact of the corrupt' prevailed.

Eva Herschinger and Martin Koch (Chapter 3) deal with UN-EU interaction in counterterrorism governance. Interested in both organizations' embeddedness in and interaction with their environments, they study how the UN and the EU use terrorist watch lists to shape a common understanding of their surroundings and explore the governance effects of these lists. Combining sociological neo-institutionalism and post-structuralist discourse theory, Herschinger and Koch understand the terrorist watch lists as a governing mode that rests on discursive closure and thus reduces uncertainty. The hegemonic practices of listing and delisting produce a binary differentiation that draws a line between individuals and organizations considered terrorist and those that are not. Through delisting, the UN and EU turn individuals and organizations from threating to unthreatening, further institutionalize the practice of listing, underpin the legitimacy of lists, and stabilize the current order. Referring to organizational fields and isomorphism, Herschinger and Koch explain why the EU adopted the UN listing procedure without being a UN member required to do so and why both organizations have, in 'back and forth', followed each other's lead, adopting and adapting lists at different points in time. Processes of development and mimicry, of adaptation and adjustment resulted in the UN and EU largely acting 'in symbiosis' regarding counterterrorism.

Anna Geis and Louise Wiuff Moe (Chapter 4) study IOR as inter-mission relations between the UN, the EU, the French-led Operation Barkhane and the G5 Sahel Joint Force in Mali. The shift from humanitarian interventions and interventions in line with the responsibility-to-protect norm, to stabilize host states in the wake of the securitization of transnational jihadist groups after 9/11, has resulted in a loose coupling of the formally distinct regimes of counterterrorism and peacekeeping and contributed to a re-prioritization of sovereigntist agendas. This 'robust turn' of peacekeeping unfolded dynamics on the ground that have significantly limited the scope for implementing civilian-protection norms and inverted the relationship between intervention and sovereignty. Instead of undermining national sovereignty, as early post-Cold-war interventions did, interventions primed for stabilization have tended to restore state control, offering opportunities for local elites to pursue agendas of regaining territory from their non-state opponents. The negative consequences on the protection of civilians, a core norm of peacekeeping missions, constitute the 'dark side' of inter-organizational cooperation, according to Geis and Moe. In Mali, a 'division of labour' has emerged between African organizations and states on the one hand, and France, the EU and the UN on the other. The latter, pointing to new threats as common enemies, defer enforcement tasks to host-state governments that repudiate human-rights norms in dealing with these threats.

Thomas Müller (Chapter 5) explores the dynamics and effects of inter-organizational competition over epistemic authority in the policy field of statistics on military expenditure as an indicator for the worldwide level of armaments. A highly controversial political issue in the Cold War, the level of armaments gave rise to political struggles and deep East-West divides over how to govern military statistics and (dis-)armament. In Müller's terms, a 'transparency cleavage' resulted from Western governments considering transparency about military expenditures the precondition for any disarmament, while Eastern governments attached no importance to this topic. The transparency cleavage prevented the UN from providing a substantial statistical infrastructure for military expenditures and generated a field structure with weak governance only. The cleavage outlasted the end of the Cold War but is less contentious today. As has already been the case in the policy field's formative phase from the late 1950s to the late 1960s, however, all renowned producers of military statistics apart from the UN still belong to the Western camp or share its transparency goal. This holds for the Stockholm International Peace Research Institute (SIPRI), the International Institute for Strategic Studies (IISS) in London, the US Arms Control and Disarmament Agency (ACDA) and, since the latter's disbandment in 1999, the US State Department (DoS). Nevertheless, the inter-organizational dynamics in the policy field of military statistics turn out to be too weak to fully harmonize the corresponding practices.

Exploring 'the inner workings' of cooperation, Jutta Joachim and Andrea Schneiker (Chapter 6) deal with the role individuals play in the formalization of security-related relations among humanitarian NGOs, a 'hard case' because of the high level of NGO competition in this field. Specifically, Joachim and Schneiker examine the European Interagency Security Forum (EISF), a network founded in 2006 and renamed as the Global Interagency Security Forum (GISF) in 2020. Combining two concepts, the organizational life cycle from public administration and the linking pin from organizational studies, Joachim and Schneiker find that the linking pins, that is, the individuals who matter most for bringing about and preserving cooperation among humanitarian NGOs, take five specific roles in three specific phases of cooperative relations. In the initial phase, marked by outward-oriented action, linking pins serve as boundary spanners and entrepreneurs. In the expansion phase, marked by inward-oriented action, as conflict over the purpose of cooperation is most likely, the dominant roles are described as purposive practitioners and caretakers, while in the consolidation phase, linking pins act as gatekeepers and orient their action towards the inside and the outside at the same time. In addition to the various roles taken by the linking pins, humanitarian NGOs' rising awareness of having to do something about their security has been a facilitating condition for cooperation that is endangered by staff turnover.

Matthias Hofferberth (Chapter 7) argues for an understanding of the UN Global Compact, the UN's attempt, along with companies, to make economic globalization more socially and ecologically sustainable, as a site of IOR. Hofferberth strives for a conceptual expansion of these relations in a way that they consist in more than overlapping mandates of intergovernmental organizations. Inspired by relational ontology, he contends not to take corporate agency for granted; to study the compact means analysing how entities become actors. To Hofferberth, the discussion of whether the compact would lead to more inclusive and effective global governance or to companies' 'blue-washing' (an allusion to blue as the colour of the UN) results from a limited ontology of governance that ignores inter-organizational dynamics. It is the mutual recognition of the partners involved in the compact through which they become global governors. Accordingly, the compact's central contribution to world order is seen in its creation, recognition and sustenance of corporate agency. Hofferberth's focus on the oil and gas company BP and its compact-related communication confirms that the UN's paradigm shift from regulating companies to partnering up and cooperating with them mostly illustrates the limits of this approach, as it foregoes clear rules of engagement and hierarchical means of enforcement, a critique as old as the compact.

Ulrich Franke and Martin Koch (Chapter 8) study the International Olympic Committee (IOC) and the International Federation of Association Football (FIFA). First, they illustrate the diversity of both organizations' environmental relations and then, based on two press releases, examine their immediate responses to the Russian invasion of Ukraine in 2022. While both organizations condemn what has happened, their beliefs as rules for action differ significantly. The IOC criticizes the breach of the Olympic Truce, calls on political leaders to respect it, and recommends them to follow the example of peacefully competing athletes. Taking world politics as a competition between states like the Olympic Games, the IOC sees itself as an authority enabled to call on political leaders for peace and thus undermines the role of the UN. If states behaved like athletes and followed the rules, there would be no war. FIFA, on the other hand, condemns any sort of violation without distinguishing between legitimate and illegitimate forms and even refutes the right of self-defence. It claims implicit moral superiority as its position is radically pacifist. Consequently, all sides are responsible for restoring peace. FIFA's statement appears like a standardized routine response to conflicts and wars in general. It says: condemn the use of force, call for dialogue and express solidarity.

In the conclusion (Chapter 9), Ulrich Franke assesses how far the volume manages to broaden the understanding of IOR on the levels of subject matter (organization type and policy field), theory and methodology. He then lifts up the study of IOR to the level of world-order research and compiles, in the form of imperatives, the contributions to world order implicitly and explicitly contained in Chapters 2–8. Beyond clashes between diplomacy and the rule of law, human rights and security considerations, as well as counterterrorism-inspired stabilization and the traditional peacekeeping principle of impartiality, the findings point to the strengthening of an economic logic of action, of governing the world through statistics, and of cooperation through the exchange of information.

Notes

1 In the literature on IOR, *cooperation* and *competition/conflict* are often used as generic terms for all kinds of binary relations. While cooperation comes in as the productive mode of relations, competition and conflict are taken as dysfunctional modes. They are seen as the opposite to cooperation but not differentiated any further (but see Werron (2010) for such a differentiation).

2 There is no space for a systematic discussion of the numerous works on world order here, but for an overview see Kissinger, 2014; Mearsheimer, 2019; Ikenberry, 2018; Lipscy, 2017; Bially Mattern, 2005; and Acharya, 2017. This introduction is based on the assumption that all the components of world order mentioned in these works are concepts to which actors of global relevance have varying and shifting 'degree[s] of loyalty' (Roos, 2015: 187).

3 The term meta-organization refers to organizations that have other organizations as their members. Ahrne and Brunsson (2008, 2012, 2019) study relations between meta-organizations and member organizations and examine how they mutually impact on each other. IGOs and supranational organizations (the EU) can be considered meta-organizations with states as their member organizations (Ahrne et al, 2016).

4 See Franke (2017) for more detailed versions of the five subsections on resource dependence, regime complexity, network accounts, sociological neo-institutionalism and classical pragmatism.

References

Abbott, K.W., Genschel, P., Snidal, D. and Zangl, B. (eds) (2015a) *International Organizations as Orchestrators*, Cambridge: Cambridge University Press.

Abbott, K.W., Genschel, P., Snidal, D. and Zangl, B. (2015b) 'Orchestrating: global governance through intermediaries', in K.W. Abbott, P. Genschel, D. Snidal and B. Zangl (eds) *International Organizations as Orchestrators*, Cambridge: Cambridge University Press, pp 3–36.

Acharya, A. (2017) 'After liberal hegemony: the advent of a multiplex world order', *Ethics & International Affairs*, 31(3): 271–85.

Ahrne, G. and Brunsson, N. (2019) 'Organization unbound', in G. Ahrne and N. Brunsson (eds) *Organization Outside Organizations: The Abundance of Partial Organization in Social Life*, Cambridge: Cambridge University Press, pp 3–36.

Ahrne, G. and Brunsson, N. (2012) 'How much do meta-organizations affect their members?', in M. Koch (ed) *Weltorganisationen*, Wiesbaden: VS Verlag, pp 57–70.

Ahrne, G. and Brunsson, N. (2008) *Meta-Organizations*, Cheltenham: Edward Elgar.

Ahrne, G., Brunsson, N. and Kerwer, D. (2016) 'The paradox of organizing states: a meta-organization perspective on international organizations', *Journal of International Organizations Studies*, 7(1): 5–24.

Aldrich, H. (1971) 'Organizational boundaries and inter-organizational conflict', *Human Relations*, 24(4): 279–93.

Alter, K.J. and Meunier, S. (2009) 'The politics of international regime complexity', *Perspectives on Politics*, 7(1): 13–24.

Aris, S. and Snetkov, A. (2018) 'Cooperation and competition', in S. Aris, A. Snetkov and A. Wenger (eds) *Inter-Organizational Relations in International Security: Cooperation and Competition*, London and New York: Routledge, pp 1–18.

Aris, S., Snetkov, A. and Wenger, A. (eds) (2018) *Inter-organizational Relations in International Security: Cooperation and Competition*, London and New York: Routledge.

Atouba, Y. and Shumate, M. (2010) 'Interorganizational networking patterns among development organizations', *Journal of Communication*, 60(2): 293–317.

Avant, D.D., Finnemore, M. and Sell, S.K. (eds) (2010) *Who Governs the Globe? Cambridge Studies in International Relations*, Cambridge: Cambridge University Press.

Barnett, M. and Finnemore, M. (1999) 'The politics, power, and pathologies of international organizations', *International Organization*, 53(4): 699–732.

Bauer, S., Biermann, F., Dingwerth, K. and Siebenhüner, B. (2009) 'Understanding international bureaucracies', in F. Biermann and B. Siebenhüner (eds) *Managers of Global Change: The Influence of International Environmental Bureaucracies*, Cambridge and London: MIT Press, pp 15–36.

Benson, J.K. (1975) 'The interorganizational network as a political economy', *Administrative Science Quarterly*, 20(2): 229–49.

Betts, A. (2013) 'Regime complexity and international organizations: UNHCR as a challenged institution', *Global Governance*, 19(1): 69–81.

Bially Mattern, J. (2005) *Ordering International Politics: Identity, Crisis, and Representational Force*, New York and Abingdon: Routledge.

Biermann, F. and Siebenhüner, B. (2009) 'The role and relevance of international bureaucracies: setting the stage', in F. Biermann and B. Siebenhüner (eds) *Managers of Global Change: The Influence of International Environmental Bureaucracies*, Cambridge and London: MIT Press, pp 1–14.

Biermann, R. (2015) 'Designing cooperation among international organizations: the quest for autonomy, the dual-consensus rule, and cooperation failure', *Journal of International Organizations Studies*, 6(2): 45–66.

Biermann, R. (2014) 'NATO's troubled relations with partner organizations: a resource-dependence explanation', in S. Mayer (ed) *NATO's Post-Cold War Politics: The Changing Provision of Security*, Basingstoke: Palgrave Macmillan, pp 215–33.

Biermann, R. (2008) 'Towards a theory of inter-organizational networking', *Review of International Organizations*, 3(2): 151–77.

Biermann, R. and Koops, J.A. (2017) 'Studying relations among international organizations in world politics: core concepts and challenges', in R. Biermann and J.A. Koops (eds) *Palgrave Handbook on Inter-Organizational Relations*, London: Palgrave Macmillan, pp 1–46.

Brosig, M. (2020) 'Whither a theory of inter-organisational relations: a burgeon field of research between conceptual innovation and fragmentation', *Journal of Intervention and Statebuilding*, 14(2): 171–86.

Brosig, M. (2014) 'EU peacekeeping in Africa: from functional niches to interlocking security', *International Peacekeeping*, 21(1): 74–90.

Brosig, M. (2011) 'Overlap and interplay between international organisations: theories and approaches', *South African Journal of International Affairs*, 18(2): 147–67.

Commission for Global Governance (ed) (1995) *Our global Neighbourhood*, Oxford: Oxford University Press.

Cook, K.S. (1977) 'Exchange and power in networks of interorganizational relations', *The Sociological Quarterly*, 18(1): 62–82.

Daft, R.L. and Weick, K.E. (1984) 'Toward a model of organizations as interpretation systems', *Academy of Management Review*, 9(2): 284–95.

Dai, X. (2015) 'Orchestrating monitoring: the optimal adaptation of international organizations', in K.W. Abbott, P. Genschel, D. Snidal and B. Zangl (eds) *International Organizations as Orchestrators*, Cambridge: Cambridge University Press, pp 139–65.

Dewey, J. (1991 [1927]) *The Public and Its Problems*, Athens, Ohio: Swallow Press and Ohio University Press.

Dijkstra, H. (2012) 'Agenda-setting in the Common Security and Defence Policy: an institutionalist perspective', *Cooperation and Conflict*, 47(4): 454–72.

DiMaggio, P.J. and Powell, W.W. (1991) 'Introduction', in P.J. DiMaggio and W.W. Powell (eds) *The New Institutionalism in Organizational Analysis*, Chicago: University of Chicago Press, pp 1–38.

DiMaggio, P.J. and Powell, W.W. (1983) 'The iron cage revisited: institutional isomorphism and collective rationality in organizational fields', *American Sociological Review*, 48(2): 147–60.

Dingwerth, K. and Pattberg, P. (2009) 'World politics and organizational fields: the case of transnational sustainability governance', *European Journal of International Relations*, 15(4): 707–44.

Ebers, M. and Maurer, I. (2014) 'Netzwerktheorie', in A. Kieser and M. Ebers (eds) *Organisationstheorien*, Stuttgart: Kohlhammer, pp 386–406.

Eckl, J. and Hanrieder, T. (2023) 'The political economy of consulting firms in reform processes: the case of the World Health Organization', *Review of International Political Economy*, online first.

Evan, W.M. (1965) 'Toward a theory of inter-organizational relations', *Management Science*, 11(10): B-217–30.

Faude, B. (2015) 'Zur Dynamik interorganisationaler Beziehungen: Wie aus Konkurrenz Arbeitsteilung entsteht', *Politische Vierteljahresschrift*, special issue 49, 294–321.

Finkelstein, L.S. (1995) 'What is global governance?', *Global Governance*, 1(3): 367–72.

Finnemore, M. (1993) 'International organizations as teachers of norms: the United Nations' educational, scientific, and cultural organization and scientific policy', *International Organization*, 47(4): 565–96.

Finnemore, M. and Sikkink, K. (1998) 'International norm dynamics and political change' *International Organization*, 52(4): 887–917.

Franke, U. (2018) 'The United Nations and regional security organizations in Africa, Europe and the North-Atlantic region', in S. Aris, A. Snetkov and A. Wenger (eds) *Inter-Organizational Relations in International Security: Cooperation and Competition*, London and New York: Routledge, pp 21–37.

Franke, U. (2017) 'Inter-organizational relations: five theoretical approaches', in R. Marlin-Bennett (ed) *Oxford Research Encyclopedia of International Studies*, New York: International Studies Association and Oxford University Press, available from oxfordre.com/internationalstudies/view/10.1093/acrefore/9780190846626.001.0001/acrefore-9780190846626-e-99 [accessed 30 March 2023].

Franke, U. (2015) 'Eine pragmatistische Perspektive auf interorganisationale Beziehungen: Der Ständige interinstitutionelle Ausschuss (IASC) zur Koordination humanitärer Hilfe', *Politische Vierteljahresschrift*, special issue 49, 266–93.

Franke, U. (2010) *Die Nato nach 1989: Das Rätsel ihres Fortbestandes*, Wiesbaden: Springer VS.

Franke, U. and Koch, M. (2013) 'Inter-organizational relations as structures of corporate practice', *Journal of International Organizations Studies*, special issue: Sociological Perspectives on International Organizations and the Construction of Global Order, 4: 85–103.

Franke, U. and Roos, U. (2010) 'Actor, structure, process: transcending the state personhood debate by means of a pragmatist ontological model for international relations theory', *Review of International Studies*, 36(4): 1057–77.

Fukuda-Parr, S. and Hulme, D. (2011) 'International norm dynamics and the "End of Poverty": understanding the Millennium Development Goals', *Global Governance*, 17(1): 17–36.

Gehring, T. and Faude, B. (2014) 'A theory of emerging order within institutional complexes: how competition among regulatory international institutions leads to institutional adaptation and division of labor', *Review of International Organizations*, 9(4): 471–98.

Gehring, T. and Faude, B. (2013) 'The dynamics of regime complexes: microfoundations and systemic effects', *Global Governance*, 19(1): 119–30.

Gehring, T. and Oberthür, S. (2009) 'The causal mechanisms of interaction between international institutions', *European Journal of International Relations*, 15(1): 125–56.

Gest, N. and Grigorescu, A. (2010) 'Interactions among intergovernmental organizations in the anti-corruption realm', *Review of International Organizations*, 5(1): 53–72.

Gulati, R. and Gargiulo, M. (1999) 'Where do interorganizational networks come from?', *American Journal of Sociology*, 104(5): 1439–93.

Gulati, R., Puranam, P. and M. Tushman (2012) 'Meta-organization design: rethinking design in interorganizational and community contexts', *Strategic Management Journal*, 33(6): 571–86.

Hafner-Burton, E.M. (2009) 'The power politics of regime complexity: human rights trade conditionality in Europe', *Perspectives on Politics*, 7(1): 33–7.

Haftel, Y.Z. and Hofmann, S.C. (2019) 'Rivalry and overlap: why regional economic organizations encroach on security organizations', *Journal of Conflict Resolution*, 63(9): 2180–206.

Hale, T. and Roger, C. (2014) 'Orchestration and transnational climate governance', *Review of International Organizations*, 9(1): 59–82.

Harsch, M.F. (2015) *The Power of Dependence: NATO-UN Cooperation in Crisis Management*, Oxford and New York: Oxford University Press.

Hawkins, D.G., Lake, D.A., Nielson, D.L. and Tierney, M.J. (2006) 'Delegation under anarchy: states, international organizations, and principal-agent theory', in D.G. Hawkins, D.A. Lake, D.L. Nielson and M.J. Tierney (eds) *Delegation and Agency in International Organizations*, Cambridge: Cambridge University Press, pp 3–38.

Helfer, L.R. (2009) 'Regime shifting in the international intellectual property system', *Perspectives on Politics*, 7(1): 39–44.

Hensell, S. (2015) 'Coordinating intervention: international actors and local "partners" between ritual and decoupling', *Journal of Intervention and Statebuilding*, 9(1): 89–111.

Heucher, A. (2019) 'Evolving order? Inter-organizational relations in the organizational field of food security governance in Côte d'Ivoire', *Forum for Development Studies*, 46(3): 501–26.

Hofmann, S.C. (2019) 'The politics of overlapping organizations: hostage-taking, forum-shopping and brokering', *Journal of European Public Policy*, 26(6): 883–905.

Hofmann, S.C. (2009) 'Overlapping institutions in the realm of international security: the case of NATO and ESDP', *Perspectives on Politics*, 7(1): 45–52.

Holzscheiter, A. (2015) 'Interorganisationale Harmonisierung als sine qua non für die Effektivität von Global Governance? Eine soziologisch-institutionalistische Analyse interorganisationaler Strukturen in der globalen Gesundheitspolitik', *Politische Vierteljahresschrift*, special issue 49, 322–48.

Ikenberry, G.J. (2018) 'Why the liberal world order will survive', *Ethics & International Affairs*, 32(1): 17–29.

Jakobi, A.P. (2012) 'Die Bildung einer globalen Ordnung gegen Geldwäsche: das Netzwerk der Financial Action Taskforce', in M. Koch (ed) *Weltorganisationen*, Wiesbaden: VS Verlag, pp 177–203.

James, W. (1975 [1907]) *Pragmatism*, Cambridge: Harvard University Press.

Joachim, J.M. (2007) *Agenda Setting, the UN, and NGOs: Gender Violence and Reproductive Rights*, Washington: Georgetown University Press.

Joachim, J.M., Reinalda, B. and Verbeek, B. (2008) *International Organizations And Implementation: Enforcers, Managers, Authorities?*, London: Routledge.

Joas, H. (1996) *The Creativity of Action*, Chicago: University of Chicago Press.

Jönsson, C. (1986) 'Interorganization theory and international organization', *International Studies Quarterly*, 30(1): 39–57.

Jönsson, C. and Söderholm, P. (1996) 'IGO-NGO relations and HIV/AIDS: Innovation or stalemate?', in T.G. Weiss and L. Gordenker (eds) *NGOs, the UN, and Global Governance*, Boulder: Lynne Rienner, pp 121–38.

Karns, M.P., Mingst, K.A. and Stiles, K.W. (2015) *International Organizations: The Politics and Processes of Global Governance* (3rd edn), Boulder: Lynne Rienner.

Katzenstein, P.J. (1996) 'Introduction: Alternative perspectives on national security', in P.J. Katzenstein (ed) *The Culture of National Security: Norms and Identity in World Politics*, New York: Columbia University Press, pp 1–32.

Keck, M.E. and Sikkink, K. (1998) *Activists Beyond Borders*, Ithaca: Cornell University Press.

Keohane, R.O. and Victor, D.G. (2011) 'The regime complex for climate change', *Perspectives on Politics*, 9(1): 7–23.

Kille, K.J. and Hendrickson, R.C. (2010) 'Secretary-General leadership across the United Nations and NATO: Kofi Annan, Javier Solana, and Operation Allied Force', *Global Governance* 16(4): 505–23.

Kissinger, H. (2014) *World Order*, New York: Penguin Books.

Kjøndal, K.L. (2021) 'Global governance and inter-organizational relationships in the nuclear safety sector', *Global Public Policy and Governance,* 1(4): 446–67.

Koops, J.A. (2017a) 'Inter-organizationalism in international relations: a multilevel framework of analysis', in R. Biermann and J.A. Koops (eds) *The Palgrave Handbook of Inter-Organizational Relations in World Politics*, London: Palgrave Macmillan, pp 189–216.

Koops, J.A. (2017b) 'Theorising inter-organisational relations: the "EU–NATO relationship" as a catalytic case study', *European Security*, 26(3): 315–39.

Koops, J.A. (2013) 'Inter-organisational approaches', in K.E. Jørgensen and K.V. Laatikainen (eds) *Routledge Handbook on the European Union and International Institutions*, London, Routledge, pp 71–85.

Kranke, M. (2020) 'IMF-World Bank cooperation before and after the global financial crisis', *Global Policy*, 11(1): 15–25.

Liese, A. (2010) 'Explaining varying degrees of openness in the Food and Agriculture Organization of the United Nations (FAO)', in C. Jönsson and J. Tallberg (eds) *Transnational Actors in Global Governance: Patterns, Explanations and Implications*, Basingstoke: Palgrave Macmillan, pp 88–109.

Lipscy, P.Y. (2017) *Renegotiating the World Order: Institutional Change in International Relations*, Cambridge and New York: Cambridge University Press.

Lipson, M. (2017) 'Organization theory and cooperation and conflict among international organizations', in: J.A. Koops and R. Biermann *Palgrave Handbook of Inter-Organizational Relations in World Politics*, London: Palgrave Macmillan, pp 67–96.

Lipson, M. (2007) 'Peacekeeping: organized hypocrisy?', *European Journal of International Relations,* 13(1): 5–34.

Margulis, M.E. (2018) 'Negotiating from the margins: how the UN shapes the rules of the WTO', *Review of International Political Economy*, 25(3): 364–91.

Margulis, M.E. (2013) 'The regime complex for food security: implications for the global hunger challenge', *Global Governance*, 19(1): 53–67.

Mead, G. H. (1967 [1934]) *Mind, Self, and Society: From the Standpoint of a Social Behaviorist*, Chicago: University of Chicago Press.

Mearsheimer, J.J. (2019) 'Bound to fail: The rise and fall of the liberal international order', *International Security*, 43(4): 7–50.

Meyer, J.W. and Rowan, B. (1977) 'Institutionalized organizations: formal structure as myth and ceremony', *American Journal of Sociology*, 83(2): 340–63.

Mingst, K.A. (1987) 'Inter-organizational politics: the World Bank and the African Development Bank', *Review of International Studies*, 13(4): 281–93.

Moretti, S. (2021) 'Between refugee protection and migration management: the quest for coordination between UNHCR and IOM in the Asia-Pacific region', *Third World Quarterly*, 42(1): 34–51.

Oevermann, U. (1991) 'Genetischer Strukturalismus und das sozialwissenschaftliche Problem der Erklärung der Entstehung des Neuen', in S. Müller-Doohm (ed) *Jenseits der Utopie*, Frankfurt: Suhrkamp, pp 267–336.

Orchard, P. (2010) 'Protection of internally displaced persons: soft law as a norm-generating mechanism', *Review of International Studies*, 36(2): 281–303.

Orsini, A., Morin, J.-F. and Young, O. (2013) 'Regime complexes: a buzz, a boom, or a boost for global governance?' *Global Governance*, 19(1): 27–39.

Park, S. (2010) *World Bank Group Interactions with Environmentalists: Changing International Organisation Identities*, Manchester: Manchester University Press.

Park, S. (2006) 'Theorizing norm diffusion within international organizations', *International Politics*, 43(3): 342–61.

Park, S. (2005) 'How transnational environmental advocacy networks socialize international financial institutions: a case study of the international finance corporation', *Global Environmental Politics*, 5(4): 95–119.

Pécoud, A. (2018) 'What do we know about the International Organization for Migration?', *Journal of Ethnic and Migration Studies*, 44(10): 1621–38.

Peirce, C.S. (1992 [1878]) 'How to make our ideas clear', in N. Houser and C. Kloesel (eds) *The Essential Peirce: Selected Philosophical Writings, Vol. 1 (1867–1893)*, Bloomington and Indianapolis: Indiana University Press, pp 124–41.

Petrov, P., Dijkstra, H., Đokić, K. et al (2019) 'All hands on deck: levels of dependence between the EU and other international organizations in peacebuilding', *Journal of European Integration*, 41(8): 1027–43.

Pfeffer, J. and Salancik, G.R. (1978) *The External Control of Organizations: A Resource Dependence Perspective*, New York: Harper&Row.

Raustiala, K. and Victor, D.G. (2004) 'The regime complex for plant genetic resources', *International Organization*, 58(2): 277–309.

Reinalda, B. and Kille, K.J. (2017) 'The evolvement of international secretariats, executive heads and leadership in inter-organizational relations', in R. Biermann and J.A.Koops (eds) *The Palgrave Handbook of Inter-Organizational Relations in World Politics*, London: Palgrave Macmillan, pp 217–42.

Rese, A., Gemünden, H-G. and Baier, D. (2013) '"Too many cooks spoil the broth": key persons and their roles, in inter-organizational innovations', *Creativity and Innovation Management*, 22(4): 390–407.

Roos, U. (2015) 'Beliefs and loyalties in world politics: a pragmatist framework for analysis', in G. Hellmann and K.E. Jørgensen (eds) *Theorizing Foreign Policy in a Globalized World*, Basingstoke: Palgrave Macmillan, pp 176–98.

Roos, U. (2010) *Deutsche Außenpolitik. Eine Rekonstruktion der grundlegenden Handlungsregeln*, Wiesbaden: VS Verlag.

Rosenau, J.N. (1992) 'Governance, order, and change in world politics', in J.N. Rosenau and E.-O. Czempiel (eds) *Governance without Government. Order and Change in World Politics*, Cambridge: Cambridge University Press, pp 1–29.

Schemeil, Y. (2004) 'Expertise and political competence: consensus making within the World Trade Organization and the World Meteorological Organization', in B. Reinalda and J.W. van Deth (eds) *Decision Making within International Organizations*, London: Routledge, pp 77–89.

Shriwise, A., Kentikelenis, A.E. and Stuckler, D. (2020) 'Universal Social Protection: is it just talk?', *Sociology of Development,* 6(1): 116–44.

Smith, J., Hughes, M.M., Plummer, S. and Duncan, B. (2021) 'Inter-organizational relations in transnational environmental and women's activism: multilateralists, pragmatists, and rejectionists', *Globalizations,* 18(2): 300–20.

Stein, A.A. (1982) 'Coordination and collaboration: regimes in an anarchic world', *International Organization*, 36(2): 299–324.

Struett, M.J., Nance, M.T. and Armstrong, D. (2013) 'Navigating the maritime piracy regime complex', *Global Governance*, 19(1): 93–104.

Thompson, J.D. (1967) *Organizations in Action,* New York: McGraw-Hill.

Tolbert, P. (1985) 'Institutional environments and resource dependence: sources of administration structure in institutions of higher education', *Administrative Science Quarterly*, 30(1): 1–13

van de Ven, A.H. (1976) 'On the nature, formation, and maintenance of relations among organizations', *Academy of Management Review*, 1(4): 24–36.

Vetterlein, A. and Moschella, M. (2014) 'International organizations and organizational fields: explaining policy change in the IMF', *European Political Science Review*, 6(1): 143–65.

Werron, T. (2010) 'Direkte Konflikte, indirekte Konkurrenzen. Unterscheidung und Vergleich zweier Formen des Kampfes', *Zeitschrift für Soziologie*, 39(4): 302–18.

Wodsak, V. and Koch, M. (2010) 'From three to five – The World Bank's pension policy norm', in S. Park and A. Vetterlein (eds) *Owning Development: Creating Policy Norms in the IMF and the World Bank*, Cambridge: Cambridge University Press, pp 48–69.

Young, O.R. (2010) 'Institutional dynamics: resilience, vulnerability and adaptation in environmental and resource regimes', *Global Environmental Change*, 20(3), pp 378–85.

Young, O.R. (1996) 'Institutional linkages in international society: polar perspectives', *Global Governance*, 2(1): 1–23.

Young, O.R. (1982) 'Regime dynamics: the rise and fall of international regimes', *International Organization*, 36(2): 277–97.

Zelli, F., Gupta, A. and van Asselt, H. (2013) 'Institutional interactions at the crossroads of trade and environment: the dominance of liberal environmentalism?' *Global Governance*, 19(1): 105–18.

2

Hybrid Anti-Impunity Commissions and the Rule of Law

Theresa Reinold

Introduction

When the Comisión Internacional Contra la Impunidad en Guatemala (CICIG) was expelled from the country in 2019, this heralded the end of a successful experiment in international cooperation. The commission was a unique governance arrangement in the rule of law sector that was embedded in a dense web of inter-organizational relations (IOR), interacting with organizations at different layers of governance, ranging from the global to the local. Anti-impunity commissions are part of a broader global trend towards hybrid governance solutions,[1] which are located in the middle of a continuum, with purely international mechanisms (using international law, international staff and enjoying supranational powers) occupying one end of the spectrum, and domestic mechanisms (employing national law, local staff and ceding no sovereign privileges to external actors) occupying the other end.

This present contribution investigates the impact of this novel type of hybrid actor on the rule of law. More specifically, it inquires into how the new hybrids' entanglement in a web of inter-organizational relations shapes their impact on the culture of lawfulness in their host state. The study of IOR is a relatively young subfield in the discipline of international relations (IR), and within this nascent subdiscipline, the inter-organizational relations of hybrid anti-impunity commissions have not been the subject of academic scrutiny. As noted in the introductory chapter, existing studies of IOR tend to be somewhat limited in terms of organizations and issue-areas studied – privileging relations between international organizations (IOs) in the fields of economic and security governance – and with regard to forms of interaction, in that existing studies tend to assume a binary distinction between cooperative and confrontational relations. The present contribution seeks to correct these biases: first, by introducing a new issue area – judicial cooperation; second, by focusing on a new type of organization – hybrid anti-impunity commissions and their manifold relations with IOs, non-governmental organizations (NGOs) and state actors; and third, by demonstrating how hybrid anti-impunity commissions' inter-organizational relations produce variegated and ambivalent forms of interaction that defy the cooperation vs conflict dichotomy.

Hybrid anti-impunity commissions are deeply embedded in their organizational environment, as they do not seek to supplant the justice system of the target state but fight impunity from within it. Their embedded nature requires them to interact with a broad range of actors not only within the host state but also with organizations at the regional and global levels. These novel forms of governance have begun to proliferate in South and Central America (with cognates in Eastern Europe and Asia) in the past decade and a half and continue to be a highly under-researched phenomenon. This dearth of research is rather surprising, considering that the new hybrids have been praised for producing 'transcendental' effects (WOLA, 2015: 27)[2] – at least in the short-term. It remains unclear, however, to what extent they can effect a lasting transformation of the justice systems of their host state and how their interactions with other organizations shape their impact. This chapter uses the case of CICIG to shed light on these questions. The chapter is based on first-hand data generated through more than 30 semi-structured interviews conducted with commission staff, political elites, civil society members, judges, prosecutors, journalists and academics throughout 2021.

The chapter's main insights can be summarized as follows: the impact of the new hybrids is shaped by their interaction with various organizations operating at different levels of governance.[3] Three actors in particular enable a hybrid commission to carry out its mandate even in the face of host-government obstructionism; namely, support from civil-society organizations, powerful donor states and the Attorney-General's office (Ministerio Público). While the hybrid's relationship with its global or regional sponsoring organization also plays a role, it does not seem to have the same significance as these other players. The interplay of all of these factors will determine if the changes initiated by the hybrid will lead to a deeper cultural transformation, that is, if the hybrid commission will succeed in establishing a 'new way of doing things' within the host state, in that compliance with the law ceases to be an exception and becomes the norm. If no such culture of lawfulness is successfully consolidated, it is very likely that, after the hybrid's departure, a relapse into the bad old habits of impunity will occur.

State of the art

Despite their impressive achievements and innovative nature, CICIG and its counterparts in Honduras, El Salvador, Ecuador and Kosovo are barely known outside specialist circles and therefore remain largely under-researched. This is somewhat surprising, given that they have been considered to be particularly promising models of rule-of-law promotion tools worth replicating in other states (Hudson and Taylor, 2010). As pointed out in the introduction to this chapter, hybrid anti-impunity commissions are embedded in a complex web of inter-organizational relations. As such, they provide instructive examples of governance arrangements under conditions of polycentricity, which are dynamic and complex. However, the IOR of the new hybrids and, more broadly speaking, the impact of these new governance arrangements on a variety of outcomes, including the rule of law, democracy and sovereignty remain almost completely under-theorized. The following sections, therefore, first review the academic literature on hybrid governance more generally, including research on hybrid criminal tribunals, a close cognate of hybrid anti-impunity commissions. Subsequently, they discuss what we can learn from these for the study of hybrid anti-impunity commissions. The focus is then on CICIG and its replicas more specifically, in order to identify existing lacunae in the literature and explain how they might be addressed.

Conceptualizations of hybridity abound. Levi-Faur (2011), for instance, distinguishes four forms of hybridity, of which the fourth, multi-level regulation, is relevant for the purposes of this chapter. Multi-level regulation means that actors from different layers of governance are involved in the exercise of governance tasks. This involvement characterizes not only hybrid anti-impunity commissions but also hybrid criminal tribunals, which have proliferated globally in the past couple of decades (Dickinson, 2003; see also Higonnet, 2005/06; Cruvellier, 2009). Hybrid tribunals were born partly out of the realization that 'a purely international process that largely bypasses the local population does little to help build local capacity. An international court staffed by foreigners, or even a local justice system operated exclusively by the United Nations (UN) transitional administration, cannot hope to train local actors in necessary skills' (Dickinson, 2003: 304). Purely international criminal tribunals are often perceived as quick fixes that temporarily replace local mechanisms yet fail to empower local actors to handle future prosecutions themselves. They are thus quite ineffective in building a culture of lawfulness in the target state. Hybrid criminal tribunals, by contrast, seek to leave a 'legacy', that is, a more lasting imprint upon the justice systems of their host states. Unfortunately, however, even though the importance of legacy is widely recognized, its actual successes, 'although not entirely absent, have been few' (OHCHR, 2008: 5). The bottom line is: we do not really know what works and why.

This is also true for hybrid anti-impunity commissions, the effects of which are even less studied in the academic literature than those of hybrid criminal tribunals. While a number of useful policy briefs have been written about the new hybrids, hardly any theory-building work has been carried out (but see Reinold, 2020a, which focuses exclusively on institutional design aspects, however). The handful of existing scholarly publications are usually single-case studies on CICIG, which do not, however, examine its IOR and the impact on the rule of law in any detail.

Among those who have studied CICIG and its counterparts in depth are Charles Call and Jeffrey Hallock, who have published a number of insightful policy briefs on CICIG as well as its replicas in Honduras and El Salvador, including from a comparative perspective (Call, 2018; see also Call, 2019; Call and Hallock, 2020). However, these policy briefs lack theoretical reflection upon the IOR of CICIG et al or on their impact on the culture of legality. A number of think tanks have also published a range of policy briefs on CICIG and its replicas, including the International Crisis Group (2016), the Open Society Justice Initiative (2016) and the Washington Office on Latin America (WOLA, 2015). While these policy briefs are equally rich in empirical detail and often contain very interesting background information, they tend not to consider the theory-building implications of their case studies.

In addition to these policy briefs, a handful of articles has been published in scholarly journals which focus on CICIG as a single case study (Donovan, 2008; see also Hudson and Taylor, 2010; Nyberg, 2015; Krylova, 2018; Zamora, 2019). Yet these contributions are equally somewhat limited in their reflections upon broader theoretical implications and do not address the IOR of CICIG in any detail. The following section therefore examines this aspect of inter-organizational relations and discusses how they influence the ability of hybrid anti-impunity commissions to effect lasting changes in the rule-of-law culture of their host states.

Theoretical framework

The overarching objective of this chapter is to explore how hybrid commissions' inter-organizational relations shape their impact upon the culture of legality in their host states. This section first discusses what type of relations can potentially materialize between the new hybrids and their environment, and second, how the outcome under scrutiny – the culture of legality – can be conceptualized.

It has become conventional wisdom in the discipline of organizational sociology to state that organizations cannot be understood in isolation from their environment (Parsons, 1956), and that organizations mimic other organizations that they view as successful and legitimate (DiMaggio and Powell, 1983). Hybrid anti-impunity commissions are no exceptions in this regard. As they are embedded in a dense web of relations with actors at different levels of governance, their operations are continually influenced by their environment. Now, as explained in the introduction, existing studies of IOR tend to envisage a somewhat limited range of potential interactions between organizations, establishing a binary distinction between cooperative and confrontational relations. In this section, however, I want to suggest conceptualizing IOR not as a dichotomy but as a continuum, with cooperation and conflict forming merely the respective ends of this spectrum. In between these two poles, a range of potential forms of interaction exist that may also mutate over time. IOR should thus be conceived of as dynamic rather than static, and as characterized by ambivalences and many shades of grey.

Cooperative relationships range from explicit to tacit endorsement, from unconditional to qualified support. These degrees of support in turn can be disaggregated into different forms of support – ranging from material (for example, financial) to non-material (for example, diplomatic backing). Towards the more conflictive end of the spectrum, we find relationships of outright antagonism (manifested, for instance, in threats of expulsion or physical harassment), but also much more subtle forms of conflict (such as stalling the operations of the hybrid through legal and administrative manoeuvres). Another important point is that relationships may transform over time, depending on factors such as individual leadership, geopolitical changes and so on. All of these factors influence – in one way or another – the hybrid's ability to consolidate a culture of lawfulness in the host state.

This leads to the second point: the conceptual distinction between the rule of law as a technical requirement on the one hand, and, on the other, a rule of law *culture* or culture of lawfulness that arises over time from this technical adherence to core rule of law precepts. I define the rule of law in general terms as the requirement that a community be governed by legal rules, not the whims of men (or women). The concept of rule of law culture,[4] by contrast, requires more elaboration. Lawrence Friedman (1975: 193) describes 'legal culture' as encompassing 'public knowledge of and attitudes and behavior patterns toward the legal system'. Public attitudes and beliefs are thus an integral element of a rule of law culture. Brian Tamanaha (2007: 13) in turn posits that:

> For the rule of law to exist, people must believe in and be committed to the rule of law. They must take it for granted as a necessary, proper, and existing part of their political-legal system. This attitude is not itself a legal rule. It is a shared political ideal that amounts to a cultural

> belief. When this cultural belief is pervasive, the rule of law can be resilient, spanning generations, surviving episodes in which the rule of law is flouted by government officials. When this cultural belief is not pervasive, however, the rule of law will be weak or non-existent. [...] This tends to be the case in societies where the law has a long or recent history of enforcing authoritarian rule, or where legal officials are perceived to be corrupt or inept, or where legal professionals are widely distrusted, or where the content or application of the law is seen to be unfair or is identified with particular interests or the elite.

Hence there is a difference between the rule of law in a procedural sense as a technical requirement that the legal rules that govern a community be transparent, publicly promulgated, uniformly applied and so on (which can be achieved through external capacity-building, for instance) and the public consciousness, the belief system and so on that grows *over time* from such a technical adherence to legality. The rule of law is therefore not just a matter of 'detailed institutional design' but is furthermore anchored in an 'interconnected cluster of values' (Krygier (2005) quoted in Zimmermann, 2007: 25).

What is important to keep in mind is that consolidating a culture of lawfulness is not a purely technical exercise that is only about reforming laws, training personnel and fortifying institutions. It is a highly political project that will touch upon the vital interests of powerful players who had thus far benefited from the absence of a strong rule of law culture. Creating such a culture therefore 'creates high-stakes winners and losers' (McKay, 2015: 16). Building compliance constituencies with other organizations is thus vital for reform-minded actors wishing to promote the rule of law (McKay, 2015: 43).

In sum, hybrid anti-impunity commissions seeking to build a rule-of-law culture in a hostile environment will need to understand the panorama they are faced with, who wins, who stands to lose from their intervention, whom to prosecute and when, whom to ally with in order to reduce the intensity of the anticipated backlash – in short, they need to engage in a (multilevel) stakeholder analysis. However, before analysing this web of inter-organizational relations in more detail, the following section presents some basic methodological considerations and a brief overview of CICIG's genesis and functioning.

Methodology

This section adopts a qualitative, process-tracing methodology (Bennett and Checkel, 2014) by inductively identifying the weight of different factors contributing to the outcome of interest. The impact of the hybrid commission on the culture of lawfulness can be gauged from a set of indicators, ranging from quantifiable criteria to softer measures. Quantifiable indicators include case statistics and impunity rates. Note, however, that what matters is not only the sheer quantity of cases being investigated and convictions achieved. It is equally important to look at who is being investigated, prosecuted, and convicted. Do the new hybrids merely go after small fry – lower-level policy officials, petty criminals and so on, or are the big fish – those normally considered untouchable – equally targeted? Another relevant indicator for measuring impact is the new hybrids' legacy in terms of building local capacity, that is, the creation of what Ciorciari and Krasner (2018: 485) have called islands of excellence – 'entities that provide public services much more effectively and transparently than most surrounding domestic institutions. The creation of islands of excellence is a crucial mechanism by which sovereignty-sharing arrangements can have a lasting positive impact on host-state governance'. A related proxy for measuring impact is the new hybrids' contribution to legislative reform aimed at strengthening the local justice system. Have relevant initiatives (for instance those related to the creation of a specialized anti-corruption infrastructure) been successfully adopted, or are important reform measures stalled by political opposition? Finally, impact can be gauged through surveys measuring public trust in the hybrid commissions as well as the justice system in general, which suggests that a culture of lawfulness has begun to take hold.

As hybrid commissions interact with players at different levels of governance, I have sought to identify the relative weight of these factors based on more than two dozen semi-structured interviews that I conducted throughout 2021 with CICIG management and staff, judges, politicians, IO staff, civil-society representatives and academics. I recruited my interviewees through a snowballing technique, which does not generate a random sample but had the advantage of ensuring that I would interview the most relevant persons in the field. I chose a three-pronged approach. First, I interviewed CICIG management and staff, in order to get an insider's perspective into the internal workings of the organization. Second, I recruited interviewees from organizations CICIG cooperated with, in order to shed more light on CICIG's inter-organizational relations. In a third step, I cast my net even wider, reaching out to interviewees that could offer an external perspective on these relations, including academics and politicians. In selecting my interviewees, I sought moreover to ensure a certain amount of variation regarding cultural background, level of seniority, disciplinary affiliation and so on in order to obtain a balanced picture. Due to the COVID-19 pandemic, it was not possible to conduct these interviews in person; instead, all of them were carried out via video meetings. Naturally, in-person interviews differ from online conversations in a number of ways and have shortcomings of their own; yet overall, I agree with Howlett (2021: 4) that, in light of 'the significant advancements in technology, in-person interactions are [...] no longer "the gold standard against which the performance of computer-mediated interaction is judged" (Hine, 2005: 4), as online methods are indeed equally valid and legitimate approaches to research'.

I used the interview data to complement and triangulate other primary sources, such as media reporting, along with secondary sources including the (sparse) academic literature as well as a number of policy briefs that have been published on CICIG. Based on a process-tracing methodology, I thereby reconstructed the relationship between CICIG and other organizations it cooperated with, and examined how these relations were causally connected to CICIG's ability to foster a culture of lawfulness.

A final word on case selection and the generalizability of my findings: this chapter focuses on CICIG, as the commission pioneered the emergence of a novel form of governance in the judicial sector. As the first and to date most successful example of hybrid anti-impunity commissions, CICIG therefore deserves closer academic scrutiny. Naturally, as a single case study, the present chapter's causal inferences regarding the broader phenomenon of hybrid anti-impunity commissions should be treated with caution. However, while I am not in a position to claim (yet) that CICIG offers a representative case study of the inter-organizational relations of this novel form of hybrid governance, my preliminary research into other Latin American hybrids as well as the European Union Rule of Law Mission (EULEX) in Kosovo suggests that the CICIG experience is rather typical in terms of which inter-organizational relations matter most to a hybrid's successes, and in terms of the dynamics that lead to the rise and demise of this new form of hybrid governance.

Analysis: CICIG and the rule of law

The presentation of the analysis proceeds in two steps. First, I sketch the genesis of CICIG. Second, I present CICIG's inter-organizational relations at various levels including global/regional, national and societal.

The genesis of CICIG

In Central America, the problem of state capture by illegal groups is pervasive, and impunity is the norm. The region has been plagued by alarming levels of violence caused by remnants of civil-war-era clandestine intelligence and paramilitary forces, organized crime and their allies in political and business circles. An unholy alliance of these actors has by now captured almost all of the institutions of the state of Guatemala, leaving the local justice system incapable of fighting the prevailing culture of impunity. As Carlos Castresana, former head of CICIG told me: "The dark forces from the civil war had captivated all the justice system because it was the guarantee of their impunity."[5] This is thus the panorama we were faced with in Guatemala before CICIG's arrival. CICIG was established in 2006 pursuant to an agreement between the UN and the Guatemalan government and began its work in 2007 to address the threat emanating from the persistence of clandestine security networks, corruption and organized crime. CICIG was kicked out of Guatemala in 2019 after it decided to investigate President Morales and his family for corruption.

The commission was composed of both local and international staff, but it operated under Guatemalan law and in Guatemalan courts. It was mandated to investigate and co-prosecute organized crime and grand corruption. It also had the authority to remove obstructionist public officials and to contribute to longer-term structural reform, for instance through the professionalization of investigation methods, the creation of specialized high-risk tribunals (*Tribunales de Mayor Riesgo*) and the establishment of a special unit within the Attorney General's office, which has become known as FECI (*Fiscalía Especial Contra la Impunidad*). In 2015, CICIG's investigations triggered a political earthquake that offered Guatemala 'its best hope for change in 20 years' (Open Society Justice Initiative, 2016: 39). CICIG had exposed a massive corruption scandal called *La Línea*, which implicated high-level officials from President Molina's inner circle, including Vice President Baldetti – and later Molina himself. The revelations triggered large-scale street protests culminating in the resignation and arrest of Baldetti. Further investigations produced incriminating evidence that Baldetti and Molina themselves were the ringleaders of *La Línea*. Molina was ultimately forced to step down as well and is currently in jail.

Apart from bringing down a sitting president and his deputy, CICIG produced a range of other astonishing results. It achieved a 25 per cent reduction in the impunity rate and investigated more than 200 cases that led to charges against more than 160 high-level government officials. Critically, CICIG built trust in the Guatemalan justice system, trust that historically did not exist. Survey data indicate high rates of public approval, with CICIG becoming the most trusted institution in Guatemala. In addition, citizens' trust in the Guatemalan justice system as a whole increased significantly as a consequence of CICIG's work (Paredes, 2018; Zamora, 2019). As one of my interviewees stated, "CICIG allowed Guatemalans to have dreams about a better future."

So, CICIG proved wildly successful in the short to medium term, but now that the commission has left the country, most of its achievements have been undone by the dark forces running the country. This begs the question of how one can account for the impact of this new form of hybrid governance. An important structural feature of these commissions is that they are embedded in a web of inter-organizational relations. The following section therefore sheds light on this web of inter-organizational relations and discusses its impact on the hybrid's ability to foster a culture of legality in the host state.

CICIG's inter-organizational relations

Stakeholders at the global/regional level

An important question about hybrid governance arrangements that needs to be addressed at the outset is whether they should be affiliated with a global or regional sending organization. According to one of my interlocutors, the relationship between the hybrid and its sponsoring organization is a "fundamental topic". It is fundamental because the relationship between both organizations has significant repercussions for the hybrid's ability to discharge its mandate effectively. Unlike the other hybrid commissions in South and Central America, which were created through an agreement between the host state and the Organization of American States (OAS), CICIG was created through an agreement between the UN and the state of Guatemala. While the agreement bringing CICIG to life involved the UN as an external partner, in its day-to-day operations, CICIG was largely independent of its sending organization.

Not affiliating CICIG with the OAS was sensible as the OAS is widely seen as too politicized, weak and itself corrupt, and all of my interviewees agreed that it would be better to associate a hybrid commission with the UN. When asked if it had been better to affiliate CICIG with the OAS, one interviewee emphatically rejected this proposal: "No, no, not at all!" The OAS, according to her, is an organization headed by a personality who has little interest in fighting corruption and organized crime. Former Guatemalan foreign minister Edgar Gutierrez affirmed this skepticism in an interview:

> '[W]hen one sees a president or parliament approach the OAS, the Organization of American States, this already raises suspicion, because the OAS is a weak organism, in the hemisphere it does not have prestige. The United Nations at least has better capacities, experience, and has more autonomy. The OAS not, it is politically very much subjected to governments.'

This was echoed by Manfredo Marroquín, president of Acción Ciudadana, who joked that OEA (the Spanish name of the OAS) was the acronym for "olvida ese asunto" ("forget it"), stressing that the OAS was as just as corrupt as the countries it was supposed to free from corruption. This assumption is also borne out by the track record of the other hybrid commissions that operated in Honduras and El Salvador – Misión de Apoyo Contra la Corrupción y la Impunidad en Honduras (MACCIH) and the Comisión Internacional Contra la Impunidad de El Salvador (CICIES) – whose impact was significantly undermined by the lackadaisical support they received from the OAS and the lack of credibility the OAS enjoyed as a promoter of the rule of law in its member states

Privileging affiliation with a global body over affiliation with a regional organization does not mean that the relationship between the hybrid and its global partner is not going to be fraught with difficulties. CICIG and the UN found themselves in an often tense relationship, with CICIG complaining about lack of UN support towards the end of its period of operation, when the commission was under relentless attack by the dark forces that had taken over Guatemala, ultimately resulting in the commission's expulsion. Carlos Castresana, CICIG's first head, pointed out to me that, in the first years of CICIG's existence the UN strongly endorsed the commission: "We received lots of support, they were loyal with us." However, at the same time, the UN was critical of CICIG's activist stance and the political and diplomatic challenges that arose from this activism:

> 'I was creating new problems for them every day, I wanted to purchase weapons but they said no you cannot do that! According to the UN rules for ordinary missions this was impossible, the regulations were too restrictive and I was creating new problems by wanting to buy armored vehicles, etc.'

In the UN's perception, according to an unidentified CICIG staff member, the commission was rocking the boat a little too much, touching too many sensitive subjects that the UN did not want to deal with:

> '[T]he UN […] decided that it was a mistake to put the CICIG too close to the Secretary-General, it shouldn't have been under the responsibility of the Department of Political Affairs, better to be under UNODC or UNDPO because all the complaints, all the criticism came to the Secretary-General. They said we were already creating problems, but I said, sorry, the problem was there before my arrival. I'm just pointing it out to you.'

Another interlocutor called the relationship between CICIG and the UN "complex", maintaining that the UN neither understood the situation on the ground very well nor the expectations that local actors had towards CICIG. This interviewee also echoed other CICIG staff members' perception that the UN would have preferred CICIG to keep a lower profile and not go after high-ranking figures or remove obstructionist officials from power – even though both types of activity were clearly covered by CICIG's mandate.

Some of the interviewees expressed regret that the UN did not have CICIG's back in public when Guatemalan state institutions, including the

President, Congress, and the Attorney-General, did everything in their power to obstruct CICIG's work. As a variety of UN agencies and programmes were operating in Guatemala, the UN was hesitant to throw its full weight behind CICIG, as it feared retaliation from the government of Jimmy Morales against other UN programmes. Several high-ranking CICIG officials told me that, when the commission first entered Guatemala, everyone expected it to confine itself to writing a few reports but not to upset the existing balance of power in the country. The investigations of high-ranking officials and the removal of obstructionist justice operators that CICIG subsequently undertook was, according to my interviewees, very difficult to reconcile with the diplomatic approach of the UN. CICIG staff told me that the UN would have preferred CICIG to keep a low profile, writing a few reports and engaging in technical cooperation, instead of taking on the country's most powerful.

In summary, support from the sending organization is an important factor enabling a hybrid to carry out its mandate, and if such support is absent, the commission's ability to resist political backlash at the domestic level will be undermined. If a hybrid actor adopts a highly activist stance and, in discharging its mandate, approaches the nucleus of power in the host state, this is likely not only to trigger tensions domestically but also in the relationship with the hybrid's global sponsoring organization. In addition – although this may not be generalizable beyond South and Central America – it is preferrable to associate a hybrid with a global rather than a regional sending organization, as the regional organization might lack the credibility and impartiality to act as a promoter of the rule of law.

Stakeholders at the national level – host-state institutions

Alongside the international level, organizations at national level equally exert a significant impact upon the ability of hybrid governance arrangements to promote the rule of law. In Guatemala, there is a clear division between those actors who have sought to obstruct the administration of justice at every step (the *pacto de corruptos*) and the few remaining defenders of the rule of law in the country. Currently, the only state actors that are still committed to the rule of law in Guatemala are FECI, the *Tribunales de Mayor Riesgo*, the office of the Human Rights Ombudsperson, and, until spring 2021, the constitutional court. To date, FECI is valiantly continuing its anti-impunity efforts in Guatemala, but its staff are exposed to continual harassment, intimidation and obstructionism. This harassment escalated to such an extent that the Inter-American Human Rights Court felt compelled to intervene, calling upon Guatemala to reinforce security measures to protect the lives of FECI's head Juan Francisco Sandoval and other FECI prosecutors. The *Tribunales de Mayor Riesgo* are another important element of CICIG's legacy and a vital ally for FECI. They were created at the initiative of CICIG to handle complex criminal cases. Nowhere in Latin America does something similar to these high-risk courts exist, courts with specialized judges to handle complex criminal cases. The high-risk tribunals' judges are generally considered to be independent and have continued to enable FECI's investigations, but, in doing so, they put their own lives at risk. Then there is the office of the Human Rights Ombudsperson, which also offered consistent support to CICIG and continues to be one of the few pockets of resistance within Guatemala, but my interviewees agreed that its resolutions are of a merely symbolic character. Finally, the last defender of the rule of law among the state organs of Guatemala was the constitutional court. Time and again it has spoken truth to power. Meanwhile, its judges have been subjected to constant threats, influence peddling and harassment, because the court has been able to put a brake on some of the most egregious attempts at corruption and continues to challenge impunity. It has been attacked by the Supreme Court of Justice, the Office of the Prosecutor, Congress and the president himself. However, after the tainted election of new magistrates in 2021, the constitutional court also fell into the hands of the *pacto de corruptos*.

This 'pact of the corrupt' can be described as a united movement in Guatemala. It brought down CICIG in 2019 and continues to influence the executive, legislature and judiciary. By November 2022, almost all state institutions have been captured by the pact of the corrupt. The president obviously plays a critical role in determining the fate of an anti-impunity commission, inter alia, because it is the president who decides about renewing or terminating the mandate of the commission. When CICIG took up its work in Guatemala, it enjoyed strong support from then-President Alvaro Colom, whose presidency was actually saved by the commission's investigations into the Rosenberg case.[6] Then came Otto Pérez Molina, whom CICIG toppled through its investigations into the *La Línea* scandal, discussed earlier. Molina was succeeded by Jimmy Morales, who in turn refused to renew CICIG's mandate when the commission decided to investigate him and his family for corruption. We can thus observe an interesting sequence here, with CICIG saving the presidency of Colom, ending the presidency of Molina, and then being itself killed off by Morales.

Apart from the executive, the legislature also plays a critical role in shaping the impact of hybrid governance arrangements, inter alia, because they have to approve the legislative changes initiated by the hybrid commission. In a functioning democracy, the parliament should provide a check on the power of the executive, but in Guatemala, the legislature, for the most part, and the executive are both members of the pact of the corrupt. According to my interviewees, mafia coalitions had captured Congress by 2017 and have since then sabotaged any attempt at fighting impunity in Guatemala. Congress has repeatedly attacked the constitutional court, for instance by seeking the impeachment of independent-minded constitutional court judges, which has been seen as a frontal attack on judicial independence.

Turning to the judiciary, a critical organization that significantly shapes the work of hybrid anti-impunity commissions is the Attorney-General's office. In Guatemala, this is currently led by Maria Consuelo Porras who was appointed during the regime of Jimmy Morales. Her appointment was essentially based on the need of that particular president and of the sector that supported him to ensure their own impunity. My interviewees agreed that Porras is also a member of the pact of the corrupt, and that the work of the Ministerio Público suffered a serious blow when she took over the reins of the institution. The MP cannot make a move without Porras' consent, and all of FECI's investigations have to be authorized by her. FECI staff told me that Porras has used a variety of stalling tactics to obstruct their work, for instance by blocking investigations of high-level officials, removing sensitive cases from FECI and giving them to other units within the MP, where they ultimately died, and encouraging the filing of legal complaints against FECI staff.

The critical role played by the person of the Attorney-General in shaping the impact of a hybrid commission is underlined if we take into account variation in the Attorney-General's office over time. Claudia Paz y Paz and Thelma Aldana, Porras' predecessors at the helm of the MP, were highly committed prosecutors who collaborated effectively with CICIG and whose support proved crucial to enabling the commission to carry out its mandate effectively, despite the obstructionism CICIG faced from other powerful actors in Guatemala. Regrettably, however, one of the major lessons learned from CICIG is that those who become too successful in promoting the rule of law will sooner or later come to fear for their jobs, their reputations and even their lives. It comes as no surprise then, that both Aldana and Paz y Paz have had to flee Guatemala, and that they were replaced by an Attorney-General who does not upset the domestic power balance and instead acts as a guarantor of impunity.

Stakeholders at the societal level – civil society organizations

Civil society organizations form another important pillar of a hybrid's compliance constituency. Guatemalan civil society was, and still is, quite active in supporting CICIG as well as FECI, and in mobilizing against the Attorney-General, Congress, and other corrupt actors in Guatemala. However, large-scale societal mobilization against impunity in Guatemala has been hindered by a number of factors. On the one hand, people are afraid. In 2020, there were major protests against the approval of the 2021 budget, which were suppressed brutally by the government of President Alejandro Giammattei. My interviewees also pointed to Guatemala's historical legacy of terror: "He who complains will be killed; he who says something in the press will be killed."

Another relevant factor is clearly the COVID-19 pandemic, which reduced the potential for mobilization in the streets, although mobilization through social media continues. A third factor affecting societal mobilization are deteriorating socio-economic conditions. Most of my interviewees stressed that too many people in Guatemala have to be primarily concerned with everyday survival; to them the rule of law is a luxury, not an everyday necessity. And, as one interviewee put it, the government benefits from having a hungry people. While large-scale street protests supporting CICIG and the rule of law did occur in 2015, this was a somewhat singular event, prompted by CICIG's investigations into the *La Línea* scandal. *La Línea* triggered outrage among the population, who then allied with important business actors, ultimately achieving the resignation of President Molina and his deputy, Baldetti. This united front later dissipated, however, because of, among other things, the absence of a common political agenda. This undermined CICIG's ability to establish a strong rule-of-law culture in Guatemala.

Stakeholders at national level outside the host state – donor states

The hybrid's fate is not only influenced by organizations and individuals *within* the host state, but also by powerful external players, such as important donor states. The latter can help the hybrid commission to carry out its mandate effectively and shield it from political pressure. Conversely, in the absence of support from powerful donors, the hybrid will be extremely vulnerable to backlash in the host state. In the case of CICIG, it was United States' support that often tipped the scales when the fate of the commission was at stake. Considering the capture of Guatemala's Congress by the pact of the corrupt, one of my interviewees joked that the main opposition party in Guatemala was actually the Democratic Party of the US, which has displayed a much greater interest in fighting impunity in Guatemala than local parties. All of my interviewees agreed that the US had and still has a major impact upon the fate of CICIG or any future commission, and all expressed great hope that, with the change of US administration in January 2021, anti-impunity efforts in Guatemala would receive a strong boost, although there is disagreement over whether we will see a new CICIG or perhaps a commission at regional level for the entire Northern Triangle (of Guatemala, Honduras and El Salvador) that Biden announced during his electoral campaign, or none of the above.

President Obama was a staunch supporter of CICIG's work and contributed to ensuring the commission's survival, for example by convincing then-President Molina to renew its mandate. President Trump, by contrast, showed little interest in fighting impunity in Central America, and his indifference ultimately sealed the fate of the commission. While all of my interviewees accorded great weight to the United States and said that CICIG's future would have likely looked different had the Trump administration not abandoned CICIG, they disagreed on the extent to which the US could achieve the establishment of a new commission with teeth – ranging from interviewees who said that "the Gringos can achieve whatever they want" to those who argued that things had changed and that, while, in the past, the US embassy in Guatemala only had to click its fingers to get what it wanted, there was much more resistance these days. Many agreed that the great advances CICIG had made, especially under its last commissioner Iván Velásquez, critically hinged on the support from US Ambassador Todd Robinson, as well as Swedish Ambassador Anders Kompass, both of whom were said to be rather "undiplomatic" in their unequivocal and outspoken support for CICIG, and who, with Velásquez, formed a critical triangle that helped CICIG's success tremendously.

In summary, a hybrid commission's inter-organizational relations can be illustrated as in Figure 2.1.

Results

The preceding multilevel stakeholder analysis can be condensed into the following generalized assumptions about the effect of the hybrid's inter-organizational relations on its ability to promote the rule of law. First of all, when faced with backlash in the host state, a hybrid that is benefiting from:

- an alliance with powerful donor states;
- significant support from civil society organizations;
- a cooperative Attorney-General's office

Figure 2.1: The inter-organizational relations of hybrid anti-impunity commissions

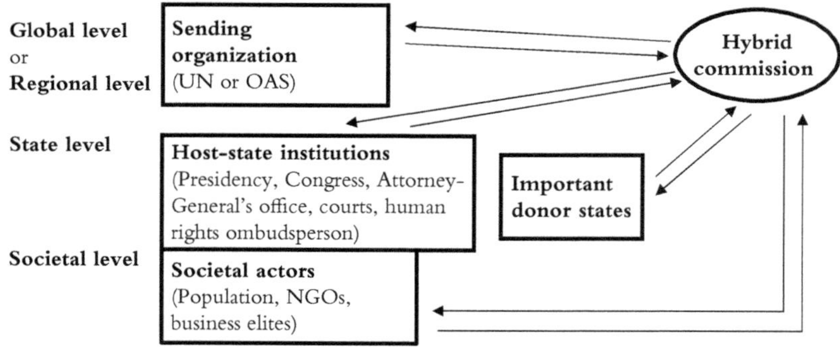

will still be able to carry out its mandate effectively. Conversely, if these actors do not have the hybrid's back, host-state obstructionism is likely to prevent the hybrid from having a significant impact upon the rule of law and might even lead to its demise. While the hybrid commission's relationship with its global (or regional) sponsoring organization is another relevant contributing factor, in comparison with the hybrid's relations with the actors just mentioned, the sending organization plays a somewhat lesser role – at least this is what the case of CICIG suggests. More in-depth research into other cases of hybrid anti-impunity commissions might yield different conclusions, however.

The forms of IOR within this case study thus ranged from explicit and unconditional support, which the hybrid received from civil society, the Attorney-General's office (for parts of its tenure) and important donor states; to qualified forms of support (offered by the UN); to outright rejection (by the host government in the later stages of CICIG's existence). The case study also demonstrates that the dynamics within a given inter-organizational relationship often change over time. Whereas CICIG had a cooperative relationship with the US under Obama, it was abandoned by the Trump administration. Similarly, while CICIG enjoyed outright support from Attorney-Generals Paz y Paz and Aldana, the relationship with the Ministerio Público turned sour when Porras took office. A similar variation could be observed in CICIG's relations with the Guatemalan government, where a supportive President Colom was succeeded by a more ambivalent President Molina, and an openly hostile President Morales. This shows how changes in individual leadership affect the nature and quality of inter-organizational relations, as do shifts in geopolitical constellations, and other factors still to be determined by future research.

Conclusion and outlook

This chapter has sought to shed light on the effects of a novel and still highly under-researched form of governance; namely, hybrid anti-impunity commissions that have proliferated in South and Central America over the past 15 years and that have produced rather impressive results during their brief lifespans. Their prototype was the Comisión Internacional Contra la Impunidad en Guatemala, which – by institutionalizing new norms related to the rule of law and socializing local actors into compliance with these norms – was able to plant the seeds for a consolidation of a culture of lawfulness in Guatemala. Yet, despite the institutionalization of a new set of norms, the creation of new infrastructure, the training of local justice operators and so on, an *internalization* of this new way of doing things by all addressees of the law, and thus the establishment of a culture of lawfulness, could not be accomplished.

So, what does the present case study imply for world order? As suggested in the introductory chapter, existing studies of IOR have given short shrift to their world-order implications, which is somewhat surprising, considering that, in these relations, fundamental norms and institutions of the present international order are being (re)negotiated and potentially transformed. The case of CICIG bears this assumption out. It suggests that inter-organizational relations have a significant impact on *the* foundational institution of the normative order since the Second World War, namely, sovereignty. The type of hybrid governance arrangement embodied by CICIG at the same time weakens *and* strengthens state sovereignty. While this might sound paradoxical at first, the paradox can be solved by disaggregating sovereignty into different components: juridical and empirical. Hybrid anti-impunity commissions – at least the comparatively intrusive variant represented by CICIG – indubitably limit juridical sovereignty, that is, the independence from outside actors that sovereigns enjoy. Hybrid anti-impunity commissions do so by formally assuming competencies for the investigation and co-prosecution of crimes, which were traditionally seen as belonging to the host state. One could of course object that the transfer of authority in and of itself can be viewed as a voluntary act of a sovereign state and thus the supreme exercise of sovereign power. After all, hybrid anti-impunity commissions are not imposed on states by the UN Security Council, for instance, but are based on an agreement between an IO (the UN or a regional IO) and the host state; an agreement that requires ratification by the host-state's legislature. Yet, even if the *process* for transferring sovereign privileges is thus entirely democratic and can be considered as an act of self-determination, in terms of *outcome*, hybrid governance arrangements result in a significant concession of sovereign privileges to outside actors. Sovereignty costs were therefore unsurprisingly a sticking point in the initial negotiations between the state of Guatemala and the UN over setting up CICIG, as, originally, an even broader transfer of sovereign privileges was envisaged. According to the original proposal, the commission was supposed to have not only independent investigatory, but equally independent prosecutorial powers. However, Guatemala refused such a far-reaching conferral of sovereign powers and thus ultimately ceded less of its juridical sovereignty than originally planned.

Regarding the implications for the host state's empirical sovereignty, that is, its ability to effectively provide core public goods such as the rule of law, the case of CICIG clearly demonstrates a strengthening of this facet of sovereignty, at least in the short to medium term. Hybrid anti-impunity commissions are not created to assume sovereign functions indefinitely but rather to fortify local institutions and thus enable them to reassume these functions in the longer term. The limitation of juridical sovereignty in the short to medium term is thus seen as an instrument to strengthen empirical sovereignty in the long run. While this sounds appealing on paper, this chapter has identified practical obstacles to making the change induced by CICIG sustainable. In a nutshell, had CICIG's compliance constituency not disintegrated, its effects on Guatemala's empirical sovereignty would have been much more significant and, above all, sustainable. The strengthening of empirical sovereignty thus requires a coincidence of factors in the absence of which a more effective provision of public goods by the host state will not occur.

As a single case study, this chapter has only limited generalization potential. Future comparative studies should examine in more detail the relative weight of these different factors in order to identify how exactly a hybrid's inter-organizational relations impact upon its work: whether, for instance, the assumption really holds across cases that the hybrid's relationship with the global or regional sponsoring organization is not as crucial as its interaction with domestic players and important donor states. Comparing the findings from the CICIG case with other hybrid governance arrangements will therefore help us to derive generalized theoretical assumptions about the inter-organizational relations of hybrid anti-impunity commissions. Potential case studies include MACCIH, which was shut down in 2020 after it got in the way of the Honduran political elite, including ex-President Hernández (who was arrested on drug-trafficking charges and extradited to the US in 2022). Its Salvadoran counterpart, CICIES, was kicked out of the country in 2021, after investigating the Bukele government's alleged misuse of COVID-19 funds. The envisaged Comisión de Expertos Internacionales de lucha Contra la Corrupción en Ecuador (CEICCE) never really got off the ground, due to a lack of political will. Finally, EULEX, which in contrast to the Latin American hybrids was equipped with rather far-reaching competencies, has been considered relatively ineffective, despite its executive powers. None of these hybrid governance arrangements has received much academic scrutiny and thus little is known about their inter-organizational relations or their impact upon the rule of law. Future research should therefore address each of these cases individually as well as from a comparative perspective, in order to arrive at a better understanding of this novel form of hybrid governance.

Notes

1. This global trend towards hybridity has inspired a burgeoning scholarly literature. See Dickinson (2003); Higonnet (2005/06); Cruvellier (2009); Peterson (2012); Millar (2014); Lemay-Hebert and Freedman (2017); Bargués-Pedreny and Randazzo (2018); Reinold (2020a, 2020b).
2. See the 'Methodology' section for a discussion of how to measure these effects.
3. While the impact of the new hybrids on the rule of law is obviously not only contingent upon *external* factors – that is, its inter-organizational relations with other stakeholders at different levels of governance – the internal factors shaping the successes and failures of hybrid anti-impunity commissions (such as their institutional design, case selection strategies and so on) will not be the subject of this chapter.

[4] In this chapter, I use the terms *rule of law culture, culture of lawfulness, legal culture* and *culture of legality* interchangeably.

[5] Direct quotes in this section are drawn from interviews conducted in February and March 2021.

[6] Rodrigo Rosenberg was a Guatemalan lawyer who sought to topple Colom by blaming his own suicide on the president. Rosenberg himself had hired hitmen to kill him; but beforehand had recorded a video saying that if he were to be assassinated, the president would be responsible for his death. CICIG investigations subsequently exposed the plot and thereby saved Colom's presidency.

References

Bargués-Pedreny, P. and Randazzo, E. (2018) 'Hybrid peace revisited: an opportunity for considering self governance?', *Third World Quarterly*, 39(8): 1543–60.

Bennett, A. and Checkel, J.T. (eds) (2014) *Process Tracing: From Metaphor to Analytic Tool*, Cambridge: Cambridge University Press.

Call, C.T. (2019) 'International anti-impunity missions in Guatemala and Honduras: what lessons for El Salvador?', CLALS Working Paper Series No. 21, American University.

Call, C.T. (2018) 'From steady progress to severely wounded: a two-year report on the performance of the OAS mission in support of the fight against corruption and impunity in Honduras', CLALS Working Paper Series No. 18, American University.

Call, C.T. and Hallock, J. (2020) 'Too much success? The legacy and lessons of the International Commission Against Impunity in Guatemala', CLALS Working Paper Series No. 24, American University.

Ciorciari J.D. and Krasner, S.D. (2018) 'Contracting out, legitimacy, and state building', *Journal of Intervention and Statebuilding*, 12(4): 484–505.

Cruvellier, T. (2009) 'From the Taylor trial to a lasting legacy: putting the special court model to the test', International Centre for Transitional Justice and Sierra Leone Court Monitoring Programme.

Dickinson, L. (2003) 'The promise of hybrid courts', *American Journal of International Law*, 97(2): 295–310.

DiMaggio, P.J. and Powell, W.W. (1983) 'The iron cage revisited: institutional isomorphism and collective rationality in organizational fields', *American Sociological Review*, 48(2): 147–60.

Donovan, M. (2008) 'The International Commission Against Impunity in Guatemala: will accountability prevail?', *Arizona Journal of International & Comparative Law*, 25(3): 779–824.

Friedman, L. (1975) *The Legal System*, New York: Russell Sage Foundation.

Higonnet, E. (2005/06) 'Restructuring hybrid courts: local empowerment and national criminal justice reform', *Arizona Journal of International and Comparative Law*, 23(2): 347–435.

Howlett, M. (2021) 'Looking at the "field" through a Zoom lens: methodological reflections on conducting online research during a global pandemic', *Qualitative Research*, 22(3): 387–402.

Hudson, A. and Taylor, A. (2010) 'The International Commission Against Impunity in Guatemala: a new model for international criminal justice mechanism', *Journal of International Criminal Justice*, 8(1): 53–74.

International Crisis Group (2016) 'Crutch to catalyst? The International Commission Against Impunity in Guatemala', Latin America Report No. 56, International Crisis Group.

Krygier, M. (2005) 'The rule of law: an abuser's guide', paper presented at the 13th Annual Conference on 'The individual vs. the state', Central European University, 10–11 June, Budapest.

Krylova, Y. (2018) 'Outsourcing the fight against corruption: lessons from the International Commission Against Impunity in Guatemala', *Global Policy*, 9(1): 95–101.

Lemay-Hebert, N. and Freedman, R. (eds) (2017) *Hybridity: Law, Culture and Development*, London: Routledge.

Levi-Faur, D. (2011) 'Regulation and regulatory governance', in D. Levi-Faur (ed) *Handbook on the Politics of Regulation*, Cheltenham: Edward Elgar, pp 3–25.

McKay, L. (2015) 'Toward a rule of law culture: exploring effective responses to justice and security challenges', Washington, DC: United States Institute of Peace, available from: www.usip.org/sites/default/files/Toward%20a%20Rule%20of%20Law%20Culture_Practical%20Guide_0.pdf [accessed 30 March 2023].

Millar, G. (2014) 'Disaggregating hybridity: why hybrid institutions do not produce predictable experiences of peace', *Journal of Peace Research*, 51(4): 501–14.

Nyberg, T. (2015) 'International Commission Against Impunity in Guatemala: a non-transitional justice effort', *Revue Québécoise de Droit International*, 28(1): 157–84.

OHCHR (Office of the United Nations High-Commissioner for Human Rights) (2008) 'Rule-of-law tools for post-conflict states: maximizing the legacy of hybrid courts', available from: ohchr.org/sites/default/files/Documents/Publications/HybridCourts.pdf [accessed 30 March 2023].

Open Society Justice Initiative (2016) 'Against the odds: CICIG in Guatemala', available from: justiceinitiative.org/uploads/88ffafc0-09bf-4998-8ef3-e2a175e3f455/against-odds-cicig-guatemala-20160321.pdf [accessed 30 March 2023].

Paredes, L. (2018) 'Comisión Internacional Contra la Impunidad, la mas confiable institucion en el 2017: Latinobarometro', *El Periódico*, online, available from: https://elperiodico.com.gt/nacion/2018/04/20/comision-internacional-contra-la-impunidad-la-mas-confiable-institucion-en-el-2017-latinobarometro [accessed 30 March 2023].

Parsons, T. (1956) 'Suggestions for a sociological approach to the theory of organizations-I', *Administrative Science Quarterly*, 1(1): 63–85.

Peterson, J. (2012) 'A conceptual unpacking of hybridity: accounting for notions of power, politics and progress in analyses of aid-driven interfaces', *Journal of Peacebuilding and Development*, 7(2): 9–22.

Reinold, T. (2020a) 'A new type of hybrid actor in global governance: anti-impunity commissions, shared sovereignty, and the rule of law', *Verfassung und Recht in Übersee*, 53(3): 245–66.

Reinold, T. (2020b) 'The causes and effects of hybrid anti-impunity commissions: outlines of a research agenda', Global Cooperation Research Paper No. 26, Centre for Global Cooperation Research, available from: gcr21.org/de/publikationen/gcr/research-papers/the-causes-and-effects-of-hybrid-anti-impunity-commissions-outline-of-a-research-agenda [accessed 30 March 2023].

Tamanaha, B. (2007) 'A concise guide to the rule of law', Legal Studies Research Paper No. 07–0082, St John's University School of Law, available from: content.csbs.utah.edu/~dlevin/conlaw/tamanaha-rule-of-law.pdf [accessed 30 March 2023].

WOLA (2015) 'The International Commission Against Impunity in Guatemala, a WOLA report on the CICIG experience', Report 6/2015, Washington Office on Latin America, available from: wola.org/wp-content/uploads/2015/07/WOLA_CICIG_ENG_FNL_extra-page.pdf [accessed 30 March 2023].

Zamora, M. (2019) 'Institutional inosculation: the International Commission Against Impunity in Guatemala (CICIG), international rule of law mechanisms, and creating institutional legitimacy in post-conflict societies', *Columbia Journal of Transnational Law*, 57(3): 535–99.

Zimmermann, A. (2007) 'The rule of law as a culture of legality: legal and extra-legal elements for the realization of the rule of law in society', *eLaw journal: Murdoch University Electronic Journal of Law*, 14(1): 10–31, available from: classic.austlii.edu.au/au/journals/MurdochUeJlLaw/2007/2.pdf [accessed 30 March 2023].

3

Inter-Organizational Relations in Counterterrorism

Eva Herschinger and Martin Koch

Introduction

> The purported blocking of Mr. Kadi's assets and his listing as a 'global terrorist' have had a serious adverse impact on Mr. Kadi's reputation, business, and his family, as well as his health. [...] it is frankly difficult to conceive of a more serious allegation against anyone than designation as a 'SDGT'. (Johnson II, 2001)

Yassin Abdullah Kadi, a Saudi Arabian businessman, is the most prominent case of what happens when one has been declared a 'specially designated global terrorist' (SDGT). In 1999 and 2000, the United Nations (UN) suspected Kadi to be an associate of Osama bin Laden and Al-Qaeda and placed sanctions against him under UN Security Council (UNSC) Resolutions 1267 and 1333 (discussed later). In October 2001, the US declared him an SDGT, which caused the blocking of all his property and interests subject to US jurisdiction. The European Union (EU) followed suit, as did Saudi Arabia, Kadi's home country. Kadi has repeatedly claimed that he has given no support to terrorism. Mired in limbo over the accusations, Kadi was forced to stay in Saudi Arabia without ever having been informed of the reasons for his listing and – before the EU endorsed the UN listing – without possibility of appeal.

While the human rights concerns are striking, the case of Yassin Abdullah Kadi draws attention to two points requiring closer scrutiny for scholars of inter-organizational relations (IOR) and world order. First, lists have been frequently used by intergovernmental organizations (IGOs) and states alike as a means in counterterrorism (Goody, 1977). For IGOs, lists are a way of governing their own remit, the IOR and an organization's environment, as lists are increasingly operating globally and across multiple jurisdictions (De Goede and Sullivan, 2016; Barnett and Finnemore, 2004). Lists represent the ways in which the external environment of IGOs is observed and internally processed. While IGOs strive to navigate this environment, they aim to reduce uncertainty by using lists that help to make the environment more predictable by explicitly naming those that are considered a threat. The second point resides in how IGOs make sense of their environment, and thereby, govern and shape this very environment – for their own further decision-making as well as for other state and non-state actors.

Against this background, we aim here to recognize how the UN and EU use terrorist watch lists to create and shape a common understanding of their environment and, thereby, making it governable. Both the UN and the EU use lists to organize their environment while acting in the same organizational field of counterterrorism governance (DiMaggio and Powell, 1983). Yet, two things are puzzling here. First, listings at the UN-level began as a reaction to the terrorist bombings on US embassies in Nairobi and Dar es Salaam in August 1998 and have been addressed by UNSC Resolutions 1267 (1999) and 1333 (2000). In 2001, the EU considered itself bound by Resolution 1333 and integrated the UN list into its Common Position 2001/930/CFSP. However, two lawsuits, known as Kadi I (2008) and Kadi II (2010) by the European Court of Justice (ECJ), overturned Kadi's listing as a terrorist,[1] and, thereby, the ECJ confirmed that the EU must at least provide the UN's justification for placing individuals on a terror list. Now, how can we grasp the UN-EU interaction, with the EU following the lead of the UN by incorporating the UN list and the UN later adapting its listing processes considering human rights concerns raised at the level of the EU? One needs to keep in mind that the EU is not a member of the UN (although it enjoys a special observer status) and thus was not required to adopt the UN list in the first place. Second, how are the UN and EU lists producing fragmented and diffuse (juridical) inter-organizational connections, yet, thereby shaping and governing these very connections and reducing uncertainty in their environment?

Exploring the governance effects of the counterterrorism lists, that is, the human rights effects exemplified by the Kadi case, gives way to our theoretical aims and arguments. First, we argue that the concepts of organizational fields and isomorphism – as advocated in sociological neo-institutionalism – explain why the UN and EU have followed each other's lead, adopting and adapting lists at different points in time. Second, we bring forward the argument that IGOs attempt to govern through discursive closure, a concept put forward from post-structuralist discourse theory. Lists are manifest, visible attempts of closure because they are ways to reduce uncertainty. Creating lists is a procedure that is institutionalized in the UN and EU and part of their working routines. By drawing up lists, by inscribing on them new persons, groups, substances and so on, IGOs aim for discursive closure. Looking into the listing processes, we argue, allows us to get hold of the specific modes of governance, of ordering organizational environments and of relations between IGOs.

The argument is organized in four steps. First, by outlining the state of the art on EU and UN counterterrorism listings we lay out the empirical background on how the EU has integrated the UN counterterrorism lists into its quiver of counterterrorism measures. Based on this step, we then introduce our theoretical combination as a different way to think about IGOs in international relations (IR). This section outlines the central aspects of a framework combining sociological neo-institutionalism and discourse theory – to study IGOs and IOR. Afterwards, we discuss our cases and the empirical data we are analysing. Finally, we go back to the UN-EU cooperation on the terrorist watch lists to explore how this theoretical approach can enrich our understanding on governance effects in terms of IOR and organizational environment.

State of the art: counterterrorism listing in the UN and EU

We aim to contribute to two strands of research closely connected with our empirical case. The first is related to the back-and-forth between the EU and UN. Predominantly, this literature evolves in the field of IR and international law. IR scholars concentrate on targeted sanctions and counterterrorism financing (see also Biersteker and Eckert, 2007; Giumelli, 2011). They criticize the EU and UN measures on different grounds, resonating with a more general criticism of EU counterterrorism policies (Argomaniz, 2009; Bures, 2011; Kaunert, 2010; Mahncke and Monar, 2006; Spence, 2007) and its efficacy, that is, whether EU and UN financial counterterrorism sanctions are functioning at all (Eckert and Biersteker, 2010; Bures, 2010, 2011; Eckes, 2009; Portela, 2009–2010). Jacobson (2007), for instance, argued that the EU's targeting of persons and entities associated with Al-Qaeda and the Taliban, and designated by the UN, was efficient, whereas targeting persons and groups outside the UN remit was largely inefficient. However, as Bures (2011) has outlined, due to a lack of publicly available official data, it remains difficult to judge the overall efficiency. Yet, the main criticism has been directed towards the negative impact on the human rights and civil liberties of the listed individuals (Almqvist, 2008; Biersteker, 2009–2010; Draghici, 2009; Eeckhout, 2007; Guild, 2008; Heupel, 2009; Vlcek, 2009; van den Herik and Schrijver, 2008). This criticism has been voiced predominantly by legal scholars interested in the conflicts between IGOs (above all the UN and EU) generated through listing procedures (De Búrca, 2010; Isiksel, 2012).

The impact of the political process has received less attention, but studies dealing with the impact are highly beneficial to our aim of conceptualizing the UN-EU interaction. Research on the political side argues that the reasons for the listing reforms reside in court proceedings and judgments (Heupel, 2009, 2012), the development of a broader security culture (De Goede, 2012) or normative processes. Regarding the UNSC, it is claimed that normative processes like shaming or learning explain the reforms, with the UNSC being exposed to and responding to pressure from a few different actors (Heupel, 2013). Regarding the EU, the literature draws a broader picture by referring to a normative commitment of the EU to 'UN-centred effective multilateralism' (Léonard and Kaunert, 2012: 473), as the EU prefers a multilateral line in international security issues – even if lists and sanctions lead to human-rights concerns. The emphasis on the constitutional nature in the Kadi rulings highlights the EU's normative commitment, since the rulings emphasized the distinctiveness of the EU's legal order from the UN and strengthened the EU's image of itself as a normative power with a clear global role (De Búrca, 2010).

The second strand of research scrutinizes security lists, leaving aside the regime they are embedded in. While much of this research is positivist or normative, conceptualizing lists as mere 'information repositories' having 'no effects on the world themselves' (Bernstein, 2013: 464), several scholars adopted a critical perspective when analysing the lists (De Goede and Sullivan, 2016). By conceptualizing lists as devices – as has been done in the field of critical security studies (Amicelle et al, 2015; De Goede et al, 2016; Guild, 2008), research focuses on how security lists are themselves productive in shaping and governing the environment as well as inter-organizational relations of IGOs. Lists are '"inscription devices" that *produce* specific material, political and legal effects' (De Goede and Sullivan, 2016: 70, italic in original). Such conceptualization of lists as devices allows analysing the productive capacities of lists (Law and Ruppert, 2013).

As will be explained later, understanding lists as devices is very important to our endeavour to analyse how lists can be considered as attempts at closure and therefore an IGO's way to govern and shape its environment to reduce uncertainty. Framing lists as devices thus emphasized their ability to provide for order. 'Lists promise order by providing concrete inventories of items in a given category, and they flatten complexity by drawing disparate items into abstract, commensurate relation' (De Goede and Sullivan, 2016: 70).

Sociological neo-institutionalism and post-structuralist discourse theory: IGOs, lists and discursive closure

To explain how IGOs use lists (Barnett and Finnemore, 2004) as a way of governing their environment, we need to conceptualize how IGOs are embedded in their (wider) environment, how they make sense of it and how they create a field of the sayable by cross-referencing other IGOs (and thereby aiming to gain legitimacy for their actions). To this end, we combine two theoretical strands: sociological neo-institutionalism and post-structuralist discourse theory. The former allows us to conceptualize how IGOs are embedded in and interacting with their environment, while the latter sheds light on how lists embody a specific way of governing and reducing uncertainty.

Sociological neo-institutionalism can be divided into two dominant strands: organizational studies and world society studies. While the former concentrates on the behaviour in and of organizations embedded in their societal environment, the latter is concerned with exploring the impact of international trends – for example norms promoted by IGOs – on the national and sub-national level. In particular, the latter strand has been used in IR social constructivism, for example Finnemore (1996). We concentrate on sociological neo-institutionalism as an organizational theory that emphasizes the divide between organizations and environments. Contrary to rationalist models, sociological neo-institutionalism argues that organizations are not sheer rational actors, and their actions and decisions are rather shaped by their social environment consisting of institutions understood as socially accepted, taken-for-granted ideas, norms, values and assumptions (DiMaggio and Powell, 1991). They are important and effective not because they are consciously reflected in actions and decisions but because they are accepted without questioning. Since organizations aim to survive in their environment and avoid any action or decision that threatens their existence, they adjust to their environment. Organizations therefore reflect elements of the institutional environment in their organizational aims, structures and means (Meyer and Rowan, 1977). They can only exist and last if they are reflected in the behaviour of organizations. They cannot be thought of in isolation from organizations. In this context, organizations often must deal with organizational fields in which they are interwoven (Aldrich, 1979). According to DiMaggio and Powell (1983: 147–48) an organizational field is constituted by 'those organizations that, in the aggregate, constitute a recognized area of institutional life', such as organizations producing similar services or products, product consumers, regulatory agencies and others.

In this regard, the UN and the EU can be seen as populating the same organizational field (DiMaggio and Powell, 1983) of counterterrorism governance, using and applying lists as a means to organize their environment. The concept of organizational fields makes it possible to relate single organizations and to focus on a structure in which organizations are embedded. Accordingly, sociological neo-institutionalism refers neither to individual organizations nor to society as a whole, but to groups of organizations that perceive one another as integrated into a shared organizational field. Thus, actions of organizations in this field are closely regarded by other organizations within the same field.

Another characteristic of organizational fields is the homogeneity of their organizations, that is, the alignment of organizational structures, processes, cultures and outcomes (DiMaggio and Powell, 1983). The structural similarity among organizations in a field is a consequence of the institutions that affect the adaptation of organizations to an organizational field. This structural similarity between organizations in a field is defined as isomorphism. Sociological neo-institutionalism distinguishes between three forms of isomorphism: first, coercive isomorphism describes an isomorphism caused by coercion resulting from the pressure of other organizations or the organizational field; second, mimetic isomorphism implies that organizations align their structures and formal processes according to dominant organizations in their field in order to be recognized as part of the organizational field; third, normative isomorphism is the collective effort of a group to define the conditions and methods of its work in order to control the 'production of producers' (Larson, 1977: 49) as well as to expand a community mindset and the justification of professional autonomy (DiMaggio and Powell, 1983).

Sociological neo-institutionalism allows us to conceptualize how IGOs are embedded in and interacting with their social environment, isomorphism – in particular mimetic and normative isomorphism – gives us an idea which processes are at play with regard to the evolution and development of the UN and EU counterterrorism lists since the end of the 1990s. Organizational fields and isomorphism explain why the UN and EU have followed each other's lead, adopting and adapting lists at different points in time. However, we still need to address how far these processes of development and mimicry, of adaptation and adjustment, between the UN and EU are processes of governing and what effects they have. Lists tie things together as they can be conceptualized as an institution and institutionalized behaviour respectively, are a taken-for-granted routine in organizations to structure the perceptions of their environment and are the devices through which IGOs govern their social environment to reduce uncertainty, namely via discursive closure, by, inter alia, excluding who belongs and who does not. In our case, lists help to organize the environment along such a binary differentiation of being either terrorist or non-terrorist. Since both organizations use lists as means and refer to each other's lists, the institution of lists and listing has been mutually reinforced.

Regarding lists as institutions, as taken-for-granted elements of and in the communication between IGOs, is the theoretical point of intersection between sociological neo-institutionalism and post-structuralist discourse theory. While the former emphasizes the importance of institutionalized elements in the organizational environment but leaves open how certain elements are institutionalized, post-structuralist discourse theory can gauge this institutionalization by understanding institutions as sedimented discourses. Sedimented discourses lose their fluidity because they are hedged in how to talk and think about issues. By crafting and using lists, IGOs aim to shape the discourse in terms of how and what the discourse is about. The 'how' refers to the way IGOs respond to the risk of identifying terrorism, that is, by crafting lists that entail those individuals and organizations supposedly having terrorist affiliations. The 'what' describes the entities and their characteristics that are listed. Thus, lists are the 'manifest', the visualized attempts at discursive closure because closure is a way to reduce uncertainty. Looking into the listing processes, we argue, allows us to get hold of the specific modes of governance, of ordering organizational environments and relations between IGOs. Before we do that, we need to briefly explain what discursive closure is, its relationship to IGOs and in how far lists as devices nicely team up with discourse theory in its post-structuralist variant.

Drawing on post-structuralist discourse theory, and on the writings of Ernesto Laclau and Chantal Mouffe, we conceptualize discourse as a 'structured totality' (Laclau and Mouffe, 2001: 105), a system of meaningful practices that relates differences to establish their meaning. These practices are routinized forms of human and societal reproduction, which are material and articulatory at the same time, since 'human beings constantly engage in the process of linking together different elements of their social lives in these continuous and projective sequences of human action' (Glynos and Howarth, 2007: 104). Among the different types of practice, we are interested in political, and more precisely hegemonic, practices. A practice can be called political when it seeks 'to generate, maintain, contain or resolve the public contestation of social norms' (Glynos and Howarth, 2007: 121). A practice can be called hegemonic in the extent to which it articulates a demand with universal dimension, since hegemony is 'the expansion of a discourse, or set of discourses, into a dominant horizon of social orientation and action by means of articulating unfixed elements into partially fixed moments in a context crisscrossed by antagonistic forces' (Torfing, 1999: 101). The dominant horizon established by hegemonies represents a specific goal, a collective demand claiming universal validity – and it is the hegemony representing itself as the single way to achieve this horizon, to reach the goal, the 'land of idle happiness' (Torfing, 2005: 24).

To be able to make representation in this way, hegemonies attempt to close a discourse to attain a fully sutured space of representation, and it is within this space that hegemonies promise to achieve the fulfilment of the demands. To this end, hegemonic practices organize the discursive space by drawing boundaries. To give an example: in her research on the South African apartheid discourse, Norval (1996) focuses on how and under what conditions the apartheid project as a project with a particular mode of social division was able to hegemonize the field of discursivity in South Africa from the 1920s onwards. Norval shows how the apartheid discourse and its institutions were the means to establish an Afrikaner identity, the dominant horizon, the goal to be achieved by overcoming those denying and aiming at preventing the establishment of the identity. Thus, forging a unity of Afrikaner was realized by reference to a series of others (predominantly Black peoples but also British imperialists) deemed to be in the way of this unity and resistant to the demand by Afrikaners to achieve their fully sutured identity, a universal Afrikaner identity.

By such hegemonic practices, IGOs attempt to close the discursive 'field of the sayable', of what can be said or not. Now, how can one perceive the delisting practice, that is, the practice both organizations have been forced to adopt when faced with human-rights concerns? Is it a way to open again the 'field of the sayable', producing uncertainty? While the listing practice is a way to reduce uncertainty by singling out terrorists, the delisting process is by no means a way to provoke uncertainty. Rather, it is stabilizing the current order: delisted persons and entities are considered 'unthreatening' or even 'safe', since they have been approved by the ombudsperson (to be discussed later) in a bureaucratic procedure. Thus, instead of uncertainty creeping back by delisting, the approval of the ombudsperson to delist a person or entity produces even greater certainty – anyone who has undergone the delisting process successfully is beyond doubt. As such, the delisting process is stabilizing the current order. Moreover – though counter-intuitively – the process stabilizes the 'field of the sayable' in a normative way, as the ability to adapt to human-rights concerns shows the viability of the institutions. Herewith the practice of listing becomes further institutionalized, since not the lists or the listing are questioned, but specific individuals and organizations are struck from the list. The processes of listing and delisting become taken for granted as a practice to organize the environment and reduce uncertainty.

Methodological remarks

To scrutinize inter-organizational interaction in the field of security, we have selected the UN and the EU, as well as their lists, as ideal cases in point for the two organizations' counterterrorism measures. These measures have been chosen for two reasons. First, fighting terrorism is 'a top priority for the EU and its member states' (EU, 2022) and 'a vital topic' for the UN (UN Office of Counter-Terrorism, nd). Second, the creation of lists of organizations and persons who are suspected of having links with international terrorism are one of the key measures in the fight against terrorism for both the EU and the UN. For the UN, the lists are an integral part of the Security Council's strategy to fight terrorism (UNSC 1267 Committee, nd). Therefore, the UN emphasizes the importance to target sanctions, moving away from comprehensive to much more tailored sanctions: 'Since 2004, all new sanctions regimes have been targeted, meaning that they are intended to have limited, strategic focus on certain individuals, entities, groups or undertakings' (UNSC, nd a: 4).

This approach towards targeting the individual and groups by the UN is very much in line with a precondition of EU counterterrorism measures (lending further credit to focus on the EU-UN interaction): to consider terrorism as being an act of individuals and of non-state actors. Accordingly, measures are needed to target the individual and such groups to produce sufficient effect (EU, 2022). In the view of the EU, to identify those persons and organizations that are suspected of committing terrorist acts or supporting terrorists, lists have been the most proper means. According to the EU Council, it is a priority 'to prevent people turning to terrorism' (EU Council, 2007). The individual is thus at the heart of the EU's counterterrorism policies: protect EU citizens from future terrorist acts, prevent terrorist acts by identifying suspicious individuals before they act, and pursue those individuals who have already committed terrorist acts (EU Council, 2007). In view of this framing, working with lists is a somewhat logical choice for EU counterterrorism policies, as lists clearly single out the targeted individuals and groups (Guild, 2008).[2] Keeping this importance of lists for the EU in mind, we have opted for the interaction of the EU and UN as, for both, the terrorist lists are cornerstones of their respective counterterrorism measures.

As our focus is on exploring the potential of the theoretical combination of sociological neo-institutionalism and discourse theory to analyse IOR, we do not carry out a fully fledged, stand-alone analysis. It would have been ideal to get hold of the various discursive processes within EU and UN, for instance, when it comes to discussions on listing or delisting. Yet, as these processes are not public, as a solution, we applied a summarizing qualitative content analysis of our material consisting of primary documents, such as narrative summaries of the UN or the Official Journal of the EU, and secondary literature. The aim of the analysis is to reduce the material in such a way that the essential content is retained, to create manageable statements through abstraction, which are still a reflection of the basic material (Mayring, 2022). This material allows us to draw conclusions on the way the EU and the UN interact when it comes to the listing and delisting processes to counterterrorism.

Shaping through closure: analysing UN-EU anti-terrorist lists

Listing as part of the counterterrorism measures at the UN was as a reaction to the terrorist bombings on the US embassies in Kenya and Tanzania. As both attacks were attributed to the Al-Qaida network, the UNSC ordered the freezing of Taliban funds, since, with Resolution 1267, the UNSC attempted to coerce the Taliban regime to extradite Osama bin Laden and to ensure that the Afghan territory was no longer 'a safe haven' for terrorists. However, the Taliban regime did not respond to the resolution and, in December 2000, the UNSC adopted Resolution 1333, which meant to tighten the measures of 1999 by specifically ordering the additional freezing of all funds and financial assets of bin Laden and of individuals and entities associated with him, including those in the Al-Qaida organization. Furthermore, the 1267 Committee (created by Resolution 1267) was given the task of drawing up a list of those persons and entities and to update this list regularly. As the sanctions of the committee are binding under international law, member states are obliged to freeze all accounts and assets of the listed individuals and bar them from leaving the country (Stoll et al, 2004).

Since then, several changes have been made. In 2006, the UN established a 'focal point for de-listing'; in 2009, the UN introduced the position of an ombudsperson – both meant to tackle the many human-rights issues produced by the listing and delisting procedures. Since 2009, the UN 1267 Sanctions Committee has released a 'Narrative Summary of Reasons for Listing' (De Goede and Sullivan, 2016: 77) concerning individuals included on the Al-Qaida targeted sanctions list, which describes in more detail why a person or entity is listed (UNSC, nd c).

With the adoption of Resolutions 1988 and 1989 in 2011, the UNSC split the list of individuals and entities subject to the measures. The committee was henceforth known as the 'Al-Qaida Sanctions Committee', mandated to oversee implementation of the measures against individuals and entities associated with Al-Qaida. A separate committee was established due to resolution 1988 (2011) to oversee the implementation of measures against individuals and entities associated with the Taliban in Afghanistan. After the advent of Islamic State in Iraq and the Levant (ISIL), Resolution 2253 (2015) expanded the listing criteria to include individuals and entities supporting ISIL; a measure supplemented by Resolution 2368 (2017) that reaffirmed the assets freeze, travel ban and arms embargo affecting all individuals and entities on the ISIL and Al-Qaida sanctions list. The resolution also extended the mandates of the monitoring team and the office of the ombudsperson to December 2021 and added eight names to the ISIL and Al-Qaida sanctions list (UNSC 1267 Committee, nd). Today, there are 255 individuals and 88 organizations designated under the ISIL (Da'esh) and Al-Qaida sanctions regime, and 135 individuals and 5 entities associated with the Taliban are designated under the 1988 sanctions regime (UNSC, nd a).

The EU considered itself bound to carry out UNSC Resolution 1333 (2000) and said so in a Common Position of 2001 (2001/931/CFSP). The EU list includes not only the UN Sanctions Committee list, as other persons and entities have been added whom the EU member states proposed.[3] At the UN, the persons and entities on the EU terrorist list are subject to the freezing of their funds and other financial assets and EU operators are prohibited from making funds and economic resources available to the listed persons and groups. The EU terrorist list is reviewed at regular intervals, at least once every six months. All in all, a total of 57 individuals and 47 entities have been added with 26 individuals and 31 entities referred to as EU 'external terrorists' (EU, 2009, 2022). Since 2016, the EU also has its own sanction regime, which allows it to apply sanctions autonomously against ISIL and Al-Qaida and against persons and entities associated with or supporting them. This is separate from the regime in which the EU implements UNSC Resolution 1989 (2011) on the freezing of funds of persons and entities associated with Osama bin Laden, the Al-Qaida network and the Taliban (including ISIL). The latest biannual review has resulted in an EU list containing 31 persons and 16 entities and they are referred to as 'internal terrorists'. They are 'subject only to enhanced measures related to police and judicial cooperation in criminal matters' (EU, 2021, 2022).

Isomorphism and mutual adjustments

From an EU perspective, the inter-organizational cooperation with the UN in countering international terrorism was driven by the EU's compliance with the UN list by stating in the Common Position that it would fully endorse the UN list. So, the EU underpinned the UN's authority and its capacity of listing. Simultaneously, the EU entered the organizational field of countering international terrorism by applying the institutionalized practice of listing (and shortly thereafter a few other measures that have been agreed upon; see EUR-Lex, 2002) as a form of mimetic isomorphism (DiMaggio and Powell, 1983). The EU changed from being merely a part of the institutional environment of the UN in the global fight against terrorism to a partner. In this sense, most visibly, the EU has not just responded to its environment of other organizations, it has rather shaped the environment both for European countries and non-state organizations in the EU. The EU endorsement of the UN list reflects how an institutional environment is reproduced within different organizations: the EU reproduced and profited from the UN's acquired knowledge on terrorism and introduced its own, independent listing as a process of mimetic isomorphism. Indeed, by incorporating the UN list, the EU redrew the borders between itself and its environment. The list, and the general idea of listing, as a means in fighting terrorism is now part of the EU and no longer part of the environment only. Through this process of discursive closure (of including the list) the identity of the EU was preserved. And at least for some time, the EU was able to legitimize the incorporation by referring to IOR with the UN and the UN's overall role as a provider of global legitimacy. During that time, the relationship between the UN and the EU becomes almost symbiotic since both organizations share the same perception of the terrorist-related environment and how to organize it by using lists, and the relationship between the UN and EU can best be characterized as mimetic isomorphism. While the UN was in the driver's seat, the EU sat comfortably in the back.

Regarding isomorphisms, the criteria for listing are particularly instructive. The way the UN list has been established and its consequences for the targeted individuals have led to several controversies. Most importantly, the procedure raised concerns of human-rights compliance since the criteria on which the selection of organizations and individuals are based have not been made public. The Security Council resolutions do not contain any substantive criteria to which the 1267 Committee can refer in its decisions on whom to include on the list. Furthermore, when updating the listing based on the information provided by member states and/or regional organizations such as the EU, the committee meets behind closed doors (Vennemann, 2004). Over the years, this secrecy has faced fierce opposition from different NGOs and other IGOs, as those persons and organizations concerned by the listing lack any protection of their elementary rights (see, above all, Statewatch, 2009).

As a reaction, paragraph 2 ofUN Resolution 2368 (2017) sets out the general criterion for listing a person or an organization that show 'acts or activities indicating association with ISIL or Al-Qaida', including 'participating in the financing, planning, facilitating, preparing, or perpetrating of acts or activities by or in support of Al-Qaida, ISIL or affiliates; supplying, selling or transferring arms and related materiel to them; and recruiting for them or otherwise supporting them' (UNSC, nd a). Persons, groups and entities identified by the UNSC as being related to terrorism and against whom it has ordered sanctions may also be included in the list. The reaction of the UN can be explained as a compliant response to an institutionalized external expectation that it must meet human-rights standards when putting people on lists. It has to disclose its information in every case and explain on what legal grounds individuals are listed.

These criteria are referred to in the narrative summaries. Looking into a randomly selected one, the summaries first introduce the individual – here, purely as an example, Muthanna Harith al-Dari – by explaining the reasons for listing the person. The UNSC continues with additional information on the individual, elaborating more closely on the activities leading to the listing. In the case of al-Dari it is explained that he:

> has provided financial support and other services to or in support of Al-Qaida in Iraq (AQI) (QDe.115). In one instance, in October 2008, Al-Dari provided $1 million to an AQI member who recruited Iraqis in Syria and Al-Anbar province, Iraq. Al-Dari told the AQI member

> to tell new AQI recruits that they would be paid up to $10,000 upon completion of their training. (UNSC, nd b)

The EU emphasizes that listings are 'drawn up from precise information indicating that a decision has been taken by a judicial or equivalent competent authority in respect of the person, group or entity concerned' (EU, 2022). Criteria are, first, the 'initiation of investigations or prosecution for a terrorist act or an attempt to carry out or facilitate such an act' and, second, the 'condemnation for any of those actions' (EU, 2022). Those entities and persons already on the UN list may be included, the Common Position states (EU, 2001). As in the case of the UN, proposals to list a person or entity can come from member states or the EU High Representative. The proposal needs to include the reasons for listing, the decision by a competent judicial national authority in line with the relevant national legal framework (EU, 2016). While less refined on the criteria than the UN, the EU makes a stronger effort to outline the judicial basis for the listings and describes the working procedure in detail in a separate document (EU, 2016). Contrary, the UN process is quite sparingly described: the ISIL and Al-Qaida Sanctions Committee must reach a consensual decision within ten days for listing and delisting proposals, though the latter are more detailed (to be discussed later).

Overall, the reaction of the UN to integrate a possibility for requesting removal from the list by creating the post of the ombudsperson clearly reflects a reaction to the institutional environment within which the respect of human rights and civil liberties has decreased considering the demands of (national) security, but which are still viable. One can plausibly accord the EU a heightened role in this process of increasing the legitimacy of the UN since the EU faced the same criticism.

Shaping through discursive closure

These processes of development, mimicry, adaptation and adjustment between the UN and the EU are processes of governing, within which lists are a crucial device to reduce uncertainty. They do so via discursive closure. Lists emerge as an institution and a way to organize the environment along a binary differentiation. The perception of both organizations that the field of counterterrorism is divided strictly into either being a terrorist or not can be explained by normative isomorphism. Furthermore, lists as institutions have some appeal with organizations in the environment of the EU and UN since they can refer to the taken-for-granted script when freezing assets or not allowing aircraft boarding, for example. At the same time, those organizations simply applying the list are not accountable for listing people; they simply refer to the authority of the UN and EU. In this respect, the EU's distinction between external and internal terrorists (mentioned earlier) is highly instructive as it clearly highlights a drawing of boundaries. Alternative ways to lists are ignored. They cannot and will not be heard in the discourse on counterterrorist measures since lists shape the discourse. Even the delisting process reinforces the existence of lists and underpins the legitimacy of lists.

The UN has successively adopted a delisting procedure as a reaction to the human-rights concerns levelled at the UN. The 1267 Committee neither hears the cases of the persons and entities concerned nor informs them of the fact that their inclusion on the list is being discussed or has been decided upon. Once on the list, there is no judicial procedure for requesting a review of the decision, for an individual to argue, for example, that they do not have links with the targeted groups or that they have been put on the list as a result of a mix-up (Vennemann, 2004). It was only in November 2002 that a possibility to reach a delisting was introduced in reaction to international criticism. A person concerned can hand in a petition at their government of residence and/or citizenship, which will eventually bring a delisting request to the attention of the Committee. The latter decides by consensus, and, if a consensual decision is impossible, the matter may be submitted to the Security Council. These peculiarities of the listing procedure can hardly be regarded as conforming to human rights (Foot, 2007).

Meanwhile (and due to many objections), the procedure is subject to regular examination and deepened monitoring by a group of experts who are advised to consider the humanitarian and personal effects of the measure as well as to allow for exceptional cases. In December 2009, the UNSC adopted Resolution 1904 to:

> fine-tune its decade-old sanctions regime imposed on Al-Qaida, Usama bin Laden and the Taliban, including through the establishment of an ombudsperson who could mediate requests from individuals, organizations and companies to be taken off the sanctions list [... and the] Council authorized the establishment of an Office of the Ombudsperson for an initial period of 18 months to assist the Sanctions Committee in its consideration of delisting requests. (UNSC, 2009)

From now on, persons and organizations listed have the possibility to file a request to be removed from the sanctions list, which the ombudsperson will have to review. Furthermore, states are requested to inform concerned individuals and organizations of discussions about their inclusion on the list and any later listing (Stoll et al, 2004; see also UNSC, 2009).

Again, the procedure of delisting and the establishment of an ombudsperson's office can be regarded as a response to institutionalized human-rights norms that IGOs have to meet otherwise they and their existence might be called into question. The delisting policy furthermore shows that the relationship between the EU and the UN is more than cooperative. They do not just exchange information but rather act in symbiosis when it comes to listing and delisting policies. The narrative summaries mentioned earlier emerged as a direct response to EU legal challenges against this list and the absence of accusatory information being made available to those targeted. Pressed to render the procedure more transparent, but reluctant to divulge classified intelligence, the genre of narrative summaries was invented and rendered public for each list entry (De Goede and Sullivan, 2016). The respective UN document (UNSC, nd a) explains that listed persons and groups may address the ombudsperson to receive a delisting. As of January 2022, 88 cases have been reviewed by the ombudsperson: 60 individuals and 29 entities have been removed, 23 delisting requests have been refused. While there is no information on how many persons and groups have been delisted in the EU, there is information provided on how to achieve a delisting process (EU, 2022).[4]

Results

Our analysis shows that IGOs produce institutionalized standards of appropriate behaviour, providing orientation for action for themselves, their members and – due to the claim for universality inherent to any hegemonic practice – those not part of the institution. Accordingly, IGOs and the order they aim to maintain represent the constant attempt to exclude specific options and elements from an organizational field and thereby, to close this field. While sociological neo-institutionalism helps us to understand how IGOs are embedded in their environment and create lists as institutionalized elements of how to observe and make sense of the environment, post-structuralist discourse theory sheds some light on both how lists emerge as institutions and how the UN and EU refer to each other's lists. In a way, post-structuralist discourse theory provides the fine tuning for IGOs' environmental embeddedness. Lists as means of organizing are such hegemonic practices since they attempt at discursive closure in the organizational field of counterterrorism.

We have shown that listing and delisting are hegemonic practices as they draw lines between those individuals and organizations considered to be terrorist in nature and those who are not. It is via the performative act of listing that individuals and organizations come into being as dangerous, terrorist 'objects'. The lists bring to light the know-how that people have acquired about the respective listed individuals and organizations. As such, lists are a strategy of using administrative and scientific knowledge meant to arrange the resources of states, security agency and civil society into a governing mode that rests on discursive closure – of reducing uncertainty by listing terrorist individuals and organizations. Via the bureaucratic procedure on delisting, the EU and UN turn individuals and groups from threating to unthreatening, and, thereby, stabilizing the current order. Delisting is as a practice to underpin the legitimacy of lists since people can be removed from that list. By listing and delisting, discursive closure is achieved – one way or the other, institutions do shape their environment via such hegemonic practices.

Both IGOs have subsequently changed their policies within the organizational field of counterterrorism and shaped their environment via discursive closure, with lists being a device of choice. The practice of listing and delisting tells us something about how both organizations order the world. First, both perceive the world as being binary, differentiated on whether somebody is a terrorist or not. This differentiation is of crucial importance, since lists are not just for internal purposes but have consequences for people. Additionally, lists create a certain understanding of the environment. Lists exhibit a perception of the world for other non-state organizations that apply the terrorist watch lists for decision-making concerning people and organizations on the list. Second, the organizations coordinate and align themselves with each other. The relations between the UN and EU are more than just cooperation; both are aiming for symbiotic co-existence. In the field of counterterrorism, the organizations are constantly observing each other and shaping the field by listing and delisting.

In this regard, it is quite astonishing that, even though the environment of each organization is by definition different, both organizations differentiate and thereby shape their environments in a similar way by applying the same devices. Thereby, both organizations mutually reinforce each other and increase the establishment of lists to organize the(ir) world.

Conclusions and outlook

This chapter has analysed the relations between the UN and EU in the field of counterterrorism. We combined two approaches: sociological neo-institutionalism and post-structuralist discourse theory. Both approaches have a similar understanding of institutions as being taken for granted or, in the terminology of post-structuralist discourse theory, sedimented discourses. In bringing together these theoretical approaches, we can combine an internal with an external perspective on IGOs. The internal perspective can be theoretically conceived with the help of post-structuralist discourse theory that explains how IGOs shape their environment by attempting to close the discursive 'field of the sayable'. The external perspective can be grasped with sociological neo-institutionalism that puts emphasis on the relations between an organization and its environment and explains how organizations can internalize environmental expectations by simultaneously buffering organizational routines and procedures from external demands. We have outlined that sociological neo-institutionalism allows us to conceptualize how IGOs are embedded in and interacting with their social environments. Mimetic and normative isomorphism let us gauge conceptually the evolution and development of the UN and EU counterterrorism lists against Al-Qaida, the Taliban and ISIL. Organizational fields and isomorphism explain why the UN and EU have followed each other's lead, adopting and adapting lists at different points in time. Moreover, the UN and EU are acting in symbiosis with as little as possible divergence on counterterrorism.

Taking our theoretical reflections to the empirical context, we used this theoretical framework to illustrate the inter-organizational relations between the UN and EU concerning the terrorist watch list. Although concentrating on two IGOs (UN and EU), we were able to scrutinize more generally their embeddedness in and interaction with their environments. It has been shown how the organizations cooperated with each other on implementing the terrorist watch list and to what extent both organizations responded to environmental objections concerning the removal of listed persons.

Along with these case-specific goals, the chapter contributes theoretically to the field of IOR by exploring the viability of combining sociological neo-institutionalism and post-structuralist discourse theory for further research as they can enrich each other's weak spots. Sociological neo-institutionalism explains how organizations are embedded in a social environment and respond to institutionalized external expectations, while post-structuralist discourse theory helps us to explicate how institutionalization takes place. We have shown how the two organizations create and close a 'field of the sayable' by using the terrorist watch lists. These lists are institutionalized devices to organize the environment for both organizations and beyond, since other organizations – be it airlines, financial institutions and the like – refer to the lists and the environmental construction they entail to justify their decisions. Thereby, listing and delisting are practices of organizing world politics and contributions to world order. Once lists are established as an institutionalized practice of IGOs, it is hard to withdraw them since they are devices to organize the world. Therefore, 'order your environment by making a list of terrorists' could be seen as an imperative strategy for IGOs to reduce uncertainty as it establishes a binary structure of the environment between those who are listed and the rest.

Further research could analyse other aspects of the counterterrorism field to grasp the overall role of lists within the counterterrorism measures of the UN and EU and how other actors in the environments of both IGOs apply those lists. Another avenue for further research is to map the organizational field of counterterrorism to see whether applying the UN/EU lists by other IGOs in that field is a characteristic of the field and whether those IGOs apply the same institutionalized practice of listing and delisting. Beside our empirical case, the fruitful combination of sociological neo-institutionalism and discourse theory could be used to investigate other instances of IOR. Relations between IGOs such as the World Bank and International Monetary Fund (IMF) on the one hand and regional or even national development organizations on the other could be a promising case. It could be analysed whether and how the World Bank and the IMF create an organizational field of economic cooperation and development assistance and how they simultaneously close the discourse of the sayable for regional and national development banks.

Notes

1. Kadi was removed from the EU (2008 and 2010), the UN (2012) and later the US list (2014). He learnt of the reasons for him being listed only after the EU Commission had sent him the justification that the UN had furnished the EU with beforehand.
2. Irrespective of well-known problems like confusing names or incorrect spellings.
3. The Council is empowered to establish an EU list and impose related restrictive measures under Council common position 2001/931/CFSP and Council regulation (EC) 2580/2001.
4. The document states that: 'Persons, groups, and entities included in the list can:
   - request the Council to reconsider the case, on the basis of supporting documentation;
   - challenge the decision of the national competent authority according to national procedures;
   - if subject to restrictive measures under Council regulation 2580/2001, challenge the Council's decision before the General Court.'

References

Aldrich, H.E. (1979) *Organizations and Environments*, Englewood Cliffs: Prentice-Hall.

Almqvist, J. (2008) 'A human rights critique of European judicial review: counter-terrorism sanctions', *International and Comparative Law Quarterly*, 57(2): 303–31.

Amicelle, A., Aradau, C. and Jeandesboz, J. (2015) 'Questioning security devices: performativity, resistance, politics', *Security Dialogue*, 46(4): 293–306.

Argomaniz, J. (2009) 'Post-9/11 institutionalisation of European Union counter-terrorism: emergence, acceleration and inertia', *European Security*, 18(2): 151–72.

Barnett, M. and Finnemore, M. (2004) *Rules for the World: International Organizations in Global Politics*, Ithaca: Cornell University Press.

Bernstein, A. (2013) 'The hidden costs of terrorist watch lists', *Buffalo Law Review*, 61(3): 461–535.

Biersteker, T.J. (2009–2010) 'Targeted sanctions and individual human rights', *International Journal*, 65(1): 99–117.

Biersteker, T.J. and Eckert, S.E. (eds) (2007) *Countering the Financing of Terrorism*, London: Routledge.

Bures, O. (2011) *EU Counterterrorism Policy: A Paper Tiger?*, London: Routledge.

Bures, O. (2010) 'EU's fight against terrorist finances: Internal shortcomings and unsuitable external models', *Terrorism and Political Violence*, 22(3): 418–37.

De Búrca, G. (2010) 'The European Court of Justice and the international legal order after Kadi', *Harvard International Law Journal*, 51: 1–49.

De Goede, M. (2012) *Speculative Security: The Politics of Pursuing Terrorist Monies*, Minneapolis: University of Minnesota Press.

De Goede, M. and Sullivan, G. (2016) 'The politics of security lists', *Environment and Planning D: Society and Space*, 34(1): 67–88.

De Goede, M., Leander, A. and Sullivan, G. (2016) 'Introduction: The politics of the list', *Environment and Planning D: Society and Space*, 34(1): 3–13.

DiMaggio, P.J. and Powell, W.W. (1991) 'Introduction', in P.J. DiMaggio and W.W. Powell (eds) *The New Institutionalism in Organizational Analysis*, Chicago: University of Chicago Press, pp 1–38.

DiMaggio, P.J. and Powell, W.W. (1983) 'The iron cage revisited: institutional isomorphism and collective rationality in organizational fields', *American Sociological Review*, 48(2): 147–60.

Draghici, C. (2009) 'International organisations and anti-terrorist sanctions: no accountability for human rights violations?', *Critical Studies on Terrorism*, 2(2): 293–312.

Eckert, S.E. and Biersteker, T.J. (2010) '(Mis)Measuring success in countering the financing of terrorism', in: P. Andreas and K.M. Greenhill (eds) *Sex, Drugs, and Body Counts*, Ithaca: Cornell University Press, pp 247–63.

Eckes, C. (2009) *EU Counter-Terrorist Policies and Fundamental Rights*, Oxford: Oxford University Press.

Eeckhout, P. (2007) 'Community terrorism listings, fundamental rights, and UN Security Council resolutions: in search of the right fit', *European Constitutional Law Review*, 3(2): 183–206.

EU (2022) 'The EU's response to terrorism', available from: consilium.europa.eu/en/policies/fight-against-terrorism [accessed 30 March 2023].

EU (2021) Official Journal of the European Union, L, 43/64 (8.2.).

EU (2016) Fight against the financing of terrorism – Establishment of a Council Working Party on restrictive measures to combat terrorism (COMET WP). 14612/1/16 REV 1.

EU (2009) Official Journal of the European Union, L, 151/45 (16.6.).

EU (2001) Official Journal of the European Union, L, 344/94 (28.12).

EU Council (2007) Council factsheet: The European Union and the fight against terrorism, available from: europarl.europa.eu/factsheets/en/sheet/24/the-council-of-the-european-union [accessed 30 March 2023].

EUR-Lex (2002) Council Framework decision of 13 June 2002 on combating terrorism, available from: eur-lex.europa.eu/legal-content/EN/TXT/?uri=CELEX:32002F0475 [accessed 30 March 2023].

Finnemore, M. (1996) *National Interest in International Society*, Ithaca: Cornell University Press.

Foot, R. (2007) 'The United Nations, counter terrorism, and human rights: institutional adaptation and embedded ideas', *Human Rights Quarterly,* 29(2): 489–514.

Fromuth, P. (2009) 'The European Court of Justice Kadi decision and the future of UN counterterrorism sanctions', *American Society for International Law,* 13(20).

Giumelli, F. (2011) *Coercing, Constraining and Signalling: Explaining UN and EU Sanctions after the Cold War,* Colchester: ECPR press.

Glynos, J. and Howarth, D. (2007) *Logics of Critical Explanation in Social and Political Theory*, London: Routledge.

Goody, J. (1977) *The Domestication of the Savage Mind*, Cambridge: Cambridge University Press.

Guild, E. (2008) 'The uses and abuses of counter-terrorism policies in Europe: the case of the "Terrorist Lists"', *Journal of Common Market Studies,* 46(1): 173–93.

Heupel, M. (2013) 'With power comes responsibility: human rights protection in United Nations sanctions policy', *European Journal of International Relations,* 19(4): 773–96.

Heupel, M. (2012) 'Judicial policymaking in the EU courts: safeguarding due process in EU sanctions policy against terror suspects', *European Journal on Criminal Policy and Research,* 18(4): 311–27.

Heupel, M. (2009) 'Multilateral sanctions against terror suspects and the violation of due process standards', *International Affairs,* 85(2): 307–21.

Isiksel, T. (2012) 'On Europe's functional constitutionalism: towards a constitutional theory of specialized international regimes', *Constellations,* 19(1): 102–20.

Jacobson, M. (2007) 'Combating terrorist financing in Europe: Gradual progress', The Washington Institute for Near East Policy, Policy Watch (1213).

Johnson II, R.W. (2001) 'Re: Kadi Abdullah Yassin, 21 December', available from: de.scribd.com/document/18487799/Petition-175 [accessed 30 March 2023].

Kaunert, C. (2010) *European Internal Security: Towards Supranational Governance in the Area of Freedom, Security and Justice?*, Manchester: Manchester University Press.

Koops, J.A. (2012) 'NATO's influence on the evoluation of the European Union as a security actor', in O. Costa and K.E. Jørgensen (eds) *The Influence of International Institutions on the European Union*, Basingstoke: Palgrave Macmillan, pp 155–85.

Laclau, E. and Mouffe, C. (2001) *Hegemony and Socialist Strategy. Towards a Radical Democratic Politics* (2nd edn), London, New York: Verso.

Larson, M.S. (1977) *The Rise of Professionalism: A Sociological Analysis*, Berkeley: University of California Press.

Law, J. and Ruppert, E. (2013) 'The social life of methods: Devices', *Journal of Cultural Economy*, 6(3): 229–40.

Léonard, S. and Kaunert, C. (2012) '"Between a rock and a hard place?": The European Union's financial sanctions against suspected terrorists, multilateralism and human rights', *Cooperation and Conflict*, 47(4): 473–94.

Mahncke, D. and Monar, J. (eds) (2006) *International Terrorism: A European Response to a Global Threat?*, Brussels: Peter Lang.

Manners, I. (2006) 'European Union 'normative power' and the security challenge', *European Security*, 15(4): 405–21.

Mayring, P. (2022) *Qualitative Content Analysis: A Step-by-Step Guide*, London: Sage.

Meyer, J.W. and Rowan, B. (1977) 'Institutionalized organizations: formal structure as myth and ceremony', *American Journal of Sociology*, 83(2): 340–63.

Norval, A. (1996) *Deconstructing Apartheid Discourse*, London: Verso.

Portela, C. (2009–2010) 'National implementation of United Nations sanctions', *International Journal*, 65: 13–30.

Spence, D. (2007) *The European Union and Terrorism*, London: John Harper Publishing.

Statewatch (2009) 2001–2009: Terrorist blacklists: monitoring proscription, designation and asset-freezing, available from: statewatch.org/observatories/2001-2009-terrorist-blacklists-monitoring-proscription-designation-and-asset-freezing [accessed 30 March 2023].

Stoll, P.T., Mißling, S. and Juretko, B. (2004) *Doppelte Sicherheit. Über die zwischenstaatliche Zusammenarbeit im Kampf gegen den internationalen Terrorismus*, Berlin: Heinrich-Böll Stiftung.

Torfing, J. (2005) 'Discourse theory: achievements, arguments, and challenges', in D. Howarth and J. Torfing (eds) *Discourse Theory in European Politics*, Basingstoke: Palgrave Macmillan, pp 1–32.

Torfing, J. (1999) *New Theories of Discourse: Laclau, Mouffe and Zizek*, Oxford: Blackwell.

UNSC (nd a) Fact Sheet Subsidiary Organs, available from: un.org/securitycouncil/sanctions/information [accessed 30 March 2023].

UNSC (nd b) Muthanna Harith Al-Dari, available from: un.org/securitycouncil/sanctions/1267/aq_sanctions_list/summaries/individual/muthanna-harith-al-dari [accessed 30 March 2023].

UNSC (nd c) Narrative summaries of reasons for listing, available from: un.org/securitycouncil/sanctions/narrative-summaries [accessed 30 March 2023].

UNSC (2009) Resolution 1904: Threats to international peace and security caused by terrorist acts, available from: unscr.com/en/resolutions/1904 [accessed 30 March 2023].

UNSC 1267 Committee (nd) Security Council Committee pursuant to resolutions 1267 (1999) 1989 (2011) and 2253 (2015) concerning Islamic State in Iraq and the Levant (Da'esh), Al-Qaida and associated individuals, groups, undertakings and entities, available from: un.org/securitycouncil/sanctions/1267 [accessed 30 March 2023].

UN Office of Counter-Terrorism (nd) 'Countering the financing of terrorism', available from: un.org/counterterrorism/countering-financing-of-terrorism [accessed 30 March 2023].

van den Herik, L. and Schrijver, N.J. (2008) 'Eroding the primacy of the UN system of collective security: the judgment of the European Court of Justice in the cases of Kadi and Al Barakaat', *International Organizations Law Review,* 5(2): 329–38.

Vennemann, N. (2004) 'Country report on the European Union', in C. Walter, S. Vöneky, V. Roben and F. Schorkopf (eds) *Terrorism as a Challenge for National and International Law: Security versus Liberty?*, Berlin: Springer, pp 217–66.

Vlcek, W. (2009) 'Hitting the right target: EU and Security Council pursuit of terrorist financing', *Critical Studies on Terrorism,* 2(2): 275–91.

4

Changing Models of Peacekeeping and the Downsizing of Human-Rights Norms

Anna Geis and Louise Wiuff Moe

Introduction

Military interventions involve a wide array of intervening actors, ranging from international and regional organizations to nation-state actors and violent as well as non-violent non-state actors. Mali is a prominent example of a contemporary intervention site where several military missions and mandates overlap and where a large number of intervening actors have been engaged since 2012. After several *coups d'état* in Mali, the further proliferation of jihadist groups in the Sahel region and the (partial) withdrawal of European troops in 2022, the country is increasingly seen as another potential case of failure of international interventionism, shortly after the disastrous withdrawal of Western troops from Afghanistan in 2021.

This chapter will not deal with the overall question of whether the international interventions in Mali can be assessed as success or failure. Instead, it seeks to highlight a more specific 'dark side' of inter-organizational interventions in Mali during the last decade. The cooperation among international organizations (IOs) such as the United Nations (UN), the European Union (EU), and new regional coalitions of states, such as G5 Sahel Joint Force, has yielded several negative effects on the protection of civilians (PoC). Given that PoC is a core norm of peacekeeping missions, the weakening of the implementation of this norm also impacted negatively on the local perception of the UN Multidimensional Integrated Stabilization Mission (MINUSMA) in Mali.

In the fields of international peace and security governance, policy makers and analysts alike have often treated cooperation among IOs as a desirable policy objective in itself. The burgeoning rhetoric of security partnerships among organizations after the end of the Cold War is an indicator of this optimism. Franke (2017: 19) has noted in a review of theoretical approaches to IOR that 'current research is restricted by the still dominant equation of (inter-organizational) relations with cooperation, coordination, or collaboration. Examinations of competition and conflict already take place but should be strongly encouraged and expanded.'

In the spirit of this suggestion, this chapter seeks to elucidate more problematic and conflictive dimensions of inter-organizational collaboration itself: the weakening of the implementation of a core norm of peacekeeping missions. We draw on international relations (IR) debates on regime complexity and the so-called 'robust turn' of UN peace operations (Hunt, 2017) and explore how emerging forms of stabilization and counterterrorism collaboration between international and African organizations and states interact with regional and global norm dynamics and their implementation in Mali.[1]

While many interventions after 1990 were justified with a human rights and democracy-promotion agenda, a gradual shift from such liberal interventionism has started to happen in the wake of the US-led 'global war on terror' since 2001, with a growing emphasis towards the *stabilization* of regimes (Geis and Wagner, 2021). This shift in interventionist practices that is mainly built on the securitization of (transnational) jihadist groups (Sheikh, 2022) has led to an entanglement of peacekeeping and counterterrorism regimes. Mali constitutes a paradigmatic case of this wider development. Focusing on the UN, the EU and the more recently founded regional African security collaboration G5 Sahel Joint Force (FC-G5S), this chapter examines how such inter-organizational collaboration has resulted in a division of labour for the tasks of mandating, training of security forces and enforcement of military operations and missions. While enhanced collaboration across the issue areas of development, peacebuilding and counterterrorism seem to increase inter-institutional order and convergence, it also involves a weakening of the implementation of human rights norms and specifically, the protection of civilians.

The following (second) section of this chapter outlines the state of the art on IOR in African security governance. The third section introduces the conceptual framework, combining selected insights from regime complexity and norms research. In the fourth section, the methodology of the underlying research project is briefly explained. The fifth section presents the empirical analysis of the inter-organizational collaboration in Mali. In the concluding section, some broader implications of the gradual shift towards post-9/11 stabilization in intervention politics on the global order are suggested.

State of the art

Contemporary security governance in Africa is shaped by a dense web of interactions between national, (sub-)regional and international actors and organizations. Since the 2000s, the African Union (AU) and sub-regional African organizations have increasingly been interacting with the UN and the EU. The UN is currently conducting 12 peacekeeping operations, of which six are located on the African continent (Western Sahara, Central African Republic, Mali, Democratic Republic of the Congo, Abyei, South Sudan).[2] A considerable body of literature has emerged on the African Peace and Security Architecture (APSA), evaluating the institutional capacities of APSA and showing how AU peace and security mechanisms are embedded in a broad approach that includes prevention, mediation and other non-military measures of response (for example, Engel and Porto, 2013; Williams, 2014; Döring et al, 2021). Nevertheless, peace operations form a core part of APSA, and their impediments and so-far mixed records have been highlighted. The literature also addresses the interaction between the AU, regional and sub-regional organizations (for example, Murithi, 2008; Aning and Salihu, 2011; Williams and Boutellis, 2014; Gelot, 2015), as well as the agency of African organizations in the field of security and the contribution to international norm development (for example, Coleman and Tieku, 2018; Coffie and Tiky, 2021).

Most relevant for this chapter are those studies that apply the concept of regime complexity to the study of security governance in Africa, such as the special issue of African Security (Brosig, 2013). These earlier studies, however, focus on convergence and regime effectiveness, rather than normative effects of inter-organizational collaboration, which is crucial to the analysis of Mali in this chapter. As Brosig (2017) has studied in detail, within the African security complex, the analysis of individual 'lead nations', such as Nigeria, South Africa, France and the UK, is also part of a regime-complexity perspective. In addition, studies of security regime complexity in Africa have uncovered patterns of 'niche selection', whereby organizations within the increasingly crowded field of peacekeeping construct their demarcated functional niches according to their different resources and, on this basis, engage in a differentiated division of labour (Brosig, 2017). Other studies have mapped variances and complementarities between the formal norms, doctrines and legal frameworks of the key organizations and actors involved in governing peace and security in Africa (for example, de Coning, 2017).

Moe and Geis (2020b) have co-edited a special issue of the *Journal of Intervention and Statebuilding* that assembles a number of contributions on the 'messiness' of IOR in African security governance. The special issue brings the analysis of IOs into conversation with critical peace and intervention studies, discussing the 'politics' of military intervention within and around IOs active in African conflict territories. The authors suggest that IOR should not be categorized into simplified binary categories such as 'competitive' (bad relations) and 'cooperative' (good relations) (Clark, 2021: 1133; see also Margulis, 2021: 874). Such relations are far more complex in reality and change over time and in issue area in case of more encompassing IOs. In drawing on the regime-complexity literature, this chapter seeks to further elucidate the complexity of inter-organizational relations in the multi-actor intervention site of Mali and their effects on the implementation of norms. Given that rationalist perspectives dominate in the regime-complexity scholarship on African security governance, we also seek to shift the focus towards the norms that are at risk when these interventionist actors collaborate.

Conceptual framework: regime complexity and its effects on norm dynamics in peacekeeping operations

The numbers of actors, frameworks and doctrines, as well as partnerships and coordination mechanisms, have multiplied in the field of security governance in Africa. This offers a paradigmatic illustration of a global trend of organizational proliferation and growing institutional density (Abbott and Faude, 2022). Interactions, overlaps and legitimation relationships between the UN Security Council (UNSC) and regional organizations are more complex than the institutional hierarchy outlined in the UN charter suggests. One analytical perspective for studying inter-organizational security relations in Africa is provided by the concept of regime complexity (see also Chapter 1). According to Malte Brosig, the interplay of various actors, including the UN, African and sub-regional African organizations and Western collective and nation-state actors, can be considered an emerging African security regime complex, characterized as 'decentered, with multiple overlap in membership and policy, raising concerns over operative and normative interaction between elemental actors. Although a number of joint declarations, memoranda of understanding or partnerships exist, these interinstitutional links are usually only weakly institutionalized and do not proscribe hierarchical relations' (Brosig, 2013: 173).

Brosig's (2017) instructive empirical study of the cooperative peacekeeping regime on the African continent focuses on convergence between participating actors and uses the rationalist concept of dependency theory and resource exchange within a regime complex to analyse the inter-organizational relations and the role of lead nations in peacekeeping missions. The IOs' activities on peacekeeping operations are assessed as partially converging in this regime complex, which is 'structured without clear hierarchies describing processes of alignment and contestation' (Brosig, 2017: 19). The analytical framework of this chapter makes a more selective use of the regime-complexity concept by focusing on the division of labour aspect only. In the case of Mali, however, we propose to see not one large security regime complex at work, but the increasing entanglement of two more specific ones – the international peacekeeping and the counterterrorism regime complexes (to be discussed later). France, as a central lead nation, with a heavy influence on the politics of the participating IOs, is part of the security regime complex in Africa as Brosig (2017) has highlighted. Given the empirical focus of this chapter on the Mali intervention site, France's crucial role in these interventions will be discussed.

In addition, we seek to go beyond the rationalist outlook of regime-complexity scholarship by studying the negative *effects* of a division of labour on norm implementation in the field of peacekeeping. To date, only a few authors have proposed to open up the regime-complexity concept for research perspectives, usually associated with social-constructivist scholarship in IR (Struett et al, 2013; Franke, 2017; Alter, 2022). Since the much-cited definition of international regimes by Stephen Krasner as 'sets of implicit or explicit principles, norms, rules, and decision-making procedures around which actor expectations converge in a given issue-area' (Krasner, 1982: 186), does refer to *norms,* a more explicit research focus on norms in regime-complexity studies seems to be warranted. We will not deal with the question of how peacekeeping or counterterrorism norms have emerged but, instead, we focus on the *effects* of the increasing blurring of peacekeeping and counterterrorism regime complexes on one central norm of peacekeeping; namely, the protection of civilians.

The scholarly literature on regime complexity has grown substantially over the last 15 years (Alter, 2022). Alter and Meunier (2009: 13) define international regime complexity as 'the presence of nested, partially overlapping, and parallel international regimes that are not hierarchically ordered'. In a recent literature review, Karen Alter has identified several shifts in the literature over the last years; among others, the restatement that regime complexes can have 'different degrees of order and hierarchy within them' and that a very broad range of actors can be part of a regime complex (Alter, 2022: 378–9). Regimes regulating the use of force are still dominated by centralized states and IOs (Alter, 2022).

Earlier studies on international regime complexity have drawn scholarly attention to rationalist strategies that actors can apply in these institutional settings, such as forum-shopping, regime-shifting and strategic inconsistency (Alter and Meunier, 2009). The key category for this chapter derived from this scholarship is the notion of division of labour that can be an intended or unintended result of institutional overlap within regime complexes, based on mutual adaption processes of involved organizations (Faude, 2014). Gehring and Faude (2014) identify the creation of a division of labour as an inherent tendency of institutional complexes that might prevent the fragmentation of global governance arrangements. While such a division of labour can prove to be a quite stable arrangement (Faude, 2014), power relations and actors' self-interests, as well as competition between institutions, remain important so that a division of labour can 'be challenged by interested actors at any time. Yet, a prerequisite for a successful challenge of an established division of labor is a significant change of the distribution of power among the institutions involved and their proponents or of the preferences of relevant actors' (Gehring and Faude, 2014: 493). We will show that, in Mali, such a division of labour has emerged between the UN, Western actors (the EU and France) and African organizations and states, enabling the actors to minimize autonomy costs and benefit from resource pooling (Brosig, 2017). With regard to global norms, and in the context of the 'robust turn' in UN peace operations, these practices might have quite negative effects on the compliance with and implementation of human-rights norms.

In order to discuss the consequences of a division of labour for norm dynamics, it is necessary to include categories and insights from IR norms research. For some time, debates on norm dynamics in the context of inter-organizational – as well as North-South – collaboration seemed to take as given the relative stability of the wider global normative context. Specifically, the prevalence of 'good' international norms has often been assumed in the context of a predominantly liberal international order. From this perspective, IOs serve as important norm diffusers, that is, collective institutional actors promoting convergence on particular standards for appropriate behaviour, across scales (international, national) and from Global North to Global South-settings (Finnemore and Sikkink, 1998). The lively scholarly debate on 'norm localization' that modified this early optimism of liberal IR research on norm diffusion has provided many valuable insights into the 'unorderly' manner in which norms are perceived, adapted, 'pruned' or translated in different regional settings (for example, Acharya, 2004; Zimmermann, 2017).

Recent IR scholarship on norm dynamics has shifted from the earlier focus on emergence and diffusion of norms to their challenges and robustness (Panke and Petersohn, 2016). It is far from clear how the robustness of a specific norm can be measured, given that norms can be both strengthened and weakened by contestation. In addition, some norms are especially complex, such as the responsibility to protect (R2P) norm, and belong themselves, in turn, to a wider normative complex so that the robustness of one norm can often not be judged separately from the robustness of related norms. In the case of R2P, this complex norm includes certain principles of international humanitarian law, genocide prevention, accountability for international crimes, guarantees of non-recurrence and PoC in armed conflict (Welsh, 2019).

Deitelhoff and Zimmermann (2019) proposed a combination of mainly discourse-based and practice-based dimensions to assess the dynamics of norm robustness. Discourse-based dimensions include acceptance of a norm's legitimacy by state actors and the broader public as expressed in international forums or in surveys, number of ratifications and third-party reactions to norm violations such as discursive sanctioning. Practice-based dimensions include the compliance with a norm, that is, 'the level of behavior consistent with norms' and the implementation – meaning the level of 'norm inclusion' in policy papers, protocols or standards of IOs and incorporation into domestic law (Deitelhoff and Zimmermann, 2019: 8). In order to assess whether a norm is being strengthened or weakened, an empirical analysis of all dimensions is required. Not surprisingly, norm researchers differ in their assessment of when exactly a norm is being *weakened* or simply *changed* in practice (Deitelhoff and Zimmermann, 2019). Panke and Petersohn (2016: 4–5) describe the varying effects of norm challenges as follows:

> A norm may survive despite instances of non-compliance and despite the efforts of actors to delimit a norm through renegotiations. [...] A norm may be weakened if its applicatory scope is restricted through practices. In this process, actors still refer to the norm, but previously inappropriate behaviour is now considered to be in accordance with the norm. [...] By contrast, a norm can be considered dead or abolished if practices of norm violation are not an exception but the rule, while the actors no longer make any effort to use the old norm as a reference point for their action.

In addition to assessments of weakening and strengthening of a norm, Wiener (2018: 152) developed the notion of norm 'downsizing' that offers diverging perspectives. A norm may remain 'stable' as a formal 'visible norm container' while it is, simultaneously, 'downsized' in regard to its actual practical reach (Wiener, 2018: 132). This perspective is especially useful in the post-9/11 context, which is marked by normative transformations and probable erosion of human-rights norms, emanating from within what is widely assumed to be the liberal 'core' of norm diffusers.

Since our empirical study in this chapter is limited to the specific case of Mali and a rather short period of time (2012–2020), we cannot provide a deeper analysis of change of the PoC norm in peacekeeping operations in Africa. Instead, we outline an empirical trend that seems to reflect the mode of norm 'survival', but which may result in the downsizing or the overall weakening of the PoC norm in the longer term, due to enduring insufficient compliance with and implementation of the norm in multi-actor stabilization missions.

Analysing the Mali case as a 'laboratory' for stabilization interventions

The research for this chapter has been conducted within an inter-disciplinary research group on 'Overlapping Spheres of Authority and Interface Conflicts in the Global Order' (see endnote 1) so that the conceptual framework builds on theoretical work that has (to date) been published in a special issue of *Global Constitutionalism* (Kreuder-Sonnen and Zürn, 2020) and a working paper containing results from our overall project database (Fuss et al, 2021). The research group has studied interface conflicts within and across overlapping spheres of authority in the current system of global governance. Such interface conflicts refer to 'a subset of norm collisions arising in global governance', emanating from different institutions in the global governance system (Kreuder-Sonnen and Zürn, 2020: 252).

Our sub-project analysed the management of interface conflicts in African security governance, centring on military interventions on the African continent. The empirical results presented in this chapter are based on the research conducted within this framework (Moe and Geis, 2020a; Moe, 2021). We combined in-depth reviews of the academic literature and key policy documents of international and regional organizations in the field of military interventions, with semi-structured expert interviews. We interviewed experts in three settings, reflecting our interest in gaining perspectives on (and from within) organizations at the international level (UN) and the regional level (AU; Economic Community of West African States [ECOWAS]), as well as operational perspectives reflecting views (re)shaped by institutional representatives engaged in practice within a mission. The empirical research draws on a total of 54 interviews conducted during our research visits to Abuja (ECOWAS headquarters), Addis Ababa (AU headquarters), Bamako (Mali), New York (UN headquarters) and Washington, DC (George Washington University) during 2018 and 2019.

The interview guides were structured according to overarching themes within the research group (see Fuss et al, 2021), but, in the subsequent analysis, new themes emerging from the interviews were identified. This resulted in reaching out to further strands of pertinent debates, such as that on a 'robust turn' of UN peacekeeping (Hunt, 2017; also Karlsrud, 2019a and b) or norm 'downsizing' (Wiener, 2018). We sought to gain insights into how key African regional organizations and international actors coordinate their roles and comparative advantages in specific missions, the occurrence of frictions in these inter-organizational partnerships (including norm conflicts) and the management of frictions.

For this chapter, the intervention in Mali was chosen as a paradigmatic example of regime complexity, defined by multiple actors and organizations and related mandates that overlap, converge and clash. Since the situation in Mali has continuously and rapidly evolved, including two *coups d'état* in 2020 and 2021, and given that the consequences for international troops have also remained in constant flux, we have limited our period of analysis from 2012 to 2020. Mali paradigmatically brings to the fore some of the wider dilemmas and trends of contemporary international interventions, in particular pertaining to the revival of stabilization. The escalation of the conflict in Mali was shaped by multiple intertwined developments, involving liberation struggles and a coup against an ineffective and unaccountable state, offering opportunities for armed and Islamist groups to take advantage of the situation and control parts of territory and populations.

Since the series of crises culminating in 2012, Mali has evolved as a 'laboratory' for counterterrorism-inspired stabilization interventions (Charbonneau, 2017; also Cold-Ravnkilde and Nissen, 2020; Welz, 2022). In December 2012, the UNSC authorized the African-led International Support Mission (AFISMA) – a military mission organized by ECOWAS – to support the Malian state against the Islamist insurgents. AFISMA lacked adequate capacity, funding and political backing. As the insurgents advanced towards Bamako, France launched a military initiative, 'Opération Serval', to combat the insurgents in January 2013, upon the request of the transitional government in Bamako. A few months after the Serval intervention, the UNSC authorized the re-hatting of AFISMA to MINUSMA. Its mandate includes peacekeeping and stabilization, and it also authorized the French armed forces to 'use all necessary means' in their support of MINUSMA. In August 2014, Serval was replaced by the counterterrorism 'Opération Barkhane', which was led by the French armed forces, and cooperated with the G5 Sahel countries Burkina Faso, Chad, Mali, Mauritania and Niger. Additionally, the G5 states launched a regional counterterrorism task force, the G5 Sahel Joint Force (FC-G5S), in the summer of 2017.[3] The EU has also been involved in Mali, in particular through the EU Training Mission (EUTM) and the EU Capacity Building Mission, running since 2013 and 2014, respectively. The peak of military interventions in Mali (in approximately 2013–2020) thereby provides ample opportunities for analysing regime complexity 'in action'.

The politics of regime complexity: peacekeeping, protection and counterterrorism in Mali

During the 1990s, UN-led peacekeeping evolved and diversified substantially as the prevailing regime governing the domain of international peace and security, with PoC emerging as a priority mandate in peacekeeping missions. Since 1999, PoC has been systematically provided in the mandates of UN peacekeeping missions, comprising the three tiers of dialogue and engagement, physical protection and the establishment of a protective environment. However, differing interpretations, PoC's ambiguous relationship with the rise of the R2P norm and the related controversies around the rules guiding the use of force in peacekeeping have, in several instances, impeded its implementation (Williams, 2016). The subsequent global war on terror since 2001 has emphasized threat framings centred on state failure, non-state armed groups and 'Islamic terrorism' and 'extremism' (Sheikh, 2022). While international cooperation against terrorism dates back to at least the 1960s, the 9/11 attacks added unprecedented momentum to the rapid rise of a multilateral, albeit fragmented, counterterrorism regime with its own prescriptions, procedures and agreements (Council on Foreign Relations, 2011).

PoC has remained a priority mandate in UN missions. Yet, the rise and reverberations of the emerging counterterrorism regime have contributed to subtle shifts beyond the paradigm of protection centred on human security towards an emphasis on protection grounded in more traditional sovereigntist frameworks. In addition, the counterterrorism regime has expanded. While the military interventions in Iraq and Afghanistan were US-dominated, the 'long war on terror' and its extension particularly across the Middle East and Africa have involved ever greater interest convergence across states, and more related coalition-building, coordination frameworks, interagency collaboration and joint trainings and operations. In this process, the counterterrorism regime benefitted from the opportunity of a 'spill over-like expansion' (Alter and Meunier, 2009: 19) in the context of growing regime complexity. One consequence is the loose coupling of the formally distinct regimes of counterterrorism and peacekeeping. Such coupling has manifested itself in new flexible forms of collaboration, underpinned by the understanding that objectives of securing peace and protecting populations converge with objectives of countering extremism, defeating non-state terrorism threats, stabilizing territories and reinstalling state authority (Karlsrud, 2019a and b).

This emphasis on mutually reinforcing synergies between civilian and military objectives, frameworks and actors is at the core of the revival of the stabilization doctrine. The term of stabilization gained traction in the post-Cold-War era, in particular within the North Atlantic Treaty Organization (NATO) and the US military doctrine, which acquired growing momentum after 9/11. It has also increasingly been adopted by the UN, which launched its first stabilization mission in Haiti in 2004, and additional three missions during the 2010s, in the Democratic Republic of Congo (DRC, 2010), Mali (2013) and the Central African Republic (CAR, 2014). Stabilization activities are understood to contribute to a continuum of interventions, including peace support, humanitarian assistance, counterinsurgency and combat operations (NATO, 2015), as well as security cooperation and foreign internal defence, involving external support for a government in countering subversion and terrorism (US Army, 2014). Stabilization strategies propose a 'division of labour between military and civilian entities based on competencies inherent to those entities' (Robinson et al, 2018: 23), whereby military means targeting non-state 'enemies' are assumed to pave the way for the revival of state authority, rule of law, PoC and, ultimately, long-term peace (US Army, 2014; NATO, 2015).

The remainder of this chapter seeks to elucidate and problematize the inter-organizational and inter-mission relations between the UN, EU, Opération Barkhane and the G5 Sahel Force in Mali. The following section will show how *discursive* differentiation between peacekeeping and counterterrorism is maintained, while, *in practice*, allowing for substantial collaboration and convergence. Stabilization practices in Mali involve much less clear-cut differentiation than that inferred by policy discourses on a division of labour as well as in the IO literature on regime complexity as a driver of niche selection and differentiation (Brosig, 2017). The subsequent section discusses the negative effects of the division of labour on the compliance with and implementation of the PoC norm.

Counterterrorism and peacekeeping entanglements in Mali

Since the Tuareg rebellion – spearheaded by the National Movement for the Liberation of Azawad – began in northern Mali in early 2012, which triggered a coup as well as fierce armed competition over control of northern Mali, the country has occupied a central position on the international security agenda. The culmination of the 2012 crisis must be understood against a wider backdrop of long-standing structural and historical developments; from the role of colonial policies in spurring marginalization and competition over resources and territory, to more recent but related dynamics of aid-dependency, rivalries over the control of smuggling networks, the absence of a functioning state as well as the 2011 disintegration of Libya and the subsequent return of armed Tuareg groups (who had served Gaddafi) to Mali. Concerns over terrorism and migration, however, were key to placing the Malian crisis at the centre of international, and especially European, attention.

Initially, optimism regarding the possibilities for addressing the crisis tended to prevail. The multiple new intervention alliances that formed in the wake of the crisis were seen as particularly illustrative of the potentials of international and regional inter-organizational collaboration. Mali was considered as a site of innovation for intervention models forming a new networked pattern of multi-stakeholder cooperation and partnership (Freear and De Coning, 2013). Along these lines, a 2015 report of the UN Secretary-General conceived of interventions in Mali, CAR and Somalia as 'successful cases of cooperation [which] may provide a framework for a further rationalization of efforts in future cases' (UNSC, 2015: 2). Notions of an organizational division of labour and comparative advantages framed the efforts of creating synergies across the spectrum of UN peacekeeping, European defence packages and regional 'robust action' to counter extremist groups and protect civilians (UNSC, 2015: 1–3).

The different interventions in Mali are often understood as operating separately from one another with distinct, if presumably complimentary, tasks. Specifically, intervention in Mali has commonly been framed as divided between a UN-led peacekeeping regime on the one hand, and a French-led counterterrorism regime on the other (Charbonneau, 2017). Accordingly, MINUSMA officials emphasized the difference between their activities and the tasks of Opération Barkhane and its allies, in particular emphasizing that the "UN does *not* do counterterrorism".[4] EUTM officials also underlined that "we are not executive" in regard to undertaking military action against armed non-state actors.[5] This aligns with the official UN stance expressed in the High-Level Independent Panel on Peace Operations report (HIPPO, 2015), and with the definition of EUTM as a 'non-executive military mission'.[6] Such discursive distancing to military executive practices and counterterrorism combat efforts affirms the institutional identities of the UN as the established international peacekeeper and the EU as a civilian and normative power.

However, the collaboration on the ground in Mali is more ambiguous. The inter-organizational interactions maintain formal discursive distinctions between peacekeeping and counterterrorism, while, in practice, collaboration and convergence have deepened substantially. One of the mechanisms enabling collaboration, while allowing the 'non-executives' to maintain formal strategic distance to the execution of enforcement activities, is *deference*. Deference is the process by which an IO selectively confers authority to another actor or organization to mitigate a rule conflict (Pratt, 2018). Deference of enforcement tasks to regional actors, in particular, is an increasingly common feature of international stabilization and peacekeeping operations. It serves to help international actors in reducing contentions related to risk-taking and the use of force.

An illustrative example is the international support to the counterterrorism force FC-G5S. The force was formed in July 2017 by the heads of the G5 Sahel states, with strong support from France. It received further international backing, including from the EU, which provided an initial €100 million for its establishment. The international support for the force, as well as the endorsement of its counterterrorism mandate, took place against the backdrop of a French call for more active international counterterrorism support and a more robust UN mandate to allow international and regional burden-sharing with Opération Barkhane.

FC-G5S became the regional mechanism through which this request could be mediated. Specifically, both the EU and the UN could channel support through FC-G5S while keeping strategic distance to the military executive aspects. Consequently, UNSC Resolution 2423, which extended MINUSMA's mandate in 2018, welcomed the signing of 'a technical agreement between the United Nations, the EU and the G5 Sahel with a view to providing specified operational and logistical support through MINUSMA to the FC-G5S' (UNSC, 2018). Furthermore, the EUTM mandate of May 2020 expanded its area of operation to include all the countries of the G5 Sahel, thereby allowing it to conduct capacity-building activities with the armed forces of the FC-G5S states.[7]

The latter was, in turn, commonly viewed as an instrumental part of France's 'exit strategy' for Opération Barkhane (Van der Lijn et al, 2019: 45). These developments show how international regime complexity may project military power and enable the use of force at a distance. Notably, the international embrace of African solutions – FC-G5S in this case – enables a deferral of counterterrorism combat tasks from the EU and the UN to African regional actors, allowing the former to act as 'non-executive' enablers of the 'executive' latter.

In turn, Malian armed forces (FAMA) have been a central entry point for enabling the use of force at the host-state level (while FAMA also contributes to FC-G5S). The mandate of EUTM clarifies that the mission is exclusively involved in training Malian forces and capacity-building efforts in the defence sector, but *not in combat*.[8] When asked how and for what purposes the provided training is used, mission staff responded that the mission sticks to its mandate and "sphere of responsibility" and did not follow up on or account for how and where the military training and capacities are subsequently used, since EUTM is "not involved" in the "executive aspects".[9] While the mission in principle is 'non-executive', the training does, however, take place in a context of ongoing armed conflict, in which FAMA 'trainees' are a conflict party. Such training, therefore, has been described as a mode of international 'counterinsurgency by proxy' (Skeppström et al, 2015).

Protection of civilians and peacekeeping under pressure

The intervention alliances discussed here illustrate terrorism and extremism as prevailing threat definitions within the field of contemporary international security governance (Sheikh, 2022). They also speak to the tensions within the normative structures of the UN and the EU, facing new demands and conflict scenarios that push the limits of their mandates, norms and institutional identities. The emerging forms of mediated collaboration reflect institutional adaptation of the peacekeeping regime, whereby the UN seeks to remain a relevant actor within a wider field defined by increasing institutional density and gravitation towards military responses. Such adaptation notwithstanding, current UN frameworks and mandates reflect a sustained commitment to peacekeeping norms and objectives. This includes the PoC agenda, which remains the core obligation and yardstick for the worth of peacekeeping. However, as suggested by references to the norms research scholarship in IR (previously discussed), norms and formal policy commitments can remain fully stable on a discursive level while their reach and purchase simultaneously change in practice. Hence, examining practices and implementation dynamics on the ground is necessary in order to identify potential transformations resulting from regime complexity. Adopting such a perspective, this section outlines two sets of broader implications of the peacekeeping-counterterrorism regime complexity for PoC that will be discussed in the following subsection: the subtle militarization of PoC and the undermining of the impartiality norm with a direct negative effect on PoC norm implementation.

Enhancing coercive state power and the militarization of the protection of civilians

A first factor affecting the implementation of PoC is that interventions increasingly side squarely with the interests and powers of states' armed forces. This can be observed in the increased assistance to host governments' defence sectors or the reliance on ad hoc military coalitions such as FC-G5S. While the consent of, and collaboration with, host governments are long-standing guiding rules in UN interventions, siding with the armed forces of these governments to defeat a designated enemy adds new strains on peacekeeping in general, and on PoC implementation specifically.

The mission concept of stabilization integrates PoC. Yet, it also tends to reframe it by focusing narrowly on non-state armed actors as the main threat to civilians. Accordingly, supporting states' stabilization efforts is cast as the key means for civilian protection.[10] Crudely put, this refashioning of protection to an anticipated outcome of counterterrorism-inspired stabilization indicates the subtle "militarisation of PoC".[11] Moreover, while abuses committed by non-state armed actors are a genuine concern, the presumption that support for state forces automatically translates into the protection of civilians is inaccurate and risks underplaying human-rights abuses and violations committed by these forces themselves.

Accordingly, the UN's increasing alignment with governments' security forces may over time involve a 'high price' to be paid for the organization's human rights architecture when 'the very governments the UN relies upon for access and action become abusive and/or threaten to withdraw consent' (Hunt, 2017: 122), as has been the case in Mali. Interviewees in our research also mentioned instances where state forces, supported through MINUSMA as well as through FC-G5S, were arming "allied" civilian groups against "enemy" civilian groups and directly targeting civilians – allegedly as part of their stabilization and counterterrorism efforts.[12]

MINUSMA's mandate does include provisions for confronting such abuses, and, in line with the mission's PoC mandate 'third tier' of supporting the establishment of a protective environment, the PoC team engages in cross-sector activities towards strengthening the government's capacity to protect civilians and improve the rule of law. Yet, according to MINUSMA PoC staff, the fact that MINUSMA simultaneously "outsources" and supports counterterrorism efforts is not lost on Malian counterparts. This "completely blurs a line" and brings ambiguity in regard to which guidelines apply, thereby undermining the effective implementation of PoC.[13]

Specifically, such ambiguities widen opportunities for state forces and allies to defend contentious practices by drawing on resonant frames of the need to respond to new threats, and to rely on the status of counterterrorism partners as the basis for securing continuous support despite abusive behaviour. Illustrating such trends, one prominent Malian political observer explained how the arrival of Opération Serval (signifying the international priority of counterterrorism in Mali) affected the conflict dynamics whereby FAMA more frequently started to label its opponents as "terrorists". This, in turn, came with increasing abuses by the state and its allied forces against those being labelled.[14]

This scenario, in a nutshell, captures how 'international regime complexity contributes to rule ambiguity' by creating opportunities for state actors 'to shift framings' (Alter and Meunier, 2009: 18), to enable political strategies across different yet overlapping international collaboration venues, and thereby to circumvent or even 'abandon an inconvenient obligation' (Alter and Meunier, 2009: 20). The overall result in the Malian context is that the overlapping intervention regimes ultimately serve more to push towards the extension of *coercive state power* aimed at defeating non-state competitors than to sufficiently prioritize support for the extension of *legitimate state authority* centred on the provision of human security. The regime complexity underpinning the counterterrorism-inspired stabilization collaborations has clearly added new layers to the existing dilemmas that the UN faced regarding cooperation with governments; in particular, impacting negatively on PoC implementation and decreasing the practical reach of the norm.

Loss of impartiality and the effects on the protection of civilians

A second (closely related) effect of the UN becoming embedded within the wider 'whole' of stabilization alliances is that its impartiality has become profoundly compromised (Karlsrud, 2019b). This, in turn, has contributed to reshaping the conditions for implementing PoC. While MINUSMA maintains discursively its distinction from the counterterrorism regime, this distinction is far from clear, in practice, to the Malian population and the armed groups operating in the country.[15] The formal status of MINUSMA and the EU as non-executive in regard to military combat does not alter on-the-ground perceptions of the missions bearing responsibility in practice "when a family member has been killed or abused by forces they know have received training and support".[16] The undermining of impartiality has, moreover, made MINUSMA – and in extension, people perceived as collaborators to the mission – a target of the armed actors opposing the government. This produces the paradoxical situation where MINUSMA's patrols of villages are not straightforwardly experienced as a protective measure, as communities fear attacks by armed groups after MINUSMA visits.[17] The association of MINUSMA with FC-G5S and Opération Barkhane has made MINUSMA itself the soft target for retaliations against the counterterrorism coalition. As one MINUSMA staff explained, "There was a communiqué this week, from JNIM,[18] [...] saying that they attacked MINUSMA so that they can show France that they don't have their place here."[19]

Against this backdrop, MINUSMA became known as the UN's most dangerous mission due to the high number of casualties among its staff. This threat to peacekeepers not only renders PoC activities – which require presence within communities – more difficult, it has also led to a reprioritization of resources to force protection. Conversely, this harms MINUSMA's reputation, since the mission is increasingly seen to focus more on protecting its own personnel than Malian civilians.[20] The heightened threat to peacekeepers has also led to new operational adjustments and partial reframing of operational rules, which run counter to established peacekeeping norms. The 2017 UN-commissioned report (Dos Santos Cruz and Phillips, 2017) on how to optimize operations and protect mission staff in 'high security-risk' contexts is particularly illustrative of this. The report, produced under the leadership of the 'hawkish' Brazilian General Santos Cruz, caused 'a stir for its vocal demands for greater use of force' (Harig and Jenne, 2022: 14). The report offers recommendations pointing towards a substantially more 'robust posture', in arguing that '(u)nfortunately, hostile forces do not understand a language other than force', and further recommends that the UN 'should provide an updated interpretation of [its] basic principles' so the latter would not constitute 'restrictions on the initiative and the use of force'. In fact, it states, the UN needs to use force proactively: 'Missions should go where the threat is, in order to neutralise it' (Dos Santos Cruz and Phillips, 2017). The report has been taken up as a strategic guide by mission staff across 'high risk' missions. However, others, especially officials with PoC expertise, have been highly critical, arguing that the report "does not take into account the civilians [...] or the population" and as such does not give any serious priority in regard to addressing the poor record of MINUSMA in regard to PoC.[21] Additionally, the report's proposed 'update' of UN principles, in the words of a UN PoC official, "dismiss any [...] tool we can have to engage with an armed group"[22] as part of the PoC efforts to further dialogue and sensitization to human rights.

Conclusions and outlook

The empirical analysis of the interventions in Mali highlights a trend that is also visible in other military interventions on the African continent, notably a 'growing convergence between African and international actors around a reworked "intervention as stabilisation" regime' (Soares and Verhoeven, 2018: 8, 19). Such convergence has translated into a division of labour, structured by a logic whereby regional African actors, with training and support from international actors, take on 'first responder' enforcement activities, while the UN (ideally) engages when there is a peace to keep and/or to engage in parallel stabilization tasks. Contemporary military missions on the African continent convey different configurations of such a division of labour. These range from, for example, the African Union Mission in Somalia (AMISOM) that fights against al-Shabaab under a UN mandate, supported by the UN Support Office for AMISOM and with funding from the EU to the direct integration of an African-led UN Force Intervention Brigade into the UN mission in the DRC as well as the division of labour in Mali that has been studied in this chapter.

The case of Mali clearly conveys that, despite the discursive division – reflected in mandates, doctrines and organizational frameworks – stabilization, in practice, involves a deepening entwinement of peacekeeping and counterterrorism actors and activities. This also signifies a pragmatic consensus and cooperation among African and external actors regarding the use of force shaping the so-called 'robust turn'. Such consensus may be partly explained by the pressures, as well as newly emerging opportunities, facing these sets of actors within the context of wider normative change. First, in a reconfigured global normative context where the UN struggles to both delimit and 'update' its roles to new 'exceptional threat scenarios', the mobilization of African actors through strategic partnerships offers new leeway. As de Waal (2015: 189) puts it, the UN:

> has a set of principles that determine peacekeeping operations that can only be worked around with difficulties, including reluctance to deploy troops from one country in a neighboring country, restrictions on rules of engagements, and onerous political and human rights reporting requirements. These constraints became a problem as the US sought to merge peacekeeping and counterterrorism. ... By comparison, African countries contributing troops through the AU, ECOWAS and Intergovernmental Authority on Development (IGAD) are more

> flexible on the political purpose and mandate … [and] more ready to take casualties.

Against this backdrop, the division of labour discourse, commonly justified with reference to the established principle of subsidiarity, in practice corresponds to what Pratt (2018) terms *deference*, whereby one IO selectively confers authority to another IO or actor to mitigate divergences over norms and rules. In the present case, deference helps the UN (and to some extent also the EU) to mitigate a tension *within* its own normative structure and allows for transferring risks, as well as some of the contentious use of force tasks, to African actors. While this indicates considerable ethical issues pertaining to inequalities in North-South cooperation (Cold-Ravnkilde et al, 2017), such deference offers African elites new leverage as 'strategic partners'. Moreover, whereas post-Cold-War interventions – in particular humanitarian intervention and the R2P norm – were often conflicting with norms of sovereignty, stabilization interventions offer opportunities for African elites pursuing agendas of regaining territory from non-state opponents and thereby re-asserting or remaking sovereignty (Moe, 2017). As such, the re-conceptualization of intervention as stabilization – and the agency of African elites to make use of this shift (Soares de Oliveira and Verhoeven, 2018) – have inverted the relationship between intervention and sovereignty, as the latter is increasingly pursued and produced through the *presence* of, rather than the *barring* of, external interveners (Moe, 2017).

To be sure, human rights and protection norms remain stable within the frameworks of contemporary UN and AU stabilization missions. The protection of civilians and of human rights is part of most, if not all, contemporary AU and UN mission mandates, and the UN works under a Human Rights Due Diligence Policy to prevent collaboration with abusive elements of allied armed forces. Accordingly, a discourse-based assessment of norm robustness (see Deitelhoff and Zimmermann, 2019) of PoC indicates that the norm remains stable and influential. Yet, in zooming in on the actual dynamics of intervention – the practice-based dimension – a growing amount of empirically informed research is pointing out that the turn to post-9/11 counterterrorism and stabilization has significantly limited the scope for implementation of civilian protection norms (and the wider cluster of human-rights and human-security norms – see Dunne, 2007; Hunt, 2017; Karlsrud, 2019b), and thereby reduced their practical reach. In this regard, our analysis of military interventions in Mali demonstrates that cooperation and convergence across IOs, as well as across Global North and Global South intervention actors, need not be normatively desirable.

Some of the core dynamics observed in our case study of Mali bears resonance with wider world-order transformations, such as the regionalization of security policy (including a growing significance of coalitions of the willing), increasing (re)prioritization of *state* security in international politics and profound questioning of the previously presumed (almost) universal appeal of Western liberal norms. Our analysis also highlights current complexities of norm dynamics that unfold beyond the prevailing focus on diffusion of 'good' international norms and involve adaptation and transformations of presumed 'norm diffusers' themselves – be it IOs or states commonly assumed to be part of the liberal core of international politics.

Notes

1 The authors gratefully acknowledge the funding made available by the German Research Foundation (Deutsche Forschungsgemeinschaft, DFG) for this research (within the research group 'Overlapping Spheres of Authority and Interface Conflicts in the Global Order' (OSAIC), DFG No. 277531170). We are very grateful to Lena Pollmann who contributed to undertaking the field research and interviews drawn on in this paper. Some empirical parts of this chapter are based on Moe (2021).

2 As of May 2022. Available from: peacekeeping.un.org/en/where-we-operate [accessed 30 March 2023].

3 On 15 May 2022, Mali withdrew from the Force, after contestations over the group's presidency.

4 Interviews with MINUSMA and EUTM staff, Bamako, October 2018.

5 Interview with EUTM staff, Bamako, October 2018. The EU's activities in Mali arguably occupy a grey area, or interface, between peacebuilding, security sector reform, and counterterrorism; with the EUTM providing training for both FAMA and FC-G5S.

6 See the EUTM Mali webpage at eutmmali.eu. In military language, a 'non-executive' mission is advisory and conducted in support of a so-called 'host state', while an 'executive mission'/operation can carry out military/combat actions directly, sometimes in replacement of the host state forces.

7 EUTM Mali has later been suspended, first in the context of COVID-19, then against the backdrop of the 2020 and 2021 coups, and again as Mali's military junta decided to pull out of FC-G5S, and concerns were growing in 2022 regarding Russian interference through the Wagner group.

8 Interview with EUTM officials, Bamako, October 2018. See also EUTM mandate 2013–2014 (and extended 2016–2018). Available from: eutmmali.eu/mandates [accessed 30 March 2023].

9 Interview with EUTM officials, Bamako, October 2018.

10 Interview with UN senior official, Office of Genocide Prevention and the R2P, New York, March 2019.

11 Interview with Mali/PoC analyst, New York, March 2019.

12 Interviews, October 2018, Bamako: Malian researcher/analyst; human rights INGO official; MINUSMA/PoC team official. Since these interviews were conducted, there have been a number of INGO reports detailing several further cases, in 2019 and 2020, of abuses, extrajudicial killings and unlawful arrests along with forced disappearances of civilians, by the Malian security forces.

13 Interview with MINUSMA/PoC team official, Bamako, October 2018, and with UN senior officer, Policy and Best Practice Service/DPO, New York, March 2018.

14 Interview with Malian researcher/analyst, Bamako, October 2018.

15 Interview with MINUSMA/PoC team official, Bamako, October 2018.

16 Interview with Malian researcher/analyst, Bamako, October 2018.

17 Interview with MINUSMA Military official, Bamako, October 2018.

[18] Abbreviation for one of the most active armed groups in Mali – Jama'at Nasr al-Islam wal Muslimin – also known as Nusrat al-Islam.
[19] Interview with MINUSMA/PoC team official, Bamako, October 2018.
[20] Interview with Malian researcher/analyst, Bamako, October 2018.
[21] Interview with MINUSMA/PoC team official, Bamako, October 2018.
[22] Interview with Mali/PoC analyst, New York, March 2019.

References

Abbott, K.W. and Faude, B. (2022) 'Hybrid institutional complexes in global governance', *Review of International Organizations*, 17(2): 263–91.

Acharya, A. (2004) 'How ideas spread: whose norms matter? Norm localization and institutional change in Asia regionalism', *International Organization*, 58(2): 239–75.

Alter, K.J. (2022) 'The promise and perils of theorizing international regime complexity in an evolving world', *Review of International Organizations*, 17(2): 375–96.

Alter, K.J. and Meunier, S. (2009) 'The politics of international regime complexity', *Perspectives on Politics*, 7(1): 13–24.

Aning, K. and Salihu, N. (2011) 'Accountability for intervention: negotiating civilian protection dilemmas with respect to economic community of West African states and African Union interventions', *African Security*, 4(2): 81–99.

Brosig, M. (2017) *Cooperative Peacekeeping in Africa: Exploring Regime Complexity*, Abingdon: Routledge.

Brosig, M. (2013) 'Introduction: The African security regime complex – exploring converging actors and policies', *African Security*, 6(3–4): 171–90.

Charbonneau, B. (2017) 'Intervention in Mali: building peace between peacekeeping and counterterrorism', *Journal of Contemporary African Studies*, 35(4): 415–31.

Clark, R. (2021) 'Pool or duel? Cooperation and competition among international organizations', *International Organization*, 75(4): 1133–53.

Coffie, A. and Tiky, L. (2021) 'Exploring Africa's agency in international politics', *Africa Spectrum*, 56(3): 243–53.

Cold-Ravnkilde, S.M., Albrecht, P. and Haugegaard, R. (2017) 'Friction and inequality among peacekeepers in Mali', *RUSI Journal*, 162(2): 34–42.

Cold-Ravnkilde, S.M. and Nissen, C. (2020) 'Schizophrenic agendas in the EU's external actions in Mali', *International Affairs*, 96(4): 935–53.

Coleman, K.P. and Tieku, T.K. (eds) (2018) *African Actors in International Security: Shaping Contemporary Norms*, Boulder, Co: Lynne Rienner.

Council on Foreign Relations (2011) 'The global regime for terrorism', issue brief, 31 August, available from: cfr.org/report/global-regime-terrorism [accessed 15 May 2023].

De Coning, C. (2017) 'Peace enforcement in Africa: doctrinal distinctions between the African Union and United Nations', *Contemporary Security Policy*, 38(1): 145–60.

Deitelhoff, N. and Zimmermann, L. (2019) 'Norms under challenge: unpacking the dynamics of norm robustness', *Journal of Global Security Studies*, 4(1): 2–17.

de Waal, A. (2015) *The Real Politics of the Horn of Africa: Money, War and the Business of Power*, Cambridge: Polity Press.

Döring, K., Engel, U., Gelot, L. and Herpolsheimer, J. (eds) (2021) *Researching the Inner Life of the African Peace and Security Architecture: APSA Inside-Out*, Leiden: Brill.

Dos Santos Cruz, C.A. and Phillips, William R. (2017) *Improving Security of United Nations Peacekeepers: We Need to Change the Way We Are Doing Business*, New York: UN report.

Dunne, T. (2007) '"The rules of the game are changing": fundamental human rights in crisis after 9/11', *International Politics*, 44(2–3): 269–86.

Engel, U. and Porto, J.G. (eds) (2013) *Towards an African Peace and Security Regime: Continental Embeddedness, Transnational Linkages, Strategic Relevance*, Farnham: Ashgate.

Faude, B. (2014) 'Zur Dynamik interorganisationaler Beziehungen: Wie aus Konkurrenz Arbeitsteilung entsteht', in E. da Conceição-Heldt, M. Koch and A. Liese (eds) *Internationale Organisationen: Autonomie, Politisierung, Interorganisationale Beziehungen und Wandel*, Baden-Baden: Nomos, pp 294–321.

Finnemore, M. and Sikkink, K. (1998) 'International norm dynamics and political change', *International Organization*, 52(4): 887–917.

Franke, U. (2017) 'Inter-organizational relations: five theoretical approaches', *Oxford Research Encyclopedia*, Oxford University Press, pp 1–28.

Freear, M. and de Coning, C. (2013) 'Lessons from the African Union Mission for Somalia (AMISOM) for peace operations in Mali', *Stability*, 2(2): 1-11.

Fuss, J., Kreuder-Sonnen, C., Saravia, A. and Zürn, M. (2021) 'Managing regime complexity: introducing the Interface Conflicts 1.0. Dataset', Berlin: WZB Discussion Paper No. SP IV 2021–101, available from: hdl.handle.net/10419/233472 [accessed 15 May 2023].

Gehring, T. and Faude, B. (2014) 'A theory of emerging order within institutional complexes: how competition among regulatory international institutions leads to institutional adaptation and division of labor', *Review of International Organizations*, 9(4): 471–98.

Geis, A. and Wagner, W. (2021) '"What we are fighting for": democracies' justifications of using armed force since the end of the Cold War', in L. Brock and H. Simon (eds) *The Justification of War and International Order*, Oxford: Oxford University Press, pp 293–310.

Gelot, L. (2015) 'African regional organizations, peace operations and the UN: legitimacy and disengagement', in P. Wallensteen and A. Bjurner (eds) *Regional Organizations and Peacemaking: Challengers to the UN?*, London: Routledge, pp 137–59.

Harig, C. and Jenne, N. (2022) 'Whose rules? Whose power? The Global South and the possibility to shape international peacekeeping norms through leadership appointments', *Review of International Studies*, online first: 1–22.

HIPPO (High-Level Independent Panel on Peace Operations) (2015) 'Uniting our strengths for peace: politics, partnership and people', final report, New York: United Nations.

Hunt, C.T. (2017) 'All necessary means to what ends? The unintended consequences of the "robust turn" in UN peace operations', *International Peacekeeping*, 24(1): 108–31.

Karlsrud, J. (2019a) 'From liberal peacebuilding to stabilization and counterterrorism', *International Peacekeeping*, 26(1): 1–21.

Karlsrud, J. (2019b) 'For the greater good? "Good states" turning UN peacekeeping toward counterterrorism', *International Journal*, 74(1): 65–83.

Krasner, S.D. (1982) 'Structural causes and regime consequences: regimes as intervening variables', *International Organization*, 36(2): 185–205.

Kreuder-Sonnen, C. and Zürn, M. (2020) 'After fragmentation: norm collisions, interface conflicts, and conflict management', *Global Constitutionalism*, 9(2): 241–67.

Margulis, M.E. (2021) 'Intervention by international organizations in regime complexes', *Review of International Organizations*, 16(4): 871–902.

Moe, L.W. (2021) 'The dark side of institutional collaboration: how peacekeeping-counterterrorism convergences weaken the protection of civilians in Mali', *International Peacekeeping*, 28(1): 1–29.

Moe, L.W. (2017) 'Counterinsurgent warfare and the decentering of sovereignty in Somalia', in L.W. Moe and M.-M. Müller (eds) *Reconfiguring Intervention: Complexity, Resilience and the 'Local Turn' in Counterinsurgent Warfare*, Basingstoke: Palgrave Macmillan, pp 119–40.

Moe, L.W. and Geis, A. (2020a) 'From liberal interventionism to stabilization: a new consensus on norm-downsizing in interventions in Africa', *Global Constitutionalism*, 9(2): 387–412.

Moe, L.W. and Geis, A. (2020b) 'Hybridity and friction in organizational politics: new perspectives on the African regime complex', *Journal of Intervention and Statebuilding*, 14(2): 148–70.

Murithi, T. (2008) 'The African Union's evolving role in peace operations: the African Union Mission in Burundi, the African Union Mission in Sudan and the African Union Mission in Somalia', *African Security Review*, 17(1): 69–82.

NATO (North Atlantic Treaty Organization) (2015) *Allied Joint Doctrine for the Military Contribution to Stabilization and Reconstruction (AJP–3.4.5)*, Brussels: NATO.

Panke, D. and Petersohn, U. (2016) 'Norm challenges and norm death: the inexplicable?', *Cooperation and Conflict*, 51(1): 3–19.

Pratt, T. (2018) 'Deference and hierarchy in international regime complexes', *International Organization*, 72(3): 561–90.

Robinson, L., Mann, S., Martini, J. and Pezard, S. (2018) 'Finding the right balance: Department of Defense roles in stabilization', Santa Monica: RAND Cooperation, available from: rand.org/pubs/research_reports/RR2441.html [accessed: 30 March 2023].

Sheikh, M.K. (2022) 'Transnational jihad as a bundled conflict-constellation', *Studies in Conflict & Terrorism*, online first.

Skeppström, E., Hull, C. and Jonsson, M. (2015) 'European Union training missions: security sector reform or counterinsurgency', *European Security*, 24(2): 353–67.

Soares de Oliveira, R. and Verhoeven, H. (2018) 'Taming intervention: sovereignty, statehood and political order in Africa', *Survival*, 60(2): 7–32.

Struett, M.J., Nance, M.T. and Armstrong, D. (2013) 'Navigating the maritime piracy regime complex', *Global Governance*, 19(1): 93–104.

UNSC (United Nations Security Council) (2018) Resolution 2423, 28 June, available from: securitycouncilreport.org/atf/cf/%7B65BFCF9B-6D27-4E9C-8CD3-CF6E4FF96FF9%7D/s_res_2423.pdf [accessed 30 March 2023].

UNSC (2015) 'Partnering for peace: moving towards partnership peacekeeping', report of the Secretary-General, New York: United Nations, available from: digitallibrary.un.org/record/790913 [accessed 30 March 2023].

United States (US) Army (2014) *Field Manual FM 3–07 Stability*, Washington, DC: Headquarters, Department of Army, available from: globalsecurity.org/military/library/policy/army/fm/3-07/fm3-07_2014.pdf [accessed 30 March 2023].

Van der Lijn, J., Abouelnasr, N., Ahmed, T. et al (2019) *Assessing the Effectiveness of the United Nations Mission in Mali / MINUSMA*, Oslo: Norwegian Institute of International Affairs.

Welsh, J.M. (2019) 'Norm robustness and the responsibility to protect', *Journal of Global Security Studies*, 4(1): 53–72.

Welz, M. (2022) 'The African Union, France, and conflict management in Mali: preferences, actions, and narrations', *Journal of Intervention and Statebuilding*, online first.

Wiener, A. (2018) *Contestation and Constitution of Norms in Global International Relations*, Cambridge: Cambridge University Press.

Williams, P.D. (2016) 'The R2P, Protection of Civilians, and UN peacekeeping operations', in A.J. Bellamy and T. Dunne (eds) *The Oxford Handbook of the Responsibility to Protect*, Oxford: Oxford University Press, pp 524–44.

Williams, P.D. (2014) 'Reflections on the evolving African peace and security architecture', *African Security*, 7(3): 147–62.

Williams, P.D. and Boutellis, A. (2014) 'Partnership peacekeeping: challenges and opportunities in the United Nations-African Union relationship', *African Affairs*, 113(451): 254–78.

Zimmermann, L. (2017) 'More for less: the interactive translation of global norms in postconflict Guatemala', *International Studies Review*, 61(4): 774–85.

5

Political Cleavages and the Competition over Epistemic Authority

Thomas Müller

Introduction

This chapter zooms in on the dynamics of competition that shape inter-organizational relations (IOR) in world politics. More specifically, it probes into the competition over authority that pervades global governance: the quest by various actors to become epistemic authorities – the key knowledge producers – on the objects that are governed in world politics, such as international security, the global economy or the climate. Does this competition make the epistemic practices of these actors more similar or more distinct?

This question is key to understanding how IOR affect the ordering of world politics. If the competition fosters a diversity in the epistemic practices, this may make the objects more ambiguous, thus complicating efforts to develop frameworks and tools for their governance. One example for such an ambiguity is the world-wide level of armaments, for which military expenditures are a prominent indicator. Several organizations produce international statistics on military expenditures, vying for attention and influence in debates about security politics. Their statistics, though, diverge. The Stockholm International Peace Research Institute (SIPRI), for instance, estimates that the military spending of the US in 2019 (US$732 billion) far surpassed the combined spending of China (US$261 billion) and Russia (US$65 billion) (Tian et al, 2020). The US State Department, in turn, publishes a range of estimates on the patterns of military expenditures for the same year, with the upper end of the estimates suggesting that the combined spending of China (US$417 billion) and Russia (US$170 billion) was much closer to the US spending (US$730 billion) than the SIPRI figures indicate (US State Department, 2021a).

The chapter builds on and further develops theorizing on organizational fields to explain the effects of the competition over authority. Sociological neo-institutionalists have developed and used the concept of organizational fields to study how the interaction of organizations generates field dynamics that shape the form and practices of these organizations (for overviews, see Scott, 2008: 181–209; Wooten and Hoffman, 2017). Isomorphism, for instance, denotes field dynamics that make the forms and practices of the organizations more similar over time (see Boxenbaum and Jonsson, 2017). Scholars in international relations (IR) have drawn on this theorizing to probe into different aspects of world politics, such as isomorphism among states (Farrell, 2005) or among governance institutions (Dingwerth and Pattberg, 2009), processes of policy change (Vetterlein and Moschella, 2014) and the evolution of ecologies of governance institutions (Lake, 2021). They have not yet, however, probed into the limits of the isomorphic dynamics. This chapter posits that policy fields are a special type of organizational field coalescing around governance objects and that the political struggles over the governance of the objects may give rise to cleavages – that is, deep political divides – that modulate the field dynamics.

By teasing out the effects of these cleavages, we can better understand how competition structures and affects IOR. Research on IOR has a tendency to equate '(inter-organizational) relations with cooperation, coordination, or collaboration' (Franke, 2017). When it focuses on competition, IOR research treats it mainly in two ways: as discord among states that prevents cooperation among international organizations (Biermann and Koops, 2017) or as regulatory overlap in which two or more organizations compete over the governance of an object and negotiate a division of labour (Gehring and Faude, 2014; see also Chapter 4 in this volume). The literature on organizational fields, in contrast, regards competitive dynamics as one key factor that fosters isomorphism among organizations. This chapter shows that cleavages shape how isomorphic processes play out. Cleavages are a form of discord among states that structures the fields into durable camps with opposing political preferences. By doing so, cleavages complicate governance arrangements involving all camps and, moreover, sustain divergent attitudes towards certain practices. Put differently, cleavages make governance-related forms of field-wide isomorphism less likely, while limiting the spread of practices that are politically contested, thus fostering persistent diversity in the practices.

After introducing the notion of organizational fields and discussing the isomorphic dynamics that the competition over epistemic authority generates in the following section, the chapter re-conceptualizes organizational fields as policy fields structured by cleavages, and specifies the potential effects of these cleavages on the field dynamics afterwards. The chapter then analyses the organizational field that has coalesced around the issue of military expenditures in world politics. This field constitutes a useful case study for theory development for two reasons. It enables study of the effects of both high and low levels of political contention, as the level of military expenditures was a much more contentious issue during the Cold War than it is today. It moreover underscores that cleavages may not only relate to how an object is governed but also – important for epistemic practices – to how knowledge about the object is produced and published. After briefly describing the research strategy used to reconstruct the field and its dynamics, the chapter teases out the effects of the cleavage relating to the transparency of military expenditures. The field-structuring effects of the cleavage have persisted beyond the period of high political contention in which it emerged. The chapter finally reflects on the implications for future research on IOR.

State of the art

The notion of organizational fields was developed by sociological neo-institutionalists to explain why organizations become more similar in their form and practices over time. In their classical definition, DiMaggio and Powell (1983: 148) describe an organizational field as consisting of 'those organizations that, in the aggregate, constitute a recognized area of institutional life' and employ the vocabulary of markets to illustrate what they mean: 'key suppliers, resource or product consumers, regulatory agencies, and other organizations that produce similar services or products'. They identify three mechanisms that make the form and practices of the organizations more similar over time. The first mechanism, coercive isomorphism, denotes political and regulatory processes that prescribe certain organizational forms and practices. The second mechanism, mimetic isomorphism, happens when organizations 'model themselves on other organizations' (DiMaggio and Powell, 1983: 151). In response to uncertainty about what works best in their environment, organizations search for practices that have worked for other organizations and imitate these practices. The third mechanism, normative isomorphism, relates to processes of 'professionalization' that foster the diffusion of certain practices (DiMaggio and Powell, 1983: 152). Organizations, for instance, adopt similar practices when their staffs share the same repertoire of practices. Their staffs, in turn, prefer and use the same practices when they have the same educational or professional background and/or when they form part of the same networks.

Subsequent research has argued that the focus on isomorphism is too narrow and that organizational fields are 'capable of moving towards something other than isomorphism' (Wooten and Hoffman, 2017: 60). This argument has gone hand in hand with another; that organizational fields do not have to be markets – the intuition underpinning DiMaggio and Powell's conceptualization – but can, for instance, also form around political issues (see Hoffman, 1999). One crucial idea, though, has remained: the field dynamics are assumed to be underpinned by a considerable element of competition within the field population. This assumption is shared among field theories, though sociological neo-institutionalists emphasize it less strongly than Bourdieu's field theory (Bourdieu and Wacquant, 1992) or the theory of strategic action fields (Fligstein and McAdam, 2012).

In world politics, actors compete over, among other things, political authority, that is, the recognized competence to decide which objects are to be governed in what ways (Sending, 2015). These objects include international security, the balance of power, the global economy, the climate and global development. The meaning of these objects is socially negotiated, which makes epistemic authority – recognized expertise in producing knowledge about the objects – a key resource in the competition over political authority (see also Zürn, 2018). How the objects are widely interpreted affects how they are debated politically and governed. The debate about climate change, for instance, would be different if the current efforts of states were widely considered to be sufficient rather than insufficient to curb global warming.

To produce knowledge on the governance objects, actors use various epistemic practices. Examples are the compilation of lists (see Chapter 3), the production of statistics, the construction of rankings of how well or poorly states govern the objects, or computer simulations of how the objects are likely to change over time. These epistemic practices are also the key tools in the competition over authority. Actors use them to substantiate their claims to special knowledge about the governance objects and to thus position themselves as epistemic authorities.

What field dynamics does the competition over authority generate? Does it make the epistemic practices in a given policy field – or, for that matter, across policy fields – more similar over time? The literature on epistemic authority in world politics does not generally engage with these questions. It develops, though, arguments that suggest isomorphism will not take place as well as arguments that suggest that it will. The argument against isomorphic dynamics is that the competition over authority involves clashing policy preferences. Political actors are likely to promote those interpretations of the objects that best suit their policy preferences (see Sending, 2015). The more their policy preferences diverge, the more likely the actors are to promote dissimilar interpretations. If this is the case, the competition over authority fosters not isomorphism but persistent diversity in the representation and interpretation of the governance objects.

The literature also makes arguments that suggest the inverse, however; that the competition over authority fosters isomorphic dynamics. Notably, the IR literature on quantification argues that political contention is one key factor that has spurred the proliferation of indicators and rankings – particular epistemic practices that package knowledge in quantitative and comparative ways – in the last three decades (Kelley and Simmons, 2019). The emergence of this 'indicator culture' (Merry, 2016: 9) can be described as a process of mimetic isomorphism. Some intergovernmental organizations (IGOs) and non-governmental organizations (NGOs) started to publish benchmarks and rankings, thereby gaining attention and political influence, which in turn led other IGOs and NGOs to emulate them and likewise use these epistemic practices.

Put differently: while the actors may strive to promote diverging interpretations of a given governance object, they may nonetheless choose the same epistemic practices to substantiate and communicate these interpretations. The two arguments are in this sense not incompatible. Rather, in combination, they imply a limit to the isomorphic processes: isomorphism in the epistemic practices, but not in the knowledge that the actors produce through these epistemic practices. This ties in with the literature on organizational fields that likewise does not assume an isomorphism all the way down. While the literature argues that companies competing in the same market become more similar over time in their organizational structures, it does not argue that they come to produce identical goods. In fact, the companies are likely to seek to produce goods that are distinct and stand apart from those of their competitors.

That said, research on the competition over authority has so far not debated the limits of the isomorphic dynamics. Nor has research on IOR in world politics inquired into the extent to which epistemic practices become more similar in global governance. We do not know, therefore, whether the isomorphic dynamics only apply to the epistemic practices but not to the knowledge produced through them. Yet, we cannot fully understand the interplay between IOR and the ordering of world politics without tackling this question. After all, epistemic practices – be it the compilation of statistics, the anticipation of trends, or the modelling of phenomena such as climate change – are crucial to many, if not all, processes of global governance.

Theory: organizational fields and their cleavages

It is interesting that authors emphasizing the diversity of interpretations and authors emphasizing isomorphism in epistemic practices point to the same factor: political contention, that is, disputes about the governance of issues. It seems therefore to be productive to unpack the interplay between political contention and field dynamics in organizational fields.

Conceptualizations of organizational fields as policy fields are a good starting point. Sociological neo-institutionalists have proposed various amendments to the initial conceptualization of organizational fields (for a recent overview see Wooten and Hoffman, 2017). As mentioned, one of these proposals is to treat these fields as being organized around political issues. Hoffman (1999: 352) notably argues that organizational fields do not form 'around common technologies or common industries' but 'around issues that bring together various field constituents with disparate purposes'. In IR, Vetterlein and Moschella (2014: 149) similarly stress that organizational fields feature a 'constant struggle over the respective object that is at stake'.

Sending (2015: 11) has so far developed the most elaborate field-theoretical approach to the competition over authority in world politics. He treats 'global governance' as being 'made up of more or less distinct and autonomous fields'. While drawing on Bourdieu's field theory rather than on the literature on organizational fields, Sending likewise conceptualizes these fields as policy fields. The fields, he argues, are 'organized around governance objects' and constitute the social settings in which 'actors compete with each other to be recognized as authorities on what is to be governed, how, and why' (Sending, 2015: 28, 11). The various organizations involved in the competition over authority may, but do not have to, mutually recognize each other as competent participants in the political debate about the object and its governance. Even if they do mutually accept each other as competent participants, however, these organizations nonetheless compete over which of them – or which subgroup of them – is and remains widely recognized as the relevant and decisive expert(s) on how to interpret and govern the objects.

An understanding of organizational fields as policy fields puts political contention front and centre. If fields are organized around issues, the political struggles over the governance of these issues are crucial to the dynamics that structure the respective fields. Political contention may fuel field-wide dynamics, such as isomorphism among field constituents. The already-mentioned 'indicator culture' is a good example. But political contention may also give rise to durable divisions in a political field, with two or more political camps fundamentally differing on how to govern the object(s). If this is the case, political contention has to be treated not as a factor fuelling field-wide dynamics but as a *process that divides fields into different political camps*, thus hampering field-wide dynamics and opening up the possibility that the dynamics generated by the competition over authority affect these camps differently.

This field-structuring effect has yet to be explored in a substantial manner. The present proposal is to borrow the notion of a 'cleavage' from cleavage theory and use it denote a durable division that emerges in an organizational field and that fragments it into different camps of organizations that fundamentally differ in their preferences for governing the object(s) around which the field is organized. Developed by Lipset and Rokkan (1967) to explain the structure of national party systems, the notion of cleavages is generally associated with diverging policy preferences among groups of individuals (for example, Hooghe and Marks, 2018; Ford and Jennings, 2020), though it also sometimes used to study political blocs in world politics, for instance within the United Nations (UN) General Assembly (for example, Binder and Payton, 2019). In the following paragraphs, the notion is applied in a loose sense to organizational fields; first, to highlight that durable political divisions may emerge among organizations, and second, to argue that, if they emerge, these durable divisions have an impact on whether, and to what extent, the competition over authority fosters isomorphism or differentiation, or a combination of both.

In world politics, organizational fields are generally populated by a heterogeneous cast of organizations. States arguably constitute the most influential type of organization. But the struggle over the governance of the objects also involves other types of organization, such as IGOs, NGOs, think tanks and companies. That said, cleavages in world politics are often durable divisions among states. Examples are the division into a capitalist Western bloc and a communist Eastern bloc during the Cold War, or the division into 'developed' countries mostly situated in the Global North and 'developing' countries mostly in the Global South.

Hüther and Krücken (2016) suggest that organizational fields can be nested – for example a global field including a European subfield including national subfields – and posit that such a nested structure fosters both isomorphism and differentiation. The nested structure, they argue, creates a fragmented field topography in which organizations belong to different subfields and consequently have to cope with different field dynamics. Cleavages similarly fragment organizational fields by splitting them into opposing camps of organizations. By doing so, they may shape the field dynamics in one or more of the following ways:

- By fragmenting organizational fields, cleavages may create a simultaneity of differentiation and isomorphism: a dynamic of differentiation between the camps – as they probably favour different interpretations of the objects and thus different ways of producing knowledge about them – that co-exists with isomorphic dynamics that make the organizations within each camp more similar over time in their forms and practices.
- Cleavages may hamper or prevent the work of IGOs that comprise member states from different camps. These IGOs cannot then act as governance institutions that set standards for the forms and practices, which makes coercive isomorphism an unlikely field-wide dynamic.
- Cleavages may influence which types of organization are prevalent in the production of knowledge on the objects around which the fields are organized. By making the work of IGOs more difficult, cleavages

also create opportunities for other types of organization, such as NGOs or think tanks, to establish themselves as (epistemic) authorities in the debates about the objects. Ecological theories describe this effect as a 'double-negative regulation' in which struggles among states prevent IGOs from governing the objects, thus leaving open 'a niche' for other, non-governmental types of organization (Lake, 2021: 349). Cleavages can, however, create a situation in which only organizations from one of the camps actually fill this niche.

The effects become more complex when organizational fields are divided by more than one cleavage. The East-West conflict and the North-South divide have co-existed for some time. It is thus possible that there are two or more field-wide cleavages. Moreover, cleavages may also emerge within the camps. The more fragmented the field topography created by the cleavages, the more complex are likely to be the dynamics of differentiation and isomorphism.

Methodology

This section discusses how the effects of cleavages on organizational fields can be grasped methodologically. As mentioned, the case study will focus on the organizational field revolving around military expenditures in world politics. Military expenditures denote the money that actors – generally states – spend on training, equipping, improving, maintaining and deploying armed forces. What makes military expenditures a useful topic for an illustrative and explorative case study is that the organizational field has been characterized by a varying degree of political contention over time, which allows us to reconstruct the effects of a strong cleavage on the formation of an organizational field and to check for eventual changes in the organizational field once the cleavage becomes less pronounced (on explorative case studies, see Gerring, 2017).

The research strategy follows the general approach in the literature on organizational fields: demarcate the field population, identify differences and similarities among the actors, and then explain them with the interactional dynamics in the field (for a good example in IR, see Dingwerth and Pattberg, 2009). To tease out the effects of cleavages on epistemic practices, special attention has to be paid to the subgroup of the field population that produces statistics on military expenditures. The analysis therefore involves four steps.

The *first step* is to identify the actors that populate the organizational field. Actors form part of the field when they spend money on armed forces, when they produce and publish knowledge on these military expenditures, and/or when they participate in the debate on and governance of the issue in world politics. The primary actors maintaining armed forces and making military expenditures are states. Two types of governance institution are active in the field: on the one hand, IGOs such as the UN that seek to make military expenditures more transparent and to regulate the level of military expenditures, on the other hand, IGOs such as NATO (North Atlantic Treaty Organization) and the European Union (EU), through which states coordinate the development of their armed forces. In addition, there are non-state actors such as the International Institute for Strategic Studies (IISS) and SIPRI that compile and publish military expenditure statistics. Finally, the field includes actors such as defence companies or peace movements that seek to influence the military spending of states, as well as actors such as journalists and scholars that report on and analyse the politics of military expenditures in world politics.

As epistemic practices are crucial to the competition over authority, the *second step* is to identify the subset of these actors that dominates the production of knowledge on the issue. While there is a broader cast of actors that occasionally publish military expenditures figures, the actors that dominate the circulation of knowledge about the patterns of military expenditures are those that regularly produce statistics on these patterns. These actors – listed in Table 5.1 – were identified based on field overviews published at different points in time (Albrecht et al, 1980; Brzoska, 1981; Brzoska, 1995; Lincove, 2018). As the table shows, the set is quite small and in large parts a product of the Cold War.

The *third step* is to tease out similarities and differences in the ways in which these organizations compile, calculate and distribute their statistics. The following two sections will delve deeper into the findings, but Table 5.1 already outlines some of the similarities and differences. It shows that isomorphic processes have been at play in the field, visible notably in the widespread use of NATO's definition of military expenditures and market exchange rates (MER) – rather than purchasing power parity (PPP) – calculation methods for converting national currency figures into US dollars. At the same time, it also hints at limits of the isomorphism, with most of the IGOs adopting their own definition of military expenditures, IGOs and NGOs differing in their data collecting methods, some IGOs abstaining from converting national currencies into a common currency and the US State Department departing from the general reliance on MER-based calculations in recent years.

The *fourth step* is to look for cleavages and to trace how these structure the field and shape the dynamics of differentiation and isomorphism. Cleavages can be identified by examining whether the debates on the governance of the issue are marked by durable political divides opposing different camps of actors. Debates about military expenditures – as most matters of security politics – were overshadowed and shaped by the East-West conflict during the Cold War. Based on a combination of primary sources – such as documents

Table 5.1: Regular publishers of military expenditure statistics

Organization	Compilation	Calculation	Publication
League of Nations	Mostly open-source analysis, occasionally reports by members	Military expenditures depicted in national currencies	*Armaments Year-Book* published between 1924 and 1940
UN	Voluntary reports by members	Depicted in national currencies	Military expenditure included in *Yearbook on National Account Statistics* since 1957
IISS	Open-source analysis complemented by a questionnaire sent to states	Depicted in US dollars, calculated in MER based on NATO definition	Yearbook (*Military Balance*) since 1959
NATO	Reports by members	Depicted in US dollars, calculated in MER based on its own definition	Yearly press release since 1963
ACDA/US State Department	Open-source analysis complemented by US intelligence reports	Depicted in US dollars, calculated – since 2012 – in five formats (both MER and PPP) based on NATO definition	*World Military Expenditures and Arms Transfers* reports published annually from 1966 to the end of the Cold War; irregular publication thereafter
SIPRI	Open-source analysis complemented by a questionnaire sent to states	Depicted in US dollars, calculated in MER based on a definition that largely overlaps with NATO's	*SIPRI Yearbook* published since 1969
World Priorities (Ruth Sivard)	Reliance on statistics published by IMF, complemented by those of other organizations	Depicted in US dollars, calculated in MER based initially on NATO definition, later on IMF definition	*World Military and Social Expenditures* reports published in 16 editions between 1974 and 1996
IMF	Reports by members	Depicted in national currencies, based on a definition developed by the IMF	Figures included in *Government Finance Statistics Yearbook* published since 1977
UN	Reports by members	Developed its own definition; no conversion of national figures	Yearly report by Secretary-General since 1981
EU	Reports by members	Depicted in Euros, when necessary calculated in MER, definition agreed among EU members	Yearly press release or report since 2006

published by the producers of statistics and UN documents from the debates on military expenditures – and secondary literature, the following two sections analyse how the political struggles over the governance of military expenditures during the Cold War, as well as the waning of these struggles after the Cold War, imparted the field with dynamics that shaped the choices of the various organizations for particular ways of producing knowledge on the patterns of military expenditures.

The transparency cleavage and its effects on military expenditure statistics

The Cold War was characterized by a deep political divide between a capitalist Western camp organized around the US and NATO and a communist Eastern camp organized around the Soviet Union and the Warsaw Pact (Gaddis, 2005; Westad, 2017). This political divide structured the organizational field that formed around the issue of military expenditures. The producers of military expenditure statistics competed over epistemic authority under conditions shaped by the politico-military competition between West and East. This competition fuelled not only an arms race that prompted calls for the limitation and reduction of military expenditures. It also involved a transparency cleavage that structured the isomorphic dynamics in several ways: it obstructed field-wide governance arrangements, gave rise to a Western-dominated ecology of producers of military expenditures statistics and created uncertainty about military expenditure levels that hampered the statistical work of these actors. Although the transparency cleavage was a product of the politico-military competition between West and East, it has outlasted the Cold War and continues to shape the organizational field today.

A lack of field-wide governance

The transparency cleavage was more than a policy disagreement. It reflected a crucial difference in the political systems of the two blocs. Western democracies valued transparency as a key element of democratic accountability. They were consequently much more transparent about the activities of their governments than the Eastern autocracies. In the West, military expenditures were, to a considerable degree, public knowledge and openly debated in parliaments. In the East, in contrast, military affairs – including military expenditures – were regarded as matters of secrecy. While publishing some figures, the Eastern states did not fully disclose their military expenditures. In fact, within the Soviet political system, the true size of the defence budget was a closely guarded secret known only to a handful of people. It was only with Mikhail Gorbachev's transparency initiatives in the second half of the 1980s that the Soviet Union became more open about its military expenditures (see Harrison, 2008).

The transparency cleavage contributed to the non-emergence of a field-wide governance arrangement for military expenditures. Reductions in military expenditures were one of the disarmament proposals that were debated and negotiated in the UN in the 1950s and 1960s. In 1958, for instance, the Soviet Union proposed that the five permanent members of the UN Security Council reduce their military expenditures by 10 to 15 per cent and use the money thus saved to help developing countries (see Spies, 2019). The negotiations failed because West and East fundamentally disagreed on the timing of transparency and disarmament. For the West, full transparency was a precondition for any disarmament – including reductions in military expenditures – while the East insisted that full transparency was not necessary for disarmament and should in fact be realized only after substantial disarmament had taken place. While the West accused the East of seeking to hide its true military capabilities, the East argued that the Western insistence on prior full transparency was a tactical ploy to prevent substantial disarmament.

The transparency cleavage plagued all subsequent disarmament and arms-control negotiations between West and East during the Cold War. The disagreement was only resolved in the last decade of the Cold War when, as part of Gorbachev's transparency initiatives, the East accepted the Western demands for full transparency, first in the negotiations on intermediate-range nuclear weapons and then in the conventional arms-control negotiations (see Müller and Albert, 2021). But the two sides never agreed on a framework for the regulation and reduction of the level of military expenditures, neither inside nor outside the UN. The cleavage thus prevented the emergence of a governance arrangement that could have fuelled field-wide dynamics of coercive isomorphism.

Producers of statistics emerging in one camp but not the other

What is more, the cleavage imparted the emerging ecology of producers of statistics on military expenditures with a particular structure. The UN did not revive the League of Nations' practice of publishing statistical yearbooks on military expenditures and capabilities. It did include, however, military expenditure data provided by its members in its *Yearbook on National Account Statistics* published from 1957 onwards. Nonetheless, while the East-West arms race and the UN negotiations increased the general interest in data on military matters, such statistics were still sparse. This gap was gradually filled by the IISS, which first published its *Military Balance* in 1959; the US Arms Control and Disarmament Agency (ACDA), which started publishing military expenditure statistics in 1966; and SIPRI, which first published its

SIPRI Yearbook in 1969. Military expenditure data was also included in the International Monetary Fund (IMF)'s *Government Finance Statistics Yearbook*, published from 1977 onwards.

As the UN and IMF statistics were regarded as incomplete and insufficient to make the patterns of military expenditures transparent, the UN General Assembly initiated the development of a voluntary reporting instrument for military expenditures. None of the UN members from the Eastern camp participated in the test phase of the instrument, which the General Assembly then adopted in 1980 (Spies, 2019). The transparency instrument did not, however, improve the situation due to the low number of UN members regularly reporting military expenditures (UN Office of Disarmament Affairs, 2010). Instead, SIPRI, ACDA and, to a lesser degree, the IISS established themselves as the premier providers of data on the patterns of military expenditures. The UN convened several groups of experts on military expenditures during the Cold War and these groups primarily drew on SIPRI and ACDA statistics for the depiction and discussion of the patterns (for example UN, 1972, 1978; UN General Assembly, 1988).

High political contention thus prevented the UN from compiling reliable data, while at the same time spurring the emergence of several publishers of military expenditure statistics, which, in turn, enabled the UN's groups of experts to discuss the patterns of military expenditures by relying on the statistics of these organizations. Consistent with the cleavage, the key publishers were all either based in Western states (ACDA, IISS) or located in a neutral state but nonetheless firmly siding with the West regarding the issue of transparency (SIPRI). Moreover, no publishers from the Eastern camp entered the competition over authority. The cleavage also explains why only one of the two military alliances chose to disclose annually the military expenditures of its members: NATO has released such statistics since 1963 (see NATO, 2022).

Uncertainty about spending levels and mimetic isomorphism

The various producers of statistics were confronted with the same problem: the varying degrees of transparency among states about their military expenditures. They assembled their data in one of two ways: the IGOs through (voluntary) reports by their members, the NGOs and ACDA through open-source analysis (see Brzoska, 1981, 1995; Perlo-Freeman and Sköns, 2016; for current methodologies, see IISS, 2020; US State Department, 2021b; SIPRI, 2022). Both methods encountered problems when states did not fully disclose their military expenditures. Interestingly, the UN did not choose to offset the limits of its reporting instrument through open-source analysis as its predecessor, the League of Nations, had done – probably in order not to wade into the contentious debate between West and

East about whether or not the numbers disclosed by the East were reliable. ACDA tackled these problems by drawing on classified US intelligence estimates, a practice unavailable to the other producers of statistics. The IISS and SIPRI instead emulated the reporting instruments of the IGOs by complementing their open-source analysis with questionnaires that they sent to states, though a considerable number of states did not generally respond to these questionnaires.

The three IGOs – the UN, the IMF and NATO – each developed their own definition of military expenditures. Their definitions did, however, overlap to a considerable degree (for a discussion see Brzoska, 1995). All three organizations included the expenses for the personnel working in the armed forces, the research, procurement and maintenance of weapons systems and the costs for military operations. They differed, inter alia, with regard to pensions (which NATO and the UN included), the stockpiling of strategic goods (which only NATO included), contributions to military alliances and UN peacekeeping (which NATO and the IMF included) and civil defence (which the IMF and the UN included).

During the Cold War, the Western states were those for which most data was available on military spending, both because of their parliamentary budgeting processes and because of NATO's annual press releases. Incidentally or not, NATO's definition was the one most emulated over time. In fact, NATO's definition has influenced the statistical activities of all three of the key providers of public data on the patterns of military expenditures. The IISS and the US State Department, which has continued ACDA's statistical work after the agency was disbanded in 1999, rely on NATO's definition as far as the available data allows (see IISS, 2020; US State Department, 2021b). SIPRI's definition is likewise similar to NATO's, though partially deviating from it to better account for the limited availability of data (Perlo-Freeman and Sköns, 2016).

Mimetic dynamics have thus been at play. These dynamics also extended to the set of indicators that the various organizations used. Peace researchers, for instance, criticized SIPRI for imitating 'Western sources' by including figures about military spending in terms of Gross Domestic Product (GDP) in its *Yearbook* from 1974 onwards, as such representations seemingly suggested 'that there is nothing unreasonable in rich countries spending more on armed forces than poor countries' (Albrecht et al, 1980: 67). It nonetheless became a standard practice to depict the patterns of military expenditures not only in absolute numbers but also in the percentage of their GDP that states spent on their armed forces. This measure is conventionally known as the 'military burden' (US State Department, 2021b: 22; SIPRI, 2022: section 7).

What hampered the diffusion of some indicators was another cleavage; one between proponents and opponents of disarmament within the Western camp. A notable example is the practice of contrasting military expenditures with other forms of expenditure, such as state investment in social services, education or development. In its early reports, ACDA prominently used this practice. The Nixon administration, however, ordered it to discontinue the practice on the grounds that such statistics were 'complicating the Pentagon's task of presenting the defence budget to Congress' (quoted in Roberts, 2015), as then defence minister Melvin Laird put it. In reaction, the developer of ACDA's reports, Ruth Sivard, left the organization and set up her own publication series *World Military and Social Expenditures*, of which 16 editions were distributed between 1974 and 1996. The UN assembled several expert groups on the links between disarmament and development, which likewise used such comparisons in their reports (for example UN, 1972, 1978; UN General Assembly, 1988). The practice, though, has mostly been used by proponents of disarmament and not much by other producers of military expenditure statistics such as ACDA, the IISS and NATO.

An expert discourse pushing for purchasing power parity calculations

The West-East cleavage, though, did not prevent the emergence of a discourse among experts about the best ways of measuring and comparing military expenditures. The staffs of the organizations producing military expenditure statistics generally understood them as a subtype of economic statistics (see Omitoogun and Sköns, 2006; also Smith, 2009). This fostered normative isomorphism. The organizations drew on the established repertoire of practices for international economic statistics for the compilation of their military expenditure statistics, as did the UN expert groups that were convened on the issue of military expenditures during the Cold War. They shared the same statistical language (current prices, constant prices and so on), constructed the international statistics in terms of US dollars and used the same methods for converting national currencies into US dollars (via MER, sometimes also via PPP). The organizations, however, applied these methods differently – for example by using different base years or sets of MER – and consequently produced dissimilar statistics despite sharing the same repertoire of statistical practices.

One focal point for the methods discourse was the UN's debate on military expenditures. The Western states insisted not only on the widespread use of the UN's transparency instrument, they also argued that a precondition for negotiations on reductions in military budgets was the development of an agreed method for measuring military expenditures. The General Assembly accordingly tasked a group of experts to study the measurement of military expenditures. The report, published in 1977, recommended the use of PPP, rather than MER, to account for differences in purchasing power among the UN members (UN, 1977). A follow-up group of experts was convened to develop a purchasing-power-based calculation method

(UN, 1985). Nonetheless, due to the dispute between West and East regarding the timing of transparency – before (West) or during (East) the reductions in military budgets – the UN remained unable to agree on a method for measuring military expenditures (for example, UN General Assembly, 1986; also Spies, 2019).

The two groups of experts acknowledged that the disparate levels of transparency among the UN members meant that the publicly available data was not sufficient to calculate PPP for all UN members (UN, 1977, 1985). The transparency cleavage, in other words, hampered the shift to PPP. MER has continued to be the preferred conversion method of the IISS and SIPRI. SIPRI, has, however, experimented from the late 1990s onwards with PPP (see Perlo-Freeman and Sköns, 2016). The US State Department, meanwhile, began, in 2012, to publish five different military expenditure indicators; three based on MER calculations and two on PP calculations (see US State Department, 2012). While the IISS has indicated PPP figures for some states in the country sections of the *Military Balance* for some years, it was only in 2022 that the organization amended the graphical depiction of the top 15 defence budgets to indicate both MER and PPP figures for Chinese and Russian military spending (see IISS, 2022). Overall, the juxtaposition of methodological debate and transparency problems has thus paved the way for more ambiguity in the statistical representations of the patterns of military expenditures.

Results: the persistence of field dynamics

The politico-military competition between West and East was characterized by a cleavage between Western states pushing for more transparency about military expenditures and Eastern states opposing – or at least stalling – such a development. This cleavage generated dynamics that led to a particular field structure with weak governance, the inability of the UN to build a substantial statistical infrastructure and the dominance of SIPRI, ACDA and (to a lesser extent) the IISS in the competition over epistemic authority. This section reflects on the implications of these findings for the question of how competition – and especially the competition over authority – affects dynamics of differentiation and isomorphism in organizational fields.

First, the case study underscores that a cleavage revolving around the degree of transparency of an issue gives rise to distinctive field dynamics. As mentioned, the literature sees political contention as a factor that fuels the publication of more statistics and, relatedly, widens the circle of producers of statistics. Cold War competition indeed prompted the emergence of several producers of military statistics, with the IISS, NATO, ACDA and SIPRI all starting publishing such statistics from the late 1950s to the late 1960s. At least as important, however, as the competition over authority that emerges in a field is the competition over authority that does not emerge. Besides preventing the UN from becoming an epistemic authority on military expenditures, the transparency cleavage also created a situation in which all the producers of statistics – apart from the UN – belonged to the Western camp or shared its transparency goal. If the contentious issue is transparency, political contention may narrow the range of field constituents that take part in the competition over authority.

Second, the ecology of producers of statistics has not really changed since the Cold War. This stands in some contrast to the growing numbers of producers of data in other policy fields, such as good governance, development and human rights, in the last three decades (Broome and Quirk, 2015; Kelley and Simmons, 2019). The case of military expenditures suggests an explanation based on variations in the intensity of political contention over time. The field revolving around military expenditures was characterized by high political contention during the Cold War and low political contention thereafter. The transparency cleavage still exists; with states such as China and Russia being less transparent about their military expenditures than Western states. But military expenditures are no longer as contentious as they were during the Cold War. One exception is the debate about the spending goal that NATO's members adopted at their Wales Summit in 2014 when they pledged to work towards spending at least two per cent of their GDPs on defence by 2024 (see Müller, 2022). Meanwhile, no new initiatives for the reduction of military budgets have been started in the UN since 1989 (Spies, 2009). While high political contention spurs the entry of new producers of statistics into the competition over authority, low political contention seems to have the opposite effect and thus preserves the established epistemic authority structures.

Third, because of the cleavage, the field generated both dynamics of differentiation *and* isomorphism. The producers of the statistics remained to some degree distinct in their data-collection practices, but they adopted similar practices of representing the patterns of military expenditures in terms of absolute expenditures and expenditures in percentage of GDP. NATO's definition became the shared reference for the three organizations dominating the competition over authority: SIPRI, ACDA/the US State Department and the IISS. But differences in the statistics have nonetheless remained. Table 5.2 illustrates these differences, using as an example the military expenditure figures of the three mentioned organizations for the year 2019 (the latest year on which all three organizations have published statistics). The figures differ partly because of representational variations, with the IISS depicting the patterns of military expenditures in terms of defence budgets while SIPRI does so in terms of military expenditures, and partly because the State Department publishes, as mentioned, five different measures, some based on MER and others on PPP calculations.

Table 5.2: Differences between the IISS, SIPRI and the US State Department in the depiction of the patterns of military expenditures in 2019 (in US$ billions)

	IISS	SIPRI	State Department	
	MER	MER	MER	PPP
World total	1,730	1,917	1,940	2,960
US spending	684.6	732.0	730.0	730.0
Chinese spending	181.1	261.0	245.0	417.0
Indian spending	60.5	71.1	67.5	225.0
Russian spending	61.6	65.1	65.1	170.0
British spending	54.8	48.7	59.4	70.0
French spending	52.3	50.1	49.7	62.6

Note: IISS = International Institute for Strategic Studies, SIPRI = Stockholm International Peace Research Institute, MER = market exchange rate, PPP = purchasing power parity

Sources: US State Department, 2021a and b; IISS, 2020; Tian et al, 2020.

The isomorphic dynamics have, in other words, not been strong enough to fully harmonize their statistical practices.

One key factor hampering the isomorphic dynamics has been the persistent transparency cleavage that prevents the UN from becoming the key authority on the patterns of military expenditures and which forces the organizations publishing statistics on the patterns to make estimates for a number of states, most notably China and Russia. This 'lack of transparency is one of the main obstacles to understanding the magnitude and consequences of military expenditures', as a UN group of experts stressed (UN General Assembly, 2004: 16). The diversity of the statistics is thus not – as research on the competition over authority assumes – an effect of dissimilar policy positions but rather the product of the cleavage that still fragments the field. The cleavage has led to a situation in which statistics are available but ambiguous and in which the lack of agreed data has obstructed – or at least served as a pretext for not engaging in – more substantial governance activities, such as the regulation and reduction of the levels of military expenditures in world politics.

Conclusions and outlook

This chapter has conceptualized organizational fields as policy fields organized around political issues and structured by cleavages. These cleavages, as the case study has shown, can give rise to field dynamics that fragment organizational fields, thus limiting the isomorphic dynamics that the competition over authority generates. Cleavages shape which organizations take up certain practices and how similar these organizations become in their practices. These findings point to two avenues for further research.

The first avenue is the study of organizational ecologies that govern world politics and impart order into it. IR scholars have recently turned to organizational ecology to explain why certain types of organization – for example IGOs and NGOs – proliferate and take up governance tasks in world politics (for example, Abbott et al, 2016). As Lake (2021) notes, these ecologies are embedded in organizational fields. But the research is still at the beginning of studying how the dynamics of organizational fields shape the ecologies of organizations that emerge in them. The chapter has stressed that cleavages can have a crucial impact on the ecologies. The evolution of the ecologies is not only a question of the shifting prevalence of certain types of organization. It is also a question of whether political contention structures organizational fields in such a way that only organizations – IGOs as well as NGOs – from one of the opposing political camps, but not from the other, take up certain practices, such as the publication of statistical knowledge about the objects that are to be governed.

The second avenue is to delve deeper into the effects of cleavages. The case study points to two effects: cleavages influence how order is produced in world politics by complicating field-wide governance arrangements and by circumscribing the diffusion and convergence of governance practices. The East-West cleavage prevented the UN from becoming the key epistemic authority on and regulator of patterns of military expenditures and it limited the spread of transparency practices for patterns of military expenditures, and with them the isomorphic dynamics, to organizations within the Western camp. The Cold War, though, was characterized by a particularly strong cleavage. To what extent do weaker forms of cleavage have similar effects? The limited spread of the practice of comparing military expenditures with social expenditures suggests that weaker cleavages can have such effects as well. In other words, how polarizing does political contention have to be to fragment organizational fields and, by doing so, to shape how much governance practices converge in world politics?

Acknowledgements

I would like to thank the two editors as well as the participants of the authors' workshop for their constructive and very helpful feedback. The chapter draws on my research on military comparisons in the context of the Collaborative Research Centre 1288 'Practices of Comparing' funded by the German Research Foundation (Deutsche Forschungsgemeinschaft, DFG).

References

Abbott, K.W., Green, J.F. and Keohane, R.O. (2016) 'Organizational ecology and institutional change in global governance', *International Organization*, 70(2): 247–77.

Albrecht, U., Eide, A., Kaldor, M. et al (eds) (1980) *A Short Research Guide on Arms and Armed Forces*, New York: Facts on File.

Biermann, R. and Koops, J.A. (2017) 'Studying relations among international organizations in world politics: core concepts and challenges', in R. Biermann and J.A. Koops (eds) *The Palgrave Handbook of Inter-Organizational Relations in World Politics*, London: Palgrave Macmillan, pp 1–46.

Binder, M. and Payton, A.L. (2019) 'Cleavages in world politics: analysing rising power voting behaviour in the UN General Assembly', in M.D. Stephen and M. Zürn (eds) *Contested World Orders: Rising Powers, Non-Governmental Organizations, and the Politics of Authority Beyond the Nation-State*, Oxford: Oxford University Press, pp 345–67.

Bourdieu, P. and Wacquant, L. (1992) *An Invitation to Reflexive Sociology*, Cambridge: Polity Press.

Boxenbaum, E. and Jonsson, S. (2017) 'Isomorphism, diffusion and decoupling: concept evolution and theoretical challenges', in R. Greenwood, C. Oliver, T.B. Lawrence and R.E. Meyer (eds) *The SAGE Handbook of Organizational Institutionalism* (2nd edn), Thousand Oaks: Sage, pp 77–97.

Broome, A. and Quirk, J. (2015) 'Governing the world at a distance: the practice of global benchmarking', *Review of International Studies*, 41(5): 819–41.

Brzoska, M. (1995) 'World military expenditures', in: K. Hartley and T. Sandler (eds) *Handbook of Defense Economics, Volume 1*, Amsterdam: Elsevier, pp 45–67.

Brzoska, M. (1981) 'The reporting of military expenditures', *Journal of Peace Research*, 18(3), 261–75.

DiMaggio, P.J. and Powell, W.W. (1983) 'The iron cage revisited: institutional isomorphism and collective rationality in organizational fields', *American Sociological Review*, 48(2): 147–60.

Dingwerth, K. and Pattberg, P. (2009) 'World politics and organizational fields: the case of transnational sustainability governance', *European Journal of International Relations*, 15(3): 707–44.

Farrell, T. (2005) 'World culture and military power', *Security Studies*, 14(3): 448–88.

Fligstein, N. and McAdam, D. (2012) *A Theory of Fields*, Oxford: Oxford University Press.

Ford, R. and Jennings, W. (2020) 'The changing cleavage politics of Western Europe', *Annual Review of Political Science*, 23: 295–314.

Franke, U. (2017) 'Inter-organizational relations: five theoretical approaches', in Oxford Research Encyclopedia: International Studies, available from: oxfordre.com/internationalstudies/display/10.1093/acrefore/9780190846626.001.0001/acrefore-9780190846626-e-99;jsessionid=0F07E33C9CBE65939CE9AC25F78FF7C9 [accessed 30 March 2023].

Gaddis, J.L. (2005) *The Cold War*, London: Lane.

Gehring, T. and Faude, B. (2014) 'A theory of emerging order within institutional complexes: how competition among regulatory international institutions leads to institutional adaptation and division of labor', *Review of International Organizations*, 9(4): 471–98.

Gerring, J. (2017) *Case Study Research: Principles and Practices* (2nd edn), Cambridge: Cambridge University Press.

Harrison, M. (2008) 'Secrets, lies, and half truths: the decision to disclose Soviet defense outlays' (PERSA Working Paper No. 55), Coventry: University of Warwick.

Hoffman, A.J. (1999) 'Institutional evolution and change: environmentalism and the U.S. chemical industry', *Academy Management Journal*, 42(4): 351–71.

Hooghe, L. and Marks, G. (2018) 'Cleavage theory meets Europe's crises: Lipset, Rokkan, and the transnational cleavage', *Journal of European Public Policy*, 25(1): 109–35.

Hüther, O. and Krücken, G. (2016) 'Nested organizational fields: isomorphism and differentiation among European universities', in E. Berman and C. Paradeise (eds) *The University under Pressure*, Bingley: Emerald, pp 53–83.

IISS (2022) '*Military Balance 2022*: further assessments', available from iiss.org/blogs/analysis/2022/02/military-balance-2022-further-assessments [accessed 30 March 2023].

IISS (2020) *The Military Balance 2020*, London: Routledge.

Kelley, J.G. and Simmons, B.A. (2019) 'Introduction: the power of global performance indicators', *International Organization*, 73(3): 491–510.

Lake, D.A. (2021) 'The organizational ecology of global governance', *European Journal of International Relations*, 27(2): 345–68.

Lincove, D. (2018) 'Key sources of multinational data on conventional and nuclear armaments', *Reference & User Services Quarterly*, 58(1): 11–15.

Lipset, S.M. and Rokkan, S. (1967) 'Cleavage structures, party systems, and voter alignment: an introduction', in S.M. Lipset and S. Rokkan (eds) *Party Systems and Voter Alignments: Cross-National Perspectives*, New York: Free Press, pp 1–64.

Merry, S.E. (2016) *The Seductions of Quantification: Measuring Human Rights, Gender Violence and Sex Trafficking*, Chicago: University of Chicago Press.

Müller, T. (2022) 'Self-binding via benchmarking: collective action, desirable futures, and NATO's two percent goal', *Global Society*, 36(2): 170–87.

Müller, T. and Albert, M. (2021) 'Whose balance? A constructivist approach to balance of power politics', *European Journal of International Security*, 6(1): 109–28.

NATO (2022): 'Information on defence expenditures', available from: nato.int/cps/en/natohq/topics_49198.htm [accessed 30 March 2023].

Omitoogun, W. and Sköns, E. (2006) 'Military expenditure data: a 40-year overview', in SIPRI (ed) *SIPRI Yearbook 2006: Armaments, Disarmament and International Security*, Oxford: Oxford University Press, pp 269–94.

Perlo-Freeman, S. and Sköns, E. (2016) 'Snakes and ladders: the development and multiple reconstructions of the Stockholm International Peace Research Institute's military expenditure data', *Economics of Peace and Security Journal*, 11(2): 5–13.

Roberts, S. (2015) 'Ruth Sivard, economist who scrutinized military spending, dies at 99', New York Times, 28 August, available from: nytimes.com/2015/08/29/us/ruth-sivard-economist-who-scrutinized-military-spending-dies-at-99.html [accessed 30 March 2023].

Scott, W.R. (2008) *Institutions and Organizations: Ideas and Interests* (3rd edn), Los Angeles: Sage.

Sending, O.J. (2015) *The Politics of Expertise: Competing for Authority in Global Governance*, Ann Arbor: University of Michigan Press.

SIPRI (Stockholm International Peace Research Institute) (2022) 'SIPRI military expenditure database: sources and methods', available from: sipri.org/databases/milex/sources-and-methods [accessed 30 March 2023].

Smith, R. (2009) *Military Economics: The Interaction of Power and Money*, Houndmills: Palgrave Macmillan.

Spies, M. (2019) 'United Nations efforts to reduce military expenditures: a historical overview' (UNODA Occasional Papers No. 33), New York: United Nations Office for Disarmament Affairs.

Tian, N., Kuimova, A., Da Silva, D.L. et al (2020) 'Trends in world military expenditure, 2019' (SIPRI fact sheet), available from: sipri.org/sites/default/files/2020-04/fs_2020_04_milex_0.pdf [accessed 30 March 2023].

UN (United Nations) (1985) 'Reduction of military budgets: construction of military price indexes and purchasing-power parities for comparison of military expenditures', Report prepared by the Group of Experts on the Reduction of Military Budgets, New York: A/40/421.

UN (1978) 'Economic and social consequences of the arms race and of military expenditures', Updated report of the Secretary-General, New York: A/32/88 Rev. 1.

UN (1977) 'Reduction of military budgets: measurement and international reporting of military expenditures', Report prepared by the Group of Experts on the Reduction of Military Budgets, New York: A/31/222 Rev. 1.

UN (1972) 'Economic and social consequences of the arms race and of military expenditures', Report of the Secretary-General, New York: A/8469 Rev. 1.

UN General Assembly (2004) 'Report of the Group of Governmental Experts on the Relationship between Disarmament and Development', New York: A/59/119.

UN General Assembly (1988) 'Study on the economic and social consequences of the arms race and military expenditures', Report of the Secretary-General, New York: A/43/368.

UN General Assembly (1986) 'Report of the Disarmament Commission', New York: A/41/42.

UN Office of Disarmament Affairs (2010) 'Promoting further openness and transparency in military affairs' (UNODA Occasional Papers No. 20), New York.

US State Department (2021a) 'World military expenditures and arms transfers 2021 edition', available from: state.gov/world-military-expenditures-and-arms-transfers-2021-edition [accessed 30 March 2023].

US State Department (2021b) 'Sources, data, and methods of WMEAT 2021', available from: state.gov/wp-content/uploads/2022/01/WMEAT-2021-Sources-Data-and-Methods_508.pdf [accessed 30 March 2023].

US State Department (2012) 'Sources, data and methods for WMEAT 2012', available from: 2009-2017.state.gov/documents/organization/209519.pdf [accessed 30 March 2023].

Vetterlein, A. and Moschella, M. (2014) 'International organizations and organizational fields: explaining policy change in the IMF', *European Political Science Review*, 6(1): 143–65.

Westad, O.A. (2017) *The Cold War: A World History*, New York: Basic Books.

Wooten, M. and Hoffman, A. (2017) 'Organizational fields: past, present and future', in R. Greenwood, C. Oliver, T.B. Lawrence and R.E. Meyer (eds) *The SAGE Handbook of Organizational Institutionalism* (2nd edn), Thousand Oaks, CA: Sage, pp 55–74.

Zürn, M. (2018) *A Theory of Global Governance: Authority, Legitimacy and Contestation*, Oxford: Oxford University Press.

6

Individual Linking Pins and the Life Cycle of Inter-Organizational Cooperation

Jutta Joachim and Andrea Schneiker

Introduction

International non-governmental organizations (NGOs) have become an integral part of global governance and global world order(s). They have played an important role in the development of norms and are by now crucial players in setting agendas and standards as well as with respect to monitoring of policy issues ranging from climate change to trade and human rights (Peters et al, 2009). They have instigated and shaped international institutions such as the International Criminal Court (Pearson, 2006; Haddad, 2013), and the provision of humanitarian or development aid is meanwhile inconceivable without NGOs. In order for such activities to be successful, NGOs often engage in inter-organizational cooperation, defined as the interaction between two or more organizations with respect to information sharing, the coordination of policies, joint decision-making and other activities (Biermann and Koops, 2017). While NGO scholars have begun to inventory and characterize the types of relationship that NGOs enter into, and have studied inter-organizational cooperation regarding its form and function (Keck and Sikkink, 1998; Henry et al, 2004; Yanacopulos, 2005; Carpenter, 2007a, 2011; Ohanyan, 2012; Elbers and Schulpen, 2013; Stroup and Wong, 2013), the inner workings of such cooperation remain largely unexplored.

Therefore, we still have only scant knowledge, particularly of the processes involved and as to who instigates cooperation among NGOs and moves the involved organizations from non-cooperation to informal or formal cooperation as, for example, in the case of the Coalition for the International

Criminal Court (CICC). Starting out as a 'loosely organized coalition of NGOs, it [...] transformed into a permanent institution at the court with two headquarters, regional offices, and a secretariat with a permanent staff' (Haddad, 2013: 189; see also Pearson, 2006). While constitutive of the existing world order with respect to human rights, we know little about how the Court's transformation came about, who were the driving forces behind it, and what prompted NGOs to move from informal to formal cooperation. The same applies to the Climate Action Network (CAN), a large coalition of NGOs that has existed since 1989, and of which Duwe (2001: 182) argues that individual agents 'act as entry points for the cooperation' among the partaking NGOs. Here too we do not really know of the exact role these individuals play, as we, more generally, lack systematic knowledge of how inter-organizational cooperation among NGOs emerges and is sustained.

In this chapter, we address this blind spot in the literature by examining the role individual agents play in NGO cooperation. We combine two concepts that have not been brought into conversation with each other and rarely found entrance into the works of NGO and international organization (IO) scholars: that of the *linking pin*, originally developed by organizational studies scholars (Organ, 1971), and that of the *organizational life cycle*, stemming from public administration studies (Avina, 1993). Based on an analysis of the cooperation among humanitarian NGOs in the context of security issues, we illustrate the merit of these concepts for the study of NGO interaction.

First, the linking-pin concept allows us to adopt a more micro perspective and thus to augment the tendency of international relations (IR) scholars to treat institutions and organizations in a monolithic fashion or speak of them as if they were individuals. It reminds us that cooperation rarely involves 'organizations in their entirety but hinges on individuals in the constituent organization' (Weiss, 2011: 208) and directs our focus to the actual persons '[who] do the interacting' (Organ, 1971: 73). Second, with the linking-pin concept we can examine the role of individuals at the 'staff level' (Biermann, 2017: 260) which, contrary to that in exposed, central executive positions such as the Secretary-Generals of the United Nations or the Presidents of the European Commission (Kille and Hendrickson, 2010), remains underexposed. Yet, as we will see, these individuals are ideally suited to initiate cooperation because of their location in the organization and their skills and experience. Finally, by combining the linking-pin concept with that of the organizational life cycle, it is not only possible to distinguish different phases of inter-organizational cooperation – start-up, consolidation, expansion – but also to capture the different roles that linking pins play across these phases, including that of the entrepreneur, the boundary spanner, the gatekeeper and the purposive practitioner. Empirically, we illustrate the merit of pairing the two concepts with an analysis of the cooperation among humanitarian NGOs in the context of security issues, which, as we elaborate on later, constitutes a hard case of NGO–NGO interaction. This conflicts with these organizations' self-understanding as well as how they want to be perceived by others.

Moving the focus away from what scholars have been preoccupied with thus far – the form and function of inter-organizational relations (IOR) – and towards the inner workings of IOR as well as its movers is important for at least two reasons. First, cooperation among NGOs, while a cornerstone of their impact, may, under certain conditions and in the examined case at hand, be a lifeline for NGOs, ensuring in the literal sense the survival of their staff. Second, studying NGO cooperation, in particular, provides relevant insights about IOR more generally, with respect to the instigators and how they contribute to the formalization of these relations.

Following a brief overview of the state-of-the-art literature on NGO–NGO cooperation, the chapter introduces, drawing on diverse bodies of literature, both the linking pin and organizational life cycle concepts and discusses how they can be used in combination with each other. Based on the case of cooperation among humanitarian NGOs regarding security issues, it then illustrates the explanatory power of the paired use of these concepts. The chapter concludes with a discussion and summary of our findings.

State of the art: NGO–NGO cooperation

Cooperation among NGOs is a rather common occurrence. These organizations regularly join forces and support each other to lend force to their issue-based campaigns. While widely acknowledged among IR scholars, the relations that NGOs maintain with each other have nonetheless received comparatively little attention compared with those between these organizations and states. The works that constitute exceptions in this respect have focused on the types of arrangement that NGOs enter into and their functions, as well as the power dynamics that structure the interactions of partaking organizations.

Keck and Sikkink (1998) were among the first to provide conceptual vocabulary on NGO relations, coining the term 'transnational action networks' to describe the interactions between predominantly though not exclusively NGOs and other like-minded actors, which are united by shared 'values or principled ideas' and play a central role in the creation of new norms (Keck and Sikkink, 1998: 2). Subsequently, scholars became increasingly interested in the structural characteristics of these networks and their functioning (Duwe, 2001; Katz and Anheier, 2005) since the 'reciprocal and horizontal relations of information exchange' that Keck and Sikkink assumed to be characteristic of them (see also Appe, 2016) masked the power relations that exist among their members (Joachim, 2003; Mische, 2003; Stroup and Wong, 2013) and how they 'deal with the diversity of their members in terms of priorities, ideology, culture and capacity' (Duwe, 2001: 177; also Elbers and Schulpen, 2013).

While finding evidence that advocacy networks provide opportunities for consensus and bridge-building, research, however, also shows that cooperation not only depends upon the self-understanding and identity of the participating organizations (Cusumano, 2020; Schneiker, 2020), but also is dominated by 'a few major "hubs"' (Carpenter, 2011: 77; also Stroup and Wong, 2013). Because of how they are positioned, individual organizations – particularly Northern and large-scale NGOs – are able to set the rules that govern the partnerships between NGOs (Elbers and Schulpen, 2013) and can facilitate or impede the promotion of certain issues (Lake and Wong, 2009).

Most scholars studying the interactions of NGOs interestingly point to, though do not further investigate, the role that individuals play in this respect. Examining the relationship between Northern and Southern NGOs in CAN, Duwe (2001), for example, finds that network coordinators occupy a unique space functioning as entry points for the individual member organizations and a pivotal position for their 'identification with' and 'commitment to' the network as well as 'a deeper understanding of each other's work' (Duwe, 2001: 182). Similarly, Elbers and Schulpen (2013), interested in the power asymmetries of partnerships between Northern and Southern NGOs, attribute the room for manoeuvre that the latter enjoy to individual project officers, who can control the flow of information and are responsible for interpreting and applying the rules upon which the cooperation rests. In this respect, they also highlight that the style of the individual officers may matter, as they found some of these officers to be 'less dominant than others' and more willing of 'handing over more decision-making authorities than others' (Elbers and Schulpen, 2013: 59). Finally, concerned with issue emergence in transnational advocacy networks, Carpenter (2007b), based on her analysis, calls on scholars to pay greater attention to individual agents within these networks who, because of their location, can be important gatekeepers or facilitating entrepreneurs inside or outside the organizations and at different stages of the process.

In this chapter, we build on the work of transnational advocacy network scholars and respond to their call to focus more on individuals and the roles they play with respect to cooperation among NGOs, especially when interactions move away from being informal and temporary and towards more formal and longer-lasting relationships, a dynamic, which, as Haddad (2013) observes, has, so far, not received much attention either.

Theoretical framework: linking pins and the stages of inter-organizational cooperation

NGO cooperation has, for the most part, been treated as a rather static phenomenon in the literature, which is why questions remain regarding its drivers. Who instigates the cooperation and moves it forward? And how and under what conditions does it turn from an informal mode of interaction into a more formal and institutionalized relationship? The literatures on non-profit organizations, as well as that on public service organizations, emanating especially from administration studies[1] offer important insights and relevant conceptual vocabulary, which we employ with some modifications to shed light on these questions. First, from scholars of organization and non-profit studies as well as public administration, we extend the idea that the life of organizations can be conceived of in cyclical phases of inter-NGO relations (for an overview, see, Cameron and Whetten, 1983; Mintzberg, 1984; Avina, 1993; Bess, 1998; Phelps et al 2007).[2] Second, from the works of organization and business management scholars, we import the concepts of 'boundary spanners' (Williams, 2002), 'boundary agents' (Organ, 1971: 73; Søderberg and Romani, 2017), and 'purposive practitioners' (Bardach, 1998: 6) to develop initial propositions about the qualities and functions of individuals who play a crucial role in NGO cooperation and whom we refer to as linking pins.

Phases of inter-organizational cooperation

In their review of literature pertaining to the life cycles of organizations, and drawing on Hanks et al (1994), Phelps et al (2007: 4) conclude that 'there is a reasonable consistent pattern of organization growth' about which a certain minimal consensus exists among scholars and since the 1990s when the topic received particular attention. Similar to many of his peers, Avina (1993: 455) assumed the pattern to exhibit more or less four discriminate phases 'each [with its] own set of distinguishable characteristics': (1) a 'start-up', (2) an 'expansion', (3) a 'consolidation', and (4) a 'close-out' phase (see also Phelps et al, 2007). We apply a similar thinking to the cooperation of NGOs and use the various phases as 'metaphors' or 'descriptive devices' to capture how it evolves and proceeds (Phelps et al, 2007: 7).

Of the different phases that Avina (1993) as well as others have identified, we consider the first three to be particularly relevant when inter-organizational relations are established, beginning with the *start-up* phase. In this phase, the challenge is not only to get a critical mass of organizations together, but also to determine 'the organizational and managerial structure, organizational goals and mandate, output targets, securing adequate financing, [...] the role and obligations of beneficiaries and [...] if and when to formally incorporate' (Avina, 1993: 459). This is followed by the *expansion* phase, during which new members are to be attracted; an aim that can be challenging. At the same time as the increase in membership puts the cooperation on firmer grounds, it can also endanger an existing consensus among participants who have been there from the very beginning regarding the aims and goals of the cooperation (Avina, 1993). Monitoring the environment describes best, according to Avina, the most important task in the *consolidation* phase. Although already relevant in the expansion phase as well, it becomes ever more pertinent for organizations 'to better align [...] operative capacity to [...] external reality. This may involve a reconsideration of [...] organizational structure, programme focus, operational procedures and/or development priorities' (Avina, 1993: 466). Admittedly, these are ideal-type descriptions of the various phases, which are unlikely to be fully matched empirically.

Instead, and as Avina suggests in his study related to organizational evolution, we can expect inter-organizational cooperation to be 'neither static nor unidirectional and, as a result, [the theoretical assumptions regarding the different phases] cannot be applied mechanistically' (Avina, 1993: 455; also Phelps et al, 2007). Some interagency cooperation may 'skip stages', close-out shortly after having started, and/or consolidate before they expand and not afterwards (Avina, 1993: 455). Nonetheless, the life cycle concept, as defined by public administration and non-profit scholars, is appealing. By dividing the process of inter-organizational cooperation into different sequences, studying it becomes more manageable and the roles that individual agents play throughout and in the various phases can be identified (Avina, 1993). However, since their roles, resources and skills still remain vaguely defined in models like that of Avina, we draw on the linking-pin concept to specify these further.

Linking pins and inter-organizational cooperation

The linking-pin concept has been coined by organizational and business management scholars (Organ, 1971), but is also increasingly finding application in IR research (Gest and Grigorescu, 2010; Biermann, 2017; Koops, 2017). To define the roles that individuals may play in occupying this position in inter-organizational cooperation, we rely on terminology that has frequently been used interchangeably with that of linking pins to specify, on the one hand, their personal characteristics and qualities, and, on the other hand, their current or past position.

First, linking pins are *boundary-role occupants* and *boundary spanners* because they are located at 'the interface between organizations' (Weiss, 2011: 208) and are therefore uniquely situated to instigate and be conduits of IO interaction. Second, linking pins are *entrepreneurs* who not only 'have excellent antennae, read the windows extremely well, and move at the right moment' (Kingdon, 1984: 184), but are also able to motivate and convince others to participate in cooperative arrangements. Third, linking pins are *purposive practitioners* (Bardach, 1998: 6). In addition to relaying information from one organization to the other, they 'decode' (Organ, 1971: 77) the information emanating from outside the organization and 'encode [it] into the customary verbal repertoire of [their] own constituents' (Organ,

1971: 77). Because this task often involves 'manag[ing] differences' (Williams, 2010: 19), Organ referred to linking pins as 'activist broker[s]' (Organ, 1971: 76) who are well-versed in interpreting information in a manner that resonates with individuals inside their organizations (Aldrich and Herker, 1977). The task of translation, however, affords of linking pins that they are multilingual (Organ, 1971). At the same time as the respective individuals must be intimately familiar with the practices of their own organizations, they must speak the language of the organization(s) that they are reaching out to in order to 'project […] an image of [themselves] as an understanding ally of outsiders, making concessions to their beliefs and values […] and "talking their language"' (Organ, 1971: 75). Accordingly, linking pins must know how to frame new and frequently contested information in a credible and persuasive manner to convince initial sceptics of organizational change instead to become supporters of new policies and possibly even more far-reaching modifications of institutional procedures and structures (Organ, 1971).

Fourth, linking pins are *caretakers*, and fifth, *gatekeepers*. With respect to the former, these are individuals capable of empathy and trust-building (Williams, 2012) and able to bring to bear the 'power of friendship' (Organ, 1971: 75) that they have built throughout their careers. Regarding the gatekeeping role, linking pins, because of their situatedness, skills and personalities, can control not only the flow of information between organizations and individuals (Aldrich and Herker, 1977), but also membership in cooperative arrangements. In inter-agency cooperation, we assume all of the discussed roles to matter, though not all at once. As detailed in Table 6.1, they can be expected to be actualized during different stages of inter-IO cooperation identified earlier.

Linking pins in the phases of inter-organizational cooperation

In the start-up phase of inter-agency cooperation, we would anticipate the boundary-spanning qualities of linking pins to be most relevant given the expansive personal networks they have garnered throughout their professional lives (Seabrooke and Tsingou, 2021), although their entrepreneurial qualities also matter. This phase requires, according to Bess (1998: 47), 'a prime mover' who is 'chiefly responsible for organizing the group' or, as Avina (1993: 456) puts it, 'a single motivated leader' (to mobilize resources, especially in terms of funding (Bess, 1998). Furthermore, in this stage, when neither explicit rules nor 'standard procedures, policies, and traditions' (Organ, 1971: 76) yet exist, actors who can guide the still-informal interactions need to be 'sensory organs' who 'monitor and screen important happenings in the environment' (Organ, 1971: 74), seize windows of opportunity (Kingdon, 1984), and identify a 'niche' (Cameron and Whetten, 1983: 284) that the cooperating organizations can claim, all of which are abilities that linking pins, because of their entrepreneurial qualities, possess.

Table 6.1: The roles of linking pins depending on the phases of inter-organizational cooperation

Phase of cooperation	Roles of linking pins	Characteristics/properties
Start-up	Boundary spanners	• Strategically located at the interface of organizations • Members of different networks
	Entrepreneurs	• Move at the right moment • Able to convince others
Consolidation	Purposive practitioners	• Manage differences • Frame/decode and encode information/knowledge • Speak different 'organizational' languages
	Caretakers	• Empathy • Capacity for trust-building • Power of friendship
Expansion	Gatekeepers	• Select information • Control membership

Compared with the start-up phase, when the activities of linking pins are mainly outward-oriented, that is, directed at actors outside the emerging cooperation, for example to attract external funding, in the consolidation phase, these are mainly inward-oriented and directed at the participants of the cooperation. This is also the phase where conflicts are most likely to arise over the precise purpose and nature of the cooperation given the 'multiple and diverse ideas' of involved actors (Cameron and Whetten, 1983: 284) and where linking pins are most likely to assume the role of purposive practitioners (Bardach, 1998) 'manag[ing] differences' (Williams, 2010: 19) and forging consensus (Avina, 1993; Bess, 1998). At times, linking pins may also be required to act as caretakers of both the newly founded networks and the structures as well as individual members whose expectations of the cooperation may differ.

Finally, in the expansion phase, 'coordination and control' might still be needed (Cameron and Whetten, 1983: 283) since, with the inclusion of additional organizations, already agreed upon goals of the cooperative arrangement might be once again challenged. Linking pins therefore assume first and foremost the role of *gatekeepers* (Williams, 2013), determining the flow of information (Aldrich and Herker, 1977) between organizations and individuals including who is allowed in and privy to receive it.

In what follows, we analyse the roles that individual linking pins have played in NGO–NGO relations in the humanitarian sector on security matters and in moving the involved organizations from non-cooperation to informal and eventually formal cooperation.[3] For analytical purposes, although empirically more fluid, we conceive of informal and formal cooperation involving more than two organizations as distinct. Formal cooperation is characterized by participating parties signing official documents that stipulate the terms of cooperation or the establishment of new organizations that facilitate the cooperation. Informal cooperation, by comparison, is marked by the absence of either of these.

Methods and case selection

To study the role of individuals during the life cycle of NGO cooperation, we focus on a case in which NGOs moved from initial non-cooperation to cooperation: that of humanitarian NGO security. Being major players in the humanitarian field, though also having been faced with increased insecurity in the conflict areas in which they work (Stoddard and Harmer, 2010; Stoddard et al 2012), between 2006 and 2012, NGOs have created an impressive number of formal institutions in the forms of networks, forums or new organizations through which they cooperate on security issues (Bickley, 2006; Stoddard and Harmer, 2010; Schneiker, 2015). This cooperation involves, for example, the sharing of security-related information and/or the pooling of resources in order to produce a joint product, such as a security manual, or a service, such as security consultancy or security training (Alter and Hage, 1993). One of the first, largest and most important security networks, the European Interagency Security Forum (EISF), with headquarters in London and established in 2006, has since globalized its membership and therefore, in 2020, changed its name to the Global Interagency Security Forum (GISF). With by now 'over 140 member organizations' (GISF, 2020), its evolution is indicative of the increasing relevance of security networks for humanitarian NGOs, which, at field-level, existed or still exist in, for example, Afghanistan, Gaza, Haiti, Kenya, Pakistan, Somalia, South Sudan and Yemen (Schneiker, 2015). Humanitarian NGO cooperation on security issues can be considered a hard case because of the many barriers to cooperation.

Although '[t]he last ten years represent one of the worst decades ever in terms of attacks on humanitarian workers and lack of humanitarian access' (Egeland et al, 2011: viii), security cooperation among NGOs is not self-evident, as the organizations have a 'tendency to approach security issues with insularity' (Stoddard et al, 2012: 9). First, the humanitarian NGO sector, in general, is characterized by a high level of competition among NGOs (Cooley and Ron, 2002; Bollettino, 2008; Weiss, 2013) and 'pervasive levels of distrust' (van Brabant, 2010: 10; see also Bickley, 2006). Second, NGOs are especially reluctant to share what they consider delicate and confidential information about, for example, attacks on their convoys or compounds or the sexual assault of staff members (van Brabant, 2001; Carle and Chkam, 2006). Such information may be interpreted by donors and competitors as a failure of an organization to adequately protect its staff or compound and, consequently, may lead to a loss of external funding or even the termination of contracts, which NGOs depend upon. Third, cooperation of the kind discussed here, involving the establishment and maintenance of new institutional infrastructure, is costly (RedR UK, 2017) and not all NGOs are able or willing 'to foot the bill for collaborative initiatives and are likely to "pass the buck" to an agency that is willing to pay' (Bollettino, 2008: 268). Given these various barriers, we examine the roles that individuals in organizations play with respect to the initiation and institutionalization of security cooperation among humanitarian NGOs.

Our data includes 21 interviews with individuals involved in the security networks mentioned earlier and individuals who possess significant expertise and knowledge of these security networks because they either work for donors such as the European Civil Protection and Humanitarian Aid Operations (ECHO) and OCHA or for consultancies. Of these, a sample of 19 was used for the analysis of the establishment of EISF and of some field-level cooperation mechanisms in Afghanistan, Gaza, Kenya, Pakistan and South Sudan. Questions we asked the interviewees concerned the emergence of humanitarian NGO security networks, the transition from informal to formal cooperation, and factors that facilitated and hindered the establishment of formalized cooperation networks. Given that our research relates to the establishment of humanitarian NGO–NGO cooperation with respect to security issues, the interviews were also conducted during the early stages of such cooperation between October 2009 and May 2012.[4] However, these data continue to be relevant, as humanitarian NGOs are still facing security issues and initiate or continue to use security networks to address them. Subsequent to the transcription and anonymization of the interviews, a qualitative content analysis (Mayring, 2000) was conducted. To identify the roles that linking pins played in the different phases of the inter-organizational cooperation, we analysed and grouped the statements of our interviewees regarding the establishment of security networks using categories we derived from the theoretical literature previously discussed (see Table 6.1). To triangulate, contextualize and interpret our findings, we used the burgeoning body of policy documents and reports on humanitarian security.

The roles of linking pins in security cooperation among humanitarian NGOs

This section offers a closer look at security cooperation between NGOs. We present the roles of linking-pins in the start-up phase, the consolidation phase and the expansion phase.

The start-up phase of NGO security cooperation

In this initial phase, linking pins play a key role because of their boundary spanning capacities. We found evidence for this in the case of NGO security cooperation. Many of our interviewees considered the presence of committed individuals who were members of different networks driving the process forward "against all odds" to be "extremely" relevant. As one of them noted, it takes "a couple of people in different organizations who feel strongly about it, who'll push it through," and another interviewee observed that the establishment of security networks "really does come down to individuals caring enough to do it". Furthermore, interviewees stressed that without people

> 'who are prepared to [...] put in that extra effort, then I guess it just doesn't happen [because] you [...] need a certain amount of coordination happening before a formal body will be launched [and] have to have a critical mass of people wanting something to happen for it to happen'.

A similar argument on the important role of individuals in starting off cooperation can be found in the literature with respect to the Sphere Project, a cooperative effort of humanitarians that resulted in the publication of the *Humanitarian Charter and Minimum Standards for Disaster Response* in 2004 (Sphere Project, 2004). In order to start the initiative, some individuals were considered as 'key actors' and 'connectors' (Buchanan-Smith, 2003: v, vii) between the different agencies involved without whom, according to Buchanan-Smith having interviewed an extensive number of actors in the humanitarian field, 'Sphere would not have happened' (Buchanan-Smith, 2003: 19). This is echoed in another publication, according to which, '[a] key to the success of Sphere was this particular consortium of seven individuals [...] who formulated the first plans for a standards project and drove the process that put the initial alliance together' (Walker and Purdin, 2004: 102–3).

To absorb the initial costs of cooperation, linking pins draw on their personal networks. EISF is illustrative in this respect. It was initiated by a few individuals who already "knew each other" and started to cooperate informally and by email. EISF also is illustrative in other respects of the importance of linking pins for inter-organizational cooperation since, once the individuals met informally, their gathering did not yet yield the products and services that participants had expected. Because people had jobs and "very full commitments in their own organizations", necessary tasks such as conducting "research [...] or [...] post[ing] things on websites" were not doable in an informal way or on the basis of, for example, "working groups".

The same linking pins who had already played an instrumental role in getting the informal network off the ground, also proved crucial for obtaining funding and moving the network from informal to formal cooperation. Bringing to bear their entrepreneurial qualities, the individuals identified potential donors and convinced the "bureaucrats" within the donors' agencies to fund EISF, but also attended to "all [...] sorts of awareness raising and some work that had to be done" in connection with obtaining funding. Next to their fundraising activities, linking pins also convinced organizations that until now had participated only informally to cooperate in a more formal manner. This entailed not only "proactively [...] address[ing] the question" of cooperation, but also overcoming organizational barriers within the potential member organizations, including doubts about the prospective benefits of membership.

Quite a few scholars have noted that a change in mood or context can be conducive for linking pins to overcome resistance towards their proposals (for example, Kingdon, 1984). In the case of the security networks that humanitarian NGOs established, our interviewees lend force to this, referring to, for example, a growing realization at least "in the Anglo-Saxon countries, [...] that the world [had] changed, that it's getting more dangerous and that they [humanitarian NGOs and aid workers] just have to do something about security if [they] want to keep working in these areas" and that "there was really something in the air". "[P]eople were just ready for" the security network that NGOs established. This is not only confirmed by relevant publications according to which '[a] deterioration in the security environment leads NGOs to question their security management' (ODI, 2010: 21), but also by other individuals whom we spoke to. They remembered that, even the NGOs that initially had resisted cooperation, were suddenly "more open to dialogue, more participatory and more involved in sharing", a shift that they described as "historically [...] quite ground-breaking". With their 'excellent antennae' (Kingdon, 1984: 184; also Williams, 2012), the linking pins seized this change in organizations ('attitudes') and connected the different organizations. Again, a similar point can be found in the literature with respect to the start-up phase of the Sphere Project during which key individuals 'were also "innovators", and they spotted the policy window to take forward their ideas' (Buchanan-Smith, 2003: vii).

The consolidation phase of NGO security cooperation

In line with Avina's organizational life cycle model, we also observed a consolidation phase in the case of NGO cooperation that involved the standardization of processes, products and services as well as managing difference (Williams, 2010). This ensured that cooperation continued even when individuals were replaced, as is often the case in the humanitarian sector given the high levels of staff turnover. As was explained in a report on NGO–NGO security collaboration commissioned by the European Commission and published in 2006:

> NGO security policies and job descriptions seldom highlight the need to actively pursue security collaboration efforts with other agencies. As a consequence, the attitude of an agency towards collaboration efforts is often influenced by the interest or awareness of individual managers. As such, an NGO's commitment to collaboration can alter as individuals change roles. Even when the need for a security collaboration mechanism is recognised and pursued by staff in the field, their efforts may be hampered by a lack of commitment and support from their respective headquarters. (Bickley, 2006: 16)

The importance of standardization was highlighted by several interviewees who provided examples of the likely consequences if it was ignored, as in the case of a security network that had "four different managers" within two years who all "came in with different mindsets, different perceptions of what safety and security meant, different understandings of the [regional] context, different personal biases, all of these other things that make us human". For the network, the turnover had detrimental effects regarding its "institutional memory" and the "consistency of contacts". To prevent negative effects of this kind, one interviewee shared that his network therefore "standardized formats for all messages" and standardized "its branding more and more, [...] much like you would with a company". In his eyes, it "create[ed] a professional atmosphere [where] people know exactly what our formats are like [because] similar type of incidents [are] report[ed] in a similar manner". The standardization of procedures, services and products does not happen by itself or automatically, but requires individuals – linking pins – who are willing to subordinate their personal ideas and preferences to a broader objective and a common goal. Nor is it limited to newly created cooperation mechanisms. Instead, it is also necessary within the participating organizations, where the cooperation and activities related to it have to become part of a job description, so that "it doesn't matter if that key person retires or resigns or leaves, [...] the organization will still benefit from being a member of that forum".

Interviewees also confirmed our assumption that the consolidation stage requires linking pins who 'manage differences' (Cameron and Whetten, 2010: 19) among organizations' interests and expectations. With respect to EISF, for example, one recalled that "there have been challenges [...] around what the purpose is of EISF [...] because of the certain expectations of certain people, different expectations I should say". For these differences to be resolved, it required a purposive practitioner, a linking-pin role that the first manager of EISF assumed and who had to build, according to one interviewee, "the identity of EISF". Another manager of another security network stated that he and his organization were "meeting with all the country directors of the INGOs on [a] one-[on]-one basis and getting to know what they expect from us", while another noted that "I have to go from one NGO to another in order to trying to reach a consensus", which was considered to be "extremely time-consuming". This is also echoed in a job description mentioned in a report on humanitarian NGO cooperation published by the European Commission in 2006, according to which applicants should bring with them the following qualifications: 'Communicating effectively with a diverse group of NGOs, developing an efficient security information network, and responding to the security needs of NGOs, requires a wide range of competencies that should encompass good communication, interpersonal, negotiating and analytical skills' (Bickley, 2006: 31). Scholarly writing about the Sphere Project finds similar attributes to have been important in the case of key individuals. Buchanan-Smith (2003: 19), for example, observes that:

> When the Sphere project finally did get underway, the role of the first Sphere project manager (Susan Purdin) was critical in guiding and managing the process of putting the standards and Charter together. Many of the terms and parameters had still to be defined – for example, what is an emergency, how to differentiate between standards and indicators. Susan is credited by many for holding together this inclusive but challenging and time-pressured process.

Related to consensus-building, many of our interviewees who were also linking pins emphasized that they had to develop "mutual trust" among participating members to ensure the continuation of the cooperation. As a manager of a security network explained:

> [I]t's all about trust. [...] I was probably recruited because I was already knowing most of the country directors and most of the NGOs working in [the region]. So of course, they all know who you are, where you come from and how you work, so that helps. And I did the same [...] with my own staff. Basically, I recruited people that I knew NGOs would be comfortable with because of their background, the ways they speak and so on.

To engender trust affords, according to Bickley (2006: 20), a capacity for empathy and to '[b]uild [...] personal relationships and develop an understanding of other NGO's mandates, security concerns and constraints'.

In the words of a manager of a security network we interviewed, this meant going to the various member NGOs and "hold[ing] hands". Others illustrated what happened to their networks if a linking pin did not exhibit trust-building qualities as, for example, in the case where somebody was recruited "who wasn't really ripe for the role. And you know if you have the wrong person in post, the wrong post holder [...] then it doesn't always work out." Consequently, and as was mentioned in a report published by the Humanitarian Practice Network at the Overseas Development Institute (ODI), a '[l]ack or loss of transparency and trust, for example because sensitive information is not handled discreetly', was considered a '[f]actor that can impede security collaboration' (ODI, 2010: 21).

The expansion phase of NGO security cooperation

During the expansion phase, linking pins have to attract new members while at the same time protect the mandate of the cooperation mechanism. They act as gatekeepers, filtering information coming into and out of the network as well as monitoring who obtains access to the network. With respect to EISF, interviewees explained the difficulties of expanding the network while simultaneously ensuring that it remained effective, since it grew from five NGOs to "a year and a half later [...] around 50 European agencies". To ensure its survival and integrity, EISF's "mandate" and "vision" resulted in particular requirements for membership: "You had to be an operational European registered NGO [and] have programmes being implemented in humanitarian development situations around the world." In contrast, advocacy NGOs or NGOs that "just do different things in London, or Brussels or wherever [...] actually weren't allowed to be full members". Furthermore, EISF only allowed attendance of an organization's "security manager or a security focal point" to avoid ending up with a group:

> where the majority was simply there to receive information or knowledge or ideas, rather than contribute to those and they felt that by not having security management, or security specific roles in the room, you might run the risk of just having people who come to listen rather than to come to speak.

For this reason, "EISF [...] explicitly [does not] want the head of human resources or the head of finance turning up." This kind of gatekeeping was, according to one network member who we interviewed, necessary because of the sensitive questions that are dealt with during the meetings and for trust-building reasons. Nonetheless, and as one interviewee noted, this approach runs the risk that EISF was "perceived as being quite exclusive" because "some organization[s ...] don't have these formal positions or formal job descriptions", such as "MSF [Médecins Sans Frontières] for example". Other interviewees stressed that the gatekeeping also served to preserve the "European" character of the network and to keep EISF "different from InterAction [and its] mandate to actually represent the US NGOs". Representatives of a country-level security network explained that the control over the flow of information between members and non-members had required a change of the network's policies regarding relationships with governmental authorities. While some participating NGOs had been highly distrustful of contacts that network staff maintained with state (security) actors, other NGOs had even terminated their membership, suspecting the network to carry out some kind of intelligence work for states. Consequently, this network limited the information it exchanged with governmental authorities, deleting, for example, embassies from their mailing lists. Therefore, as another interviewee explained, the network he works for would hold official meetings for every member to join and unofficial meetings with a handful of representatives of only a few selected member organizations.

Results

The case of security cooperation of humanitarian NGOs shows that the linking-pin concept and the organizational life cycle model we imported from organization and business administration literature proved useful to study the role of individual actors with respect to the dynamics of NGO interaction, and provides initial insights into how constitutive elements of world order evolve. Yet, the case raises questions that we address in this section, beginning with whether anyone can be a linking pin and then, whether different individuals can assume this role during the different phases. Regarding the former, based on the case at hand and the interviews we conducted, it takes particular individuals with entrepreneurial and leadership qualities to instigate and move inter-organizational cooperation forward. Next to determinism and being knowledgeable, they need to be insiders, be known to others and relate to them on a personal as well as on an organizational level. This limits the number of potential linking pins whose circle becomes even smaller when considering that fluctuation among them across different cycles of the cooperation is, as the empirical evidence suggests, counter-productive.

Although different skills and traits are asked of linking pins throughout the different phases, interviewee responses suggest that continuity among those who assume this role is important. For scepticism towards cooperation to be replaced with trust by participating organizations and their staff, for purposes of institutional memory and for consensus-building, it appears crucial that it is one and the same person who acts as boundary spanner, purposive practitioner, caretaker and gatekeeper. Fluctuation, by comparison, is disruptive, as it requires organizations to adapt to someone new and their ideas, visions and character while simultaneously trying to adjust to the functional requirements of inter-agency cooperation. As one interviewee stated:

> What hinders cooperation is [...] that [...] people change jobs very quickly. [...] If trust is the essential component and if trust is something between individual persons, then this high changing of persons is a problem. Because then trust has to be built over and over again every half year.

Yet, agency alone is not enough for cooperation to become formal. While linking pins seem to be a necessary condition, the cooperation among NGOs with respect to security highlights that their presence is not a sufficient condition. Without certain structural opportunities, such as the heightening security risks with which the organizations and their staff were faced with in conflict zones, it is questionable whether the NGOs would have even found value in information exchange. The same can be said about the financial support they received from donors. NGO–NGO security cooperation after the Tsunami in Aceh in 2004, for example, never moved from an informal to a formalized stage:

> Even with high level of commitment by key individuals, the scope and activities of the forum were limited and difficult to sustain. [...] Recognising the limitations of the forum, some agencies discussed setting up a dedicated NGO security support structure, but these initial discussions failed to generate the interest of donors or the wider NGO community. Over time, as key individuals who had driven the initiative moved on, the forum broke down. (Bickley, 2006: 14)

While the forum we studied enabled participating organizations to set up their networks and thus to sustain their interaction, it also can be used by donors to shape the structure and mandate of the cooperation or to attach conditions as to who can participate. Nonetheless, despite these structural bonds, linking pins are essential for the cooperation. In the case at hand, they created awareness for their need in the first place by drawing attention to the problems in the field and by putting them into perspective; they offered solutions of how to cope with the heightened security risks, and they also put forth the effort to place the cooperation on firm ground. How generalizable these findings are to cooperation among NGOs and other issue areas is the fourth question we address.

Although there are differences among NGOs with respect to their size and budgets, which allow the respective organizations a greater or lesser degree of autonomy, cooperation among NGOs is a rather common phenomenon. They do, for example, join forces on issue campaigns or often speak with one voice in intergovernmental organizations and when exerting pressure on states. Admittedly, cooperation of this kind is different from that analysed here, as it is often more short-lived and informal. Yet, we also find examples in different issue areas where informal cooperation became more formalized, as with the already mentioned CICC or CAN. The linking-pin concept, combined with that of the organizational life cycle, we posit, can be useful to understand the change in interaction among NGOs in such cases. Taken together, the two concepts account for both the agency and dynamic mechanisms through which organizations move from resource shortages and structural impediments to a cooperative response.

Conclusion and outlook

Based on the cooperation of humanitarian NGOs with respect to security, we analysed how the concept of linking pins, together with the life cycle model of organizations, helps us to understand the emergence of inter-organizational exchange relationships. While individuals occupying the position of linking pins play important roles in defining the need for such an exchange, overcoming resistance within organizations, and the formalization of cooperation, taking note of the different phases of the cooperation reveals that each of them presents different challenges. These, in turn, require particular character traits, skills and roles of the linking pin. Given their merits when being used in tandem, the concepts open venues for future research.

While the NGO cooperation examined here resulted in the establishment of formal networks, it would be of interest to examine the role that linking pins play in less formal NGO interaction, whether they become relevant only at certain points in time or the need for them ceases to exist at other times and when perhaps the exchanges among organizations have reached a certain degree of institutionalization. Furthermore, although the roles that linking pins play are considered to facilitate cooperation, it is also conceivable that, under certain conditions, they and the individuals performing the role may be subject to controversy. Identifying and studying such cases of contestation, as well as ones where the cycle of cooperation was interrupted and did not move beyond, for example, the start-up phase, would be fruitful to further specify the scope conditions of when and how linking pins matter for inter-organizational cooperation. Finally, prospective research might also involve studying the role of linking pins in other types of cooperation in which NGOs engage in, as, for example, with intergovernmental organizations and as part of advocacy coalitions or in the case of multi-stakeholder dialogues where some of the involved actors that linking pins encounter yield, most likely, more power.

In summary, much remains to be explored with respect to inter-organizational cooperation about which we currently know rather little in terms of how it evolves and the crucial roles that individual actors play.

Notes

1 For a comparison and discussion, see Cameron and Whetten (1983).

2 While the business management literature does formulate different models of the life cycle of inter-agency cooperation (Murray and Mahon, 1993), it only identifies different phases and fails to elaborate on what happens during these different phases beyond truisms.

3 This chapter is based on the article titled 'Linking pins as drivers of interagency cooperation: humanitarian NGOs and security networks' (Schneiker and Joachim, 2021) though, in comparison, conceptualizes and illustrates the roles that linking pins play in different stages of the inter-organizational cooperation.

4 Direct quotes in the empirical and result sections of this chapter are drawn from interviews conducted during this time period.

References

Aldrich, H. and Herker, D. (1977) 'Boundary spanning roles and organization structure', *Academy of Management Review*, 2(2): 217–30.

Alter, C. and Hage, J. (1993) *Organizations Working Together*, Newbury Park: Sage.

Appe, S. (2016) 'NGO networks, the diffusion and adaptation of NGO managerialism, and NGO legitimacy in Latin America', *Voluntas*, 27(1): 187–208.

Avina, J. (1993) 'The evolutionary life cycles of non-governmental development organizations', *Public Administration and Development*, 13(5): 453–74.

Bardach, E. (1998) *Getting Agencies to Work Together: The Practice and Theory of Managerial Craftsmanship*, Washington, DC: Brookings Institution Press.

Bess, G. (1998) 'A first stage organization life cycle study of six emerging nonprofit organizations in Los Angeles', *Administration in Social Work*, 22(4): 35–52.

Bickley, S. (2006) *NGO Security Collaboration Guide*, Brussels: ECHO.

Biermann, R (2017) 'The role of international bureaucracies', in R. Biermann and J.A. Koops (eds) *The Palgrave Handbook of Inter-Organizational Relations in World Politics*, London: Palgrave Macmillan, pp 243–70.

Biermann, R. and Koops, J.A. (2017) 'Studying relations among international organizations in world politics: core concepts and challenges', in R. Biermann and J.A. Koops (eds) *The Palgrave Handbook of Inter-Organizational Relations in World Politics*, London: Palgrave Macmillan, pp 1–46.

Bollettino, V. (2008) 'Understanding the security management practices of humanitarian organizations', *Disasters*, 32(2): 263–79.

Buchanan-Smith, M. (2003) 'How the Sphere Project came into being: a case study of policy-making in the humanitarian aid sector and the relative influence of research', *Overseas Development Institute Working Paper*, 215.

Cameron, K.S. and Whetten, D.A. (2010) *Developing management skills* (8th edn), Boston: Pearson.

Cameron, K.S. and Whetten, D.A. (1983) 'Models of the organizational life cycle: applications to higher education', *Review of Higher Education*, 6(4): 269–99.

Carle, A. and Chkam, H. (2006) 'Humanitarian action in the new security environment: policy and operational implications in Iraq', London: Overseas Development Institute.

Carpenter, R.C. (2011) 'Vetting the advocacy agenda: network centrality and the paradox of weapons norms', *International Organization*, 65(1): 69–102.

Carpenter, R.C. (2007a) 'Setting the advocacy agenda: theorizing issue emergence and nonemergence in transnational advocacy networks', *International Studies Quarterly*, 51(1): 99–120.

Carpenter, R.C. (2007b) 'Studying issue (non)-adoption in transnational advocacy networks', *International Organization*, 61(3): 643–67.

Cooley, A. and Ron, J. (2002) 'The NGO scramble: organizational insecurity and the political economy of transnational action', *International Security*, 27(1): 5–39.

Cusumano, E. (2020) 'Private military and security companies' logos: between camouflaging and corporate socialization', *Security Dialogue*, 52(2): 135–55.

Duwe, M. (2001) 'The Climate Action Network: a glance behind the curtains of a transnational NGO network', *Review of European Community & International Environmental Law*, 10(2): 177–89.

Egeland, J., Harmer, A. and Stoddard, A. (2011) 'To stay and deliver: good practice for humanitarians in complex security environments', Geneva: Office for the Coordination of Humanitarian Affairs.

Elbers, W. and Schulpen, L. (2013) 'Corridors of power: the institutional design of North–South NGO partnerships', *Voluntas*, 24(1): 48–67.

Gest, N. and Grigorescu, A. (2010) 'Interactions among intergovernmental organizations in the anti-corruption realm', *Review of International Organizations*, 5(1): 53–72.

GISF (Global Interagency Security Forum) (2020) homepage at: gisf.ngo [accessed 17 May 2023].

Haddad, H.N. (2013) 'After the norm cascade: NGO mission expansion and the coalition for the International Criminal Court', *Global Governance*, 19(2): 187–206.

Hanks, S.H., Watson, C.J., Jansen, E. and Chandler, G.N. (1994) 'Tightening the life-cycle construct: a taxonomic study of growth stage configurations in high-technology organizations', *Entrepreneurship Theory and Practice*, 18(2): 5–29.

Henry, L., Mohan, G. and Yanacopulos, H. (2004) 'Networks as transnational agents of development', *Third World Quarterly*, 25(5): 839–55.

Joachim, J. (2003) 'Framing issues and seizing opportunities: the UN, NGOs, and women's rights', *International Studies Quarterly*, 47(2): 247–74.

Katz, H. and Anheier, H. (2005) 'Global connectedness: the structure of transnational NGO networks' in M. Glasius, M. Kaldor and H. Anheier (eds) *The Global Civil Society Yearbook* 2005–2006, London: Sage, pp 240–65.

Keck, M.E. and Sikkink, K. (1998) *Activists Beyond Borders: Advocacy Networks in International Politics*, Ithaca and London: Cornell University Press.

Kille, K.J. and Hendrickson, R.C. (2010) 'Secretary-General leadership across the United Nations and NATO: Kofi Annan, Javier Solana, and Operation Allied Force', *Global Governance*, 16(4): 505–23.

Kingdon, J.W. (1984) *Agendas, Alternatives, and Public Policies* (2nd edn), Boston: Longman.

Koops, J.A. (2017) 'Inter-organizationalism in international relations: a multilevel framework of analysis', in R. Biermann and J.A. Koops (eds) *The Palgrave Handbook of Inter-Organizational Relations in World Politics*, London: Palgrave Macmillan, pp 189–216.

Lake, D.A. and Wong, W.H. (2009) 'The politics of networks: interests, power, and human rights norms', in M. Kahler (ed) *Networked Politics: Agency, Power and Governance*, Ithaca and London: Cornell University Press, pp 127–50.

Mayring, P. (2000) 'Qualitative content analysis', Forum Qualitative Sozialforschung / Forum: Qualitative *Social Research*, 1(2).

Mintzberg, H. (1984) 'Power and organization life cycles', *Academy of Management Review*, 9(2): 207–24.

Mische, A. (2003) 'Cross-talk in movements: reconceiving the culture-network link', in M. Diani and D. McAdam (eds) *Social Movements and Networks: Relational Approaches to Collective Action,* Oxford: Oxford University Press, pp 258–80.

Murray, E.A. and Mahon, J.F. (1993) 'Strategic alliances: gateway to the new Europe?', *Long Range Planning*, 26(4): 102–11.

ODI (Overseas Development Institute) (2010) 'Operational security management in violent environments', *Good Practice Review*, 8.

Ohanyan, A. (2012) 'Network institutionalism and NGO studies', *International Studies Perspectives*, 13(4): 366–89.

Organ, D.W. (1971) 'Linking pins between organizations and environment: individuals do the interacting', *Business Horizons*, 14(6): 73–80.

Pearson, Z. (2006) 'Non-governmental organizations and the International Criminal Court: changing landscapes of international law', *Cornell International Law Journal*, 39(2): 243–84.

Peters, A., Koechlin, L. and Zinkernagel, G.F. (2009) 'Non-state actors as standard setters: framing the issue in an interdisciplinary fashion', in A. Peters, L. Koechlin, T. Förster, and G.F. Zinkernagel (eds) *Non-State Actors as Standard Setters*, Cambridge: Cambridge University Press, pp 1–32.

Phelps, R., Adams, R. and Bessant, J. (2007) 'Life cycles of growing organizations: a review with implications for knowledge and learning', *International Journal of Management Reviews*, 9: 1–30.

RedR UK (2017) Security Incident Information Management Handbook, available from: redr.org.uk/Our-Work/Key-Projects/Security-Incident-Information-Management-(SIIM)/The-Security-Incident-Information-Management-Handb [accessed 30 March 2023].

Schneiker, A. (2020) 'Why trust you? Security cooperation within humanitarian NGO networks', *Disasters*, 44(1): 25–43.

Schneiker, A. (2015) 'Humanitarian NGO security networks and organisational learning: identity matters and matters of identity', *Voluntas*, 26(1): 144–70.

Schneiker, A. and Joachim, J. (2021) 'Linking pins as drivers of interagency cooperation: humanitarian NGOs and security networks', *Globalizations*, 18(4): 600–16.

Seabrooke, L. and Tsingou, E. (2021) 'Revolving doors in international financial governance', *Global Networks*, 21(2): 294–319.

Søderberg, A.-M. and Romani, L. (2017) 'Boundary spanners in global partnerships: a case study of an Indian vendor's collaboration with Western clients', *Group & Organization Management*, 42(2): 237–78.

Sphere Project (2004) *Humanitarian Charter and Minimum Standards in Disaster Response*, Oxford: Oxfam.

Stoddard, A. and Harmer, A. (2010) *Supporting Security for Humanitarian Action: A Review of Critical Issues for the Humanitarian Community*, Humanitarian Outcomes, March, available from: humanitarianoutcomes.org/publications/supporting-security-humanitarian-action [accessed 30 March 2023].

Stoddard, A., Harmer, A. and Hughes, M. (2012) *Aid Worker Security Report 2012: Host States and Their Impact on Security for Humanitarian Operations*, Humanitarian Oucomes, December, available from: humanitarianoutcomes.org/publications/aid-worker-security-report-2012-host-states [accessed 30 March 2023].

Stroup, S.S. and Wong, W.H. (2013) 'Come together? Different pathways to international NGO centralization', *International Studies Review*, 15(2): 163–84.

van Brabant, K. (2010) 'Managing aid agency security in an evolving world: the larger challenge', London: European Interagency Security Forum, available from: gisf.ngo/wp-content/uploads/2010/12/2005-Koenraad-Van-Brabant-2010-EISF_Managing-Aid-Agency-Security-in-an-Evolving-World.pdf [accessed 30 March 2023].

van Brabant, K. (2001) 'Mainstreaming safety and security management in aid agencies. A review of aid agency practices and a guide for management', *HPG Report*, 9.

Walker, P. and Purdin, S. (2004) 'Birthing Sphere', *Disasters*, 28(2): 100–11.

Weiss, T. (2013) *Humanitarian Business*, Cambridge: Polity Press.

Weiss, T. (2011) *Thinking about Global Governance: Why People and Ideas Matter*, London and New York: Routledge.

Williams, P. (2013) 'We are all boundary spanners now', *International Journal of Public Sector Management*, 26(1): 17–32.

Williams, P. (2012) *Collaboration in Public Policy and Practice*, Bristol: Bristol University Press.

Williams, P. (2010) 'Special agents: the nature and role of boundary spanners', in *ESRC Research Seminar Series: Collaborative Futures – New Insights from Intra and Inter-Sectoral Collaborations*, Birmingham: University of Birmingham.

Williams, P. (2002) 'The competent boundary spanner', *Public Administration*, 80(1): 103–24.

Yanacopulos, H. (2005) 'The strategies that bind: NGO coalitions and their influence', *Global Networks*, 5(1): 93–110.

7

The UN Global Compact as Inter-Organizational Relations

Matthias Hofferberth

Introduction

Since its creation in 1999, the UN Global Compact (UNGC) has been discussed as a prime example of global governance involving multinational enterprises (MNEs) (Rasche and Gilbert, 2012; see also Ruggie, 2001). As a multi-stakeholder initiative (MSI), the UNGC is designed to bring different entities together to discuss and improve standards for human rights, labour conditions and the environment, as well as combat corruption. Fostering corporate social responsibility (CSR), transparency and dialogue, the UNGC, at least for advocates, promotes and expands fundamental responsibilities of business in a globalized economy. Such an economy, it has been argued, is 'ungovernable' through states alone (Held and McGrew, 2002). With this logic, the UNGC marks an important step towards a more inclusive and effective global governance (Brown et al, 2018). Contrary to this, critics of the UNGC have emphasized that the Compact remains limited in its current form since compliance with its principles remains voluntary and the network appears too loose (Andrews, 2019). Following this account, the UNGC, at best, has no impact. At worst, it provides an opportunity for MNEs to 'bluewash' themselves by capitalizing on the moral authority of the UN (Berliner and Prakash, 2015).

Going into its third decade, the debate between these two sides has not been settled and the overall impact of the initiative remains more uncertain than ever (Podrecca et al, 2021). In this chapter, I want to relate to and weigh in on this debate by framing the UNGC through the lens of inter-organizational relations (IOR). The rationale for this is simple: I argue that both advocates and critics rely on a similar and ultimately limited ontology of governance and the UNGC. Both assume the existence of independent global governors deliberately interacting within the Compact. The UNGC as such becomes a space to meet but otherwise does not have any transformational impact on the actors involved (Barrese et al, 2020). In other words, neither reading takes inter-organizational dynamics into consideration that potentially change how MSIs evolve over time and constitutively affect their participants. Furthermore, neither reflects how MNEs, NGOs, cities and other public-sector entities mutually recognize each other and thereby (re)produce their agency as constituents within the UNGC. Ignoring the dynamics of IOR within and through the UNGC, current assessments of the Compact in particular essentialize corporate agency and conflate *explanations for* with *implications of* the initiative. With the case for meaningful change in corporate behaviour still empirically undecided, the recognition and sustenance of corporate agency through the UNGC is potentially the initiative's most important world-order contribution as defined in the introduction to this volume (also Hofferberth and Lambach, 2022).

I contend that understanding the fluid nature of the UNGC as IOR helps us to shed light on its foundational dynamics, how it creates and sustains agency, and allows us to better assess how it contributes to world order(ing). More specifically, taking IOR seriously, I consider how corporate agency both impacts the Compact and becomes sustained by it. I do so by analysing the origins and rationale of the initiative and relate this to corporate understandings that are expressed in public statements relating to the UNGC. Overall, the UNGC has contributed to the emergence and sustenance of different *global governors*, such as MNEs, but might have been less impactful on the self-understanding and responsibilities of these actors. Framing the UNGC as IOR reveals these dynamics. It also allows us to reconcile this broader research agenda within the paradigm of global governance. In this light, I argue for a conceptual expansion of what is traditionally considered IOR (for example, conflict or cooperation between intergovernmental organizations) to include other global governors and their interactions as well. If understood and applied beyond the narrow notion of overlapping mandates of intergovernmental organizations, IOR and its emphasis on relations speaks directly to the foundational dynamics of global governance. In fact, speaking to the very core of it, a relational ontology of IOR can help us to answer *how and why* specific entities become recognized as global governors at specific points in time in order to govern specific problems in the light of each other's incapacity to govern alone (Hofferberth, 2019b).

In a first step, the chapter provides background information on the UNGC and reviews how the initiative has been discussed in the literature. This helps to sustain my claim that there are certain shortcomings in the literature as advocates and critics both rely – implicitly or explicitly – on the same ontology and fail to fully capture the dynamics of the UNGC. A second step spells out the theoretical argument of framing the UNGC as IOR in more detail by connecting this approach to global governance, agency and dynamics of recognition more broadly. In the same section, I argue that we can expand our understanding of IOR if we take into consideration its inherent fluid and dynamic character and apply it to the broader study of different entities interacting in the provision of order. The theoretical section is followed by methodological considerations on case selection and outlines the analysis. The empirical section offers illustrative insights by looking into statements during the creation of the UNGC as well as selected corporate documents reflecting how BP as an extractive MNE relates to the initiative. These insights are summarized in the results section and discussed in a broader context in the final section, concluding that reframing the UNGC as IOR reveals its most important contribution to world order(ing): the sustained recognition of corporate actors as legitimate global governors. With the broader research programme in mind, we arguably need to better theorize these dynamics of recognition if we want to further reconcile the notions of IOR and global governance.

The UN Global Compact and its ongoing assessment

Announced in 1999 by then UN Secretary-General Kofi Annan and officially launched in 2000, the UNGC, from its inception, was framed as a voluntary 'self-regulatory *guideline* that encourages organizations to monitor their social performance in the areas of human rights, labour, environment and anti-corruption' (Podrecca et al, 2021: 3, emphasis added). Framed in ten principles adapted from the Universal Declaration of Human Rights, the International Labour Organization's Declaration on Fundamental Principles and Rights at Work, the Rio Declaration on Environment and Development and the UN Convention against Corruption, the UNGC advances general ideas instead of a specific code of conduct on human rights, labour, environment and anti-corruption (UNGC, nd). It is important to understand that the principles deliberately do not translate into any obligations other than providing annual reports of 'communication on progress'. With this in mind, the UNGC stands out among the many multi-stakeholder CSR initiatives for at least two reasons. First, with currently more than 18,000 participants from more than 160 countries, it is the most-widely recognized and largest global initiative. Second, with roughly 3,000 constituents not communicating (Rasche et al, 2020), the UNGC remains rather loose and fluid. Taken together, the UNGC has become a large, dynamic initiative because it is easy to join (and difficult to be expelled from). All it takes is a letter of commitment expressing adherence to broad principles, and yet many participants fail to submit their communications on progress and hence become delisted (Orzesa et al, 2018).

Given its potential to be *the* global CSR initiative, the loose, non-compelling nature of the UNGC has polarized its academic reflection. Advocates of the Compact stressed from early on the need for dialogue between MNEs and civil society and emphasized the impact of the initiative as a flexible learning network (Kell and Ruggie, 1999; Ruggie, 2001; Kell and Levin, 2003; Williams, 2004; Kell, 2005).[1] Later contributions discussed the significant amount of growth as further evidence of how successful the UNGC was and argued that it would be a compelling force for good just by its momentum and the fact that so many members have joined, praising the overall journey as a success story (Kell, 2013; Rasche and Waddock, 2014). Critics on the other hand have argued that joining the UNGC cannot be considered meaningful CSR since the costs in doing so would be simply too low (Deva, 2006), leaving us with a loose network best characterized by its 'promise-performance gap' (Sethi and Schepers, 2014). Potentially even worse, the UNGC would allow corporate actors to 'bluewash' their CSR performance, since it does not require any change in behaviour to remain in good standing (Berliner and Prakash, 2015). Echoing a larger divide on the potential of voluntary CSR schemes and MSIs (Hofferberth, 2011), there seems to be little common ground between these two readings. While advocates argue that criticizing the UNGC for lacking bite and accountability misreads what the Compact intends to achieve (Rasche, 2009; Palazzo and Scherer, 2010), critics do not see any progress and emphasize that the UNGC fails to develop binding tools to enforce CSR (Sethi and Schepers, 2014).

These two diverging assessments of the UNGC have provided important insights into the initiative. At the same time, however, they have developed their own, rather self-referential 'niche discourse' of academics and involved practitioners. With some notable exceptions (Berliner and Prakash, 2015; Pouliot and Thérien, 2018; Andrews, 2019), the UNGC is no longer discussed and cross-referenced to broader themes and theories of global governance. Against its interdisciplinary and practice-focused nature, it seems that research on the UNGC is now mostly advanced in business ethics and regulation studies.[2] Ironically, while contrasting in their assessment, both advocates and critics rely on a similar ontology of governance. More specifically, both assume the existence of independent global governors deciding whether joining the Compact is in their interest or not. As such, while not providing a conclusive assessment, both presuppose and, through their assessment, restate the agency of the many different entities involved in the UNGC. Neither approach frames the participants relationally nor seems to be interested in the potential contribution to world order that is established by a broad range of different entities as legitimate global governors. What seems to be lacking is a willingness to work through and assess the Compact based on a relational ontology that IOR offers (Jackson and Nexon, 1999; Kurki, 2021). The starting assumption of this perspective would be not to take corporate agency for granted but focus on 'why [these] actors are authorities and are able to govern [...] to better understand their behaviors, relationships, and impacts' (Avant et al, 2010: 9). As argued next, reframing the UNGC as IOR and thereby advancing the agenda speaks precisely to this lacuna in global governance.

Framing the UN Global Compact as inter-organizational relations

More than ten years ago, Biermann (2011: 174) concluded that inter-organizational research in IR was in its infant stage, marked by 'a period of experimentation'. Arguably, despite many calls for synthesis and maturing in the meantime, this stage endures, simply because it is such a vast theme and different scholars imply different meanings or focus on different aspects (Franke, 2017; Franke and Koch, 2013). Following the inclusive conceptualization shared in the introduction to this volume, IOR is about overlap, interaction, convergence and potential conflict based on shared commitments between otherwise unrelated entities to govern particular issues. As such, inter-organizational relations include more than interaction between intergovernmental organizations. It rather reflects a core dynamic of global governance: most issues are governed by a multitude of different entities working together or against each other to provide order across borders (Weiss and Wilkinson, 2014). Each limited in their authority, global governors naturally overlap in their missions, responsibilities, interests, mandates and competencies. In addition to broadening the scope of actors in IOR, we also need to further theorize the constitutive effects that follow from it. In this light, inter-organizational relations do not only produce rules and governance. Equally important, different global governors recognize each other, confirm their agency and define their interests in relations with one another. As such, IOR can help global governance to determine *why* specific entities become recognized as global governors at specific points in time to govern specific problems in light of each other's inability to govern alone.[3]

IOR broadly conceptualized thus helps us to understand 'how IOs and *other sorts of organizations* interact, cooperate, use one another for their own purposes, and how they sometimes compete with each other' (Franke and Koch, 2013: 86, emphasis added). This already creates an affinity to core ideas of global governance, such as the absence of a final authority and multi-stakeholderism in lieu. In other words, for global governance as well as for IOR, the 'starting point is a relational one which gives analytic primacy to the links between organizations' (Biermann, 2011: 273). Taken seriously, we cannot simply presume a predefined list of actors interacting but need to consider how entities become actors in the first place. Finnemore (2014: 223) explores this theme by arguing that global governors are constituted through dynamics of cooperation/competition stemming from institutional density:

> Global governors compete, conflict, cooperate, delegate, and divide labor in a host of ways we have not always examined systematically, but should. Those trying to influence global policy may be in direct and obvious conflict as when advocacy groups clash with states or with each other. Outcomes then may range from victory for one side, to compromise of many types, to more dysfunctional eviscerations of the formally victorious policy by the losers.

Moving inter-organizational research beyond intergovernmental organizations and their formal mandates helps us to capture more holistically the range of 'public, business, or non-profit' entities and their relationships ranging 'from dyadic, involving just two organizations, to multiplicitous, involving huge networks of many organizations' (Cropper et al, 2008: 4). It also reminds us that different global governors interact in different ways to provide governance and that there are more than formal rules as outputs. Specifically, we can think of global governance and agency within it as consequences of relations instead of framing agency as an individual property or commodity based on authorization and delegation (Hofferberth, 2019b). An inter-organizational framework thus should also speak to why particular entities become recognized and consider their agency in terms of how it allowed them to be involved in the first place (Avant et al, 2010). Agency in this relational perspective is inextricably tied to recognition. Given the political nature of any governance, recognition relates to questions of authority and legitimacy, both of which are also relationally constituted and consequences of what entities bring to the interaction (Krisch, 2017). IOR thus helps us to capture how different entities advance their 'agency claims' and see that, through performing acts such as setting agendas, establishing rules, monitoring compliance, pushing for enforcement and evaluating outcomes, they not only interact but through their relations become global governors in the first place:

> Governance is not a solo act, and governors can rarely accomplish ends alone. They divide labor, delegate, compete, and cooperate with one another in many ways to produce the outcomes we observe. Almost all governing in contemporary global politics seems to be the result of governor *inter*actions of various kinds. (Avant et al, 2010: 2)

Framing the UNGC as IOR reminds us that its very institutional set-up features characteristics that are worthy of further investigation. First, given that it reflects a 'collective effort involving not only the United Nations and corporations, but also international labor and NGOs as core participants' (Ruggie, 2000: 291), the UNGC is a blueprint for how different entities come together to govern collectively and further their own agenda at the same time. Second, interaction within the UNGC is open-ended and indeterminate. In fact, with more than 18,000 participants, the Compact is indeed a rather loose network, the main contribution of which seems to be the mutual recognition of those involved as well as their convergence on broad principles. Analogous to UN membership for states, being a UNGC constituent is a requirement for and proof of corporate agency in global governance, at least in its embryonic form (Ringmar, 2016). Above and beyond the unsettled question of whether the UNGC has an impact on corporate behaviour, its immediate consequence for world order(ing) is thus a confirmation of global governance, its commitment to multi-stakeholderism, and the overall zeitgeist of bringing together different stakeholders to manage problems collectively (Ruggie, 2001). This managerial logic (Sinclair, 2012; Franke and Hofferberth, 2022) has been used to justify the UNGC in the first place. Ironically, and potentially more importantly, however, it is also reproduced, in practice and scholarship, by continuously restating the different entities involved as legitimate governors.

Using the UNGC to connect global governance and IOR, we best understand the impact of its loose design by considering how it enables participants to act in the first place. More specifically, since there is not even a shared understanding on what the UNGC is – a network, an initiative, a forum, a talk shop – its relations, just like global governance at large, produce a nebulous sphere of dispersed and ultimately limited accountability (Hirschmann, 2020). With no clear hierarchy and authority within, the UNGC remains liquid in a sense that it is likely to continue to evolve in interaction rather than follow its initial, unclear mandate (Krisch, 2017). Considering world order as defined in the introduction to this volume, the UNGC is 'meta-governance' as it constitutes actors considered to be legitimate in the first place, which makes it an important case for studying inter-organizational relations and their effects (Torfing, 2016). Including MNEs as global governors in IOR helps us to understand the nature of their agency without essentializing it. The remainder of this chapter illustrates in more depth what one gains when a) broadening the notion of IOR to include formal and informal interaction of MNEs and b) using this to frame the UNGC in a novel way, which is to reconstruct actors and their changing properties as they emerge in the process instead of taking them as given (Jackson and Nexon, 1999).

Methodology and case selection

This section advances the analysis of the UNGC on two levels. First, framing the UNGC as IOR, I highlight its contingent emergence as an MSI. Against a long history of UN attempts to regulate global business, this will help us to understand its unique rationale and novel approach as it was conceived in the 1990s. For this, I utilize UN documents and speeches from UN Secretary-General Kofi Annan (1997–2006). Together with John Ruggie as Assistant Secretary-General for Strategic Planning (1997–2001) and George Kell as Head of the UN Conference on Trade and Development (UNCTAD) from1993–97, Annan 'played a key role in this process [of UN-business rapprochement]' and thereby opened the door to allow MNEs to sit at the table (Pingeot, 2016: 194). By doing so, I will reveal moments of recognition that helped to constitute corporate agency within the UNGC. Second, I will look into a single case to illustrate how BP plc over time relates to the UNGC and makes sense of its membership. This reconstruction of corporate perception and understanding reveals what the initiative means to the enterprise and how it picks up on it. With an interest in whether continued interaction within the UNGC changes corporate perceptions and understandings over time, I chose BP because the enterprise has been involved in the UNGC since its beginning and represents a large, influential MNE that operates in the important extractive sector.

The case selection is further based on both pragmatic and substantial reasons. For the first, I have already studied extractive MNEs in other contexts (Hofferberth, 2011, 2017). BP promises to be a particularly rewarding case as it has been heavily scrutinized since the Deepwater Horizon incident, in which 11 crew members died and which also caused the largest marine oil spill in history, and furthermore has been confronted with the task of moving the sector forward in terms of its climate emissions. The extractive industry in general, and BP's operations in particular, are characterized by a high asset specificity of its investments, making it very costly if not impossible for the enterprise to divest and leave a host country when facing public scrutiny. Furthermore, BP like other MNEs from this sector, is vertically integrated and includes the full value chain from exploration to processing to distribution to sale, at least within corporate entities and subsidiaries. This makes extractive MNEs such as BP very visible in everyday consumer experiences. In other words, there are good reasons to assume that BP actively communicates its involvement in global governance at large and the UN Global Compact in particular to present a successful CSR case to consumers.

UN documents published during the 1990s are used here to reconstruct the origins of the UNGC. These include files surrounding the creation of the UN Global Compact made available through the UN Secretariat as well as some originating within the context of the UNGC and shared through its website. For both, I am specifically interested in how corporate involvement is justified and what expectations of these actors are articulated. Essentially, what rationale was advanced to bring the various entities together and in particular to reach out to MNEs? For the BP illustration, I consider letters of engagement, which are mandatory to be submitted to the UNGC in order to participate, as well as regular communications on progress and further corporate responsibility and sustainability reports (BP, 2004, 2006, 2008, 2011) as well as a more recent corporate document (BP, 2021). In these documents, I analyse sections referring to the UNGC and interpret how BP frames the Compact and perceives its dynamics. By looking at these documents in conjunction with those from the UN, I hope to capture the inter-organizational nature of the Compact from two angles. More specifically, I will determine how the UN approaches corporate agency within the UNGC, as well as how these enterprises in return look at the UN and the Compact.

Methodologically, documents were scanned for relevant sections addressing the UNGC. These were then qualitatively interpreted in terms of how they presented the UNGC and corporate involvement within it (Schwartz-Shea and Yanow, 2012). With this in mind, I am able to highlight how the UNGC allowed MNEs to become global governors and how these, in interaction, define their agency within. In other words, I will show how the inter-organizational dynamics of the UNGC contribute to world order by creating and sustaining corporate agency, and illustrate how one MNE responds to this expanded mandate. Given the shortness of the analysis and the nature of a single case, it goes without saying that this will remain mostly anecdotal, but, guided by theoretical concerns of how to reconcile IOR and global governance, hopefully insightful nevertheless.

Analysing the UN Global Compact and BP's interpretation

This section analyses the UNGC in two steps. First, I provide the context by discussing the origin and rationale of the Compact. Second, I will show – at least anecdotally – how BP has picked up on the UNGC and whether it has changed its corporate perception and (self-)understanding based on the relations they are involved in. Together, these two perspectives allow us to conclude how the UNGC, once framed as IOR, constitutes its members and whether this matters for the agency and self-understandings of those involved.

Origin and rationale of the UN Global Compact

To understand the UNGC and its unique dynamics, it is important to contextualize it within larger UN discussions on how to deal with MNEs. These discussions, initially framed in terms of regulating global business, originate in the 1960s when MNEs were first recognized in the global economy (Dell, 1990). However, the regulatory approach, argued for specifically by the then newly independent countries of the Global South, did not fly with countries from the Global North, which wanted to protect their enterprises and foreign direct investments (FDIs). Specifically, the US began to build a coalition of home countries to vocally support free markets, liberal economic policies and the protection of MNEs within the UN (Tesner and Kell, 2000). Given this clash of ideas, it is no surprise that, for the next 20 years, debates in the UN Economic and Social Council and UNCTAD became ideologically charged and could not reach any consensus. MNEs at the UN in these bodies were 'viewed as either saints or demons in an increasingly polarized and fractured global economics policy environment', with home countries being committed to the 'liberal economic dictum that FDI was on the whole positive', while host countries framed MNEs 'as exploitative, alien, and purely profit-driven' (Sagafi-nejad, 2008: 40–8).

Against these debates, the creation of the UNGC marked a turning rather than a starting point. On the one hand, it expressed the pragmatic need for compromise, knowing that further debate and disagreement would only sideline the UN. On the other hand, it marked the final win of home countries and their neoliberal ideas promoting a market-based approach of self-commitment rather than regulation and binding obligations. This 'new consensus' had been in the making since the late 1980s, when the UN Centre on Transnational Corporations (UNCTC) stated in its 1988 report that the 'era of confrontation [between states and corporations] has receded, [...] replaced by a practical search for meaningful and mutually beneficial accommodations of interests' (UNCTC, 1988: i).[4]

With this normative shift, any notion to regulate corporate actors in binding terms and potentially against their will was put to rest. Rather, for the first time, the idea of *interacting with MNEs as global governors* emerged (Sagafi-nejad, 2008). With the Washington Consensus gaining momentum, this idea quickly took hold, for example during the 1992 Rio Summit, in which many different non-state actors, including MNEs and lobby groups, participated (Kinderman, 2012). 'Following the lead of governments, which in Rio in 1992 had embraced the private sector (along with civil society) as a key actor', the UN, it seemed, was poised to include MNEs as global governors (Pingeot, 2016: 194). The UN General Assembly President in September 1992, for example, argued that the 'changed economic environment and the importance attached to encouraging foreign investment required that a fresh approach should be examined' (UNGA, 1992). This approach was further substantialized by the 1995 UN Commission on Global Governance Report, which framed MNEs as benevolent global governors willing to assume responsibilities above and beyond their core economic interests. In the attempt 'to attract capital to development projects and to benefit from private sector expertise', MNEs were framed as 'wealth creators', while states were reduced to 'facilitators' (Thérien and Pouliot, 2006: 59). More explicitly, the report presented a fait accompli as it argued:

> There is no alternative to working together and using collective power to create a better world. Governance is the sum of the many ways individuals and institutions, public and private, manage their common affairs. It is a continuing process through which conflicting or diverse interests may be accommodated and co-operative action may be taken. It includes formal institutions and regimes empowered to enforce compliance, as well as informal arrangements that people and institutions. [...] At the global level, governance has been viewed primarily as intergovernmental relationships, but it must now be understood as also involving non-governmental organizations (NGOs), citizens' movements, *multinational corporations*, and the global capital market (Commission on Global Governance, 1995: 2–3, emphasis added).

It is important to understand how this paradigm shift eventually led MNEs into different inter-organizational relations, such as the UNGC. In this initiative, presupposing the necessity of their integration, MNEs were no longer framed as the problem. Rather, they were recognized as global governors as their agency was essentialized as an undeniable 'consequence of globalization' (Whelan, 2012: 713). Framed in the emerging narrative of global governance, and spurred on by its functionalist logic, the desire to regulate enterprises, within a matter of years, had effectively been replaced by the idea to partner up and cooperate, recognizing corporate agency as 'a fact of political life world-wide' (Butler, 2000: 149). As such, their agency was confirmed and governance without them was no longer perceived as an option. In fact, it was quickly taken for granted that 'business, as a key agent driving globalization, can help to ensure that markets advance in ways that benefit society' (Rasche and Kell, 2010: 2). This new rhetoric obviously defined the creation of the UNGC and its relations. For example, in February 1997, during his first address to the World Economic Forum, UN Secretary-General Kofi Annan framed UN-business relations as a partnership and solicited for corporate input. Signalling, 'I am open to your advice and I look forward to hearing from you', he solidified the notion that MNEs are actors of global governance (United Nations, 1997). Involved in the negotiations, Tesner and Kell (2000: 84) framed the dynamics during this time as:

> [W]hile recent exchanges between the UN and the business community show signs of a strong mutual interest in this enterprise, the road ahead is paved with political hurdles, psychological roadblocks, and cultural chasms. No matter, the parties are plowing ahead, animated as they are by a sense of urgency and mission at a time of historical transition.

Kofi Annan's personal commitment to development and UN reform further drove the notion that business actors were the solution rather than the problem. A year later, again at Davos, he argued that 'the United Nations and the private sector have distinct strengths and roles, and we are still overcoming a legacy of suspicion [and] if we are bold, we can bridge those differences and turn what have been fledgling arrangements of cooperation into an even stronger force' (United Nations, 1998). Envisioned as 'a global compact of shared values and principles, which will give a human face to the global market', Kofi Annan, in rather submissive language, pleaded business leaders 'to embrace, support and enact a set of core values in the areas of human rights, labor standards, and environmental practices' (United Nations, 1999). With the blessing of the US and other FDI home countries, it was communicated on 27 July 2000, that: 'Under the leadership of United Nations Secretary-General Kofi Annan, global leaders from the world of business, labour and civil society met today to launch a joint initiative in support of universal values and responsible business operations' (United Nations, 2000). Without further consultation, other member states had to, *ex post*, endorse the UNGC, as 'UN leadership made a decision to position itself on the pro-corporate, pro-globalization side of the debate to increase its legitimacy and its authority in a neoliberal world' (Pingeot, 2016: 196).

Against this background, the UNGC emphasizes not only dialogue but creation of a specific type of IOR in which MNEs, due to their assets and on-the-ground expertise, play a leading role (Sagafi-nejad, 2008). In other words, the UNGC sustains relations in which it understands itself and its member states as facilitating an environment in which MNEs can 'lead the way'. In its own language, the Compact Guide (UNGC, 2019) states that it supports business through providing '[g]lobal reach and multi-stakeholder connections, enabling business to help shape the sustainability agenda and be a force for good'. In other words, in order to be the centrepiece of global governance, the UNGC embraced a logic of IOR that not only treats MNEs as global governors but proactively accommodates their interests. Due to this business-friendly approach, the Compact quickly gathered momentum after its creation in July 2000. With 36 enterprises joining right away, numbers over the years have grown consistently, with global business, small and large, being very supportive of the initiative. Figure 7.1 reflects the annual growth of the UNGC by displaying new members per year. It further distinguishes between different types of member, showing that, in particular, numbers of 'small and medium enterprises' as well as 'companies' grew the most. Overall, more than 23,000 companies and small and medium-sized enterprises have joined the UNGC over its 23 years of existence. Of these, 19,000 are still listed as active and constitute the majority of stakeholders among participants, putting them not only in charge but also into like-minded circles.[5]

Corporate perception and understanding of the UN Global Compact: BP

Given growing numbers on the one hand and the ongoing debate of assessing the UNGC on the other, it is important to consider perceptions and understandings of corporate actors within the Compact, specifically since these are subject to, as well as actors of, IOR. More specifically, MNEs within the UNGC interact with a range of different entities including NGOs but also other public entities. For example, with Nuremberg, Germany, being the first city to join the Compact, in May 2003, and the University of Melbourne as the first academic institution following swiftly, MNEs find themselves in relationships with very different global governors. This potentially creates dynamics that MNEs would not be exposed to otherwise and in which they, at least in theory, are challenged to reflect their own contributions to CSR and global governance. In fact, given that the UNGC, for the most part, remains rather elusive, MNEs 'must engage in a process of creating some level of a shared understanding of what constitutes the rule system' (Kostova et al, 2008: 1002). In this relational process of sense-making, MNEs frame the UNGC and thereby express beliefs that are foundational to their actions. These mark important contributions to world order(ing) and are thus a relevant consequence of the UNGC to reflect upon (Hofferberth, 2019a). Assuming that continued involvement in the Compact over time matters, the following illustration is chronologically organized and, using different BP documents published in light of the UNGC, presents findings through an interpretive reconstruction over time.

Following the 'communication on progress' requirement laid out by the UNGC (2019), the first BP document referencing the UNGC is the enterprise's *Sustainability Report* of 2003. In it, the Compact is framed as both a 'network that promotes responsible corporate behaviour in the areas of human rights, labour rights and the environment' as well as an 'international initiative that brings together companies, UN agencies and labour and civil society organizations' (BP, 2004: 32, 39). BP's commitment is to 'listen [...] to the experience of others in this network' and it assumingly has 'learned much to help us support human rights in our business interactions around the world' (BP, 2004: 32). This commitment, mostly cast through a human-rights lens, is further framed as something that BP had already incorporated, presenting membership in the UNGC not as a breakthrough moment but rather as a continuation of the enterprise's existing CSR performance. This theme of having already integrated UNGC principles in corporate decision-making is echoed throughout the following sustainability reports, stating that BP 'continue[s] to participate in Global Compact meetings in a number of countries' (BP, 2006: 67). Despite being engaged in the UNGC for several years at this point, BP's rhetorical commitment to the UNGC does not

Figure 7.1: UN Global Compact – new members by year and type

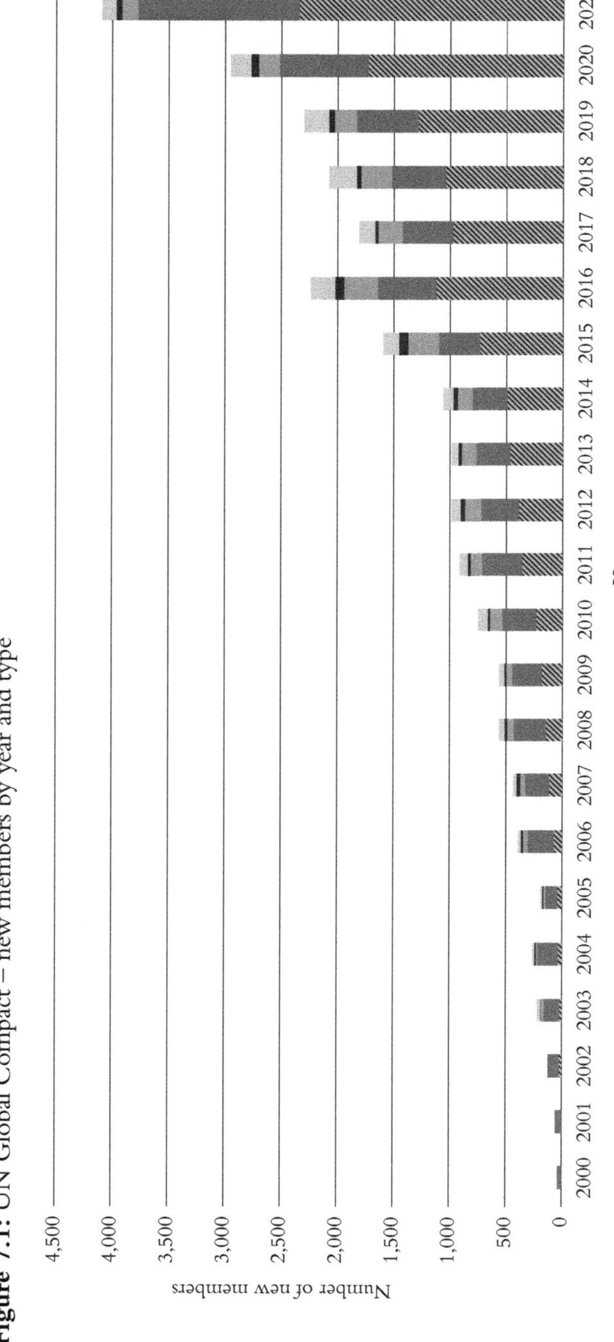

become more specific. In particular, the enterprise does not communicate a more solidified understanding of what the Compact means for its corporate action. In its 2007 *Sustainability Report*, for example, the reference to the UNGC remains open-ended, as BP states that it 'value[s] partnerships with governments, NGOs and others through membership of the UN Global Compact' (BP, 2008: 1).

While BP changes its approach to communicating on progress to the UNGC in 2008 and from thereon submits annual *Sustainability Reviews*, these documents, for the most part, remain just as generic and do not pick up on the Compact in more concrete ways. In the 2011 review, for example, BP states that, in regards to human rights and labour issues, it would 'follow guidance from the UN Global Compact', but quickly adds that 'industry practice, BP's own experience, and national and international law' are equally important (BP, 2011: 21). While the following reviews highlight BP's role as an original signatory of the UNGC, the company also emphasizes that commitments remain voluntary. What stands out in these reviews is the fact that reporting to the UNGC is presented in polished CSR language and, for the most part, remains limited to human rights.[6] What remains lacking, however, are details of how exposure to the UNGC and its wider principles matters and whether it impacts or changes corporate action on the ground. This is noteworthy since the UNGC, in its self-understanding, continues to mature at this time and expects members to expand their commitment to be 'shared publicly to stimulate mutual learning and encourage dialogue on corporate practices' (Kell, 2013: 46). Indicating yet another institutional shift, in 2015, BP switched back to annual submissions of *Sustainability Reports*. In these, the enterprise refers to the UNGC more explicitly, with the 2020 report stating that BP's 'support for the principles has been reinforced this year with the adoption of our new purpose and sustainability frame' and that the 'UN Global Compact continues to guide our approach and helps us to focus our efforts on shared principles' (BP, 2021: 92). However, these reports also lack detail as to what this means. On that note, it is important to emphasize that, even on the corporate website outlining its approach to sustainability, the UNGC is barely referenced (BP, 2022).

From 2013 on, in addition to BP's annual communication on sustainability and CSR efforts, the UNGC website lists specific letters of commitment to the Compact from BP. These letters are submitted by BP's CEO, directly addressed to the UN Secretary-General. Between 2013 and 2016, the enterprise uses a standard template, expressing strong support for the UNGC but not providing any details of what this means. Furthermore, there is no reference to interacting or collaborating with other global governors through the UNGC until 2018, when the CEO's letter states BP's desire to be recognized as a 'responsible corporate citizen and good employer'. As such, the enterprise recognizes the value of 'enduring relationships with governments, customers, partners, suppliers and communities in the countries we work' (BP, 2018). The 2020 letter, with references to 'building back better' after COVID-19, frames the UNGC as 'guid[ing] our approach and help[ing] us to focus our efforts on shared principles' as the enterprise is assumingly 'continually looking to improve our contribution across these areas and to learn from other participating businesses' (BP, 2020).[7] In addition to remaining vague in their language, these quotes do not recognize the full range of entities involved in the UNGC. Thus, they reflect a lack of awareness and an overall limited effect of the inter-organizational dynamics on BP. While there may be learning in some areas, recent documents overall do not differ from those originally published in the early 2000s.

In the big picture, if corporate rhetoric in these documents remains limited and is not making a strong(er) case for the UNGC over time, it appears unlikely that it plays a major role in corporate decision-making and action (Andrews, 2019). More specifically, the loose, fluid nature of UNGC relations does not seem to influence BP. Put differently, interaction with other stakeholders remains limited in its impact on BP, which, for the most part, seems to have its CSR policy and approaches in place. Granted, this could be because BP is one of the largest, most visible enterprises in the UNGC and arguably learned the necessity to communicate CSR issues early on during the 1990s (Avery, 2000; see also Hofferberth, 2011). That said, one can reasonably assume a larger impact of the UNGC and its inter-organizational dynamics on other enterprises, specifically smaller ones with no prior engagement in these issues. More importantly, however, evidence that corporate rhetoric in light of the UNGC remains vague does not mean that there is no agency of BP at all. In fact, being engaged in the relational dynamics of the UNGC creates an illusion of impactful action. In other words, the inter-organizational relations of the UNGC create and sustain the notion of MNEs playing a different role in global governance, but, so far, at least in the case of BP, have led to little immediate change in corporate behaviour. These insights are used to cycle back to the assessment of the UNGC and tied into a discussion on IOR more broadly in the following conclusion.

Results

As the largest MSI bringing corporate and non-corporate entities together in global governance, the Global Compact undoubtedly constitutes a milestone in global CSR. Framing the UNGC as IOR reveals important dynamics of this initiative. Looking specifically into its origins, it quickly becomes clear that the recognition of corporate agency within matters. Instead of thinking of MNEs as objects of regulation, corporate actors became increasingly viewed as partners of regulation through the dynamics of the

UNGC (Reinicke and Deng, 2000). Given the interactive nature of IOR, such recognition occurs mutually between different MNEs as members of the Compact but also by the UN and other participants at large. As such, I contend in this chapter that the main implication of the UNGC, intended or unintended, is the emergence and sustenance of corporate agency in global governance. It facilitates space for MNEs to claim agency and sustains relations in which the legitimate agency of MNEs as global governors is recognized. IOR as a lens helps us to capture these recognition dynamics and spell out their nature. As shown in the discussions surrounding the origin of this initiative, it is clear that commitments within the UNGC remain non-binding and loose. As such, the initiative is defined by specific inter-organizational relations that bring together many different entities but only loosely connects them.

As a consequence of these specific relations, when assessing the UNGC's impact on MNEs and their behaviour through the proxy of self-understandings and references to the initiative, results remain rather mixed at best. Just like membership in the UN defines statehood but does not ensure multilateralism, participation in the UNGC sustains the notion that MNEs legitimately and meaningfully contribute to global governance but does not necessarily change anything on the ground. In other words, the fact that membership in the UNGC does not seem to translate, at least not directly, into meaningful change in corporate behaviour, for now strengthens the critique voiced about the UNGC. The illustration at least suggests that corporate agency within the UNGC, due to the non-binding approach of the MSI, remains unaccounted for and does not solidify or expand over time. More specifically, while the UNGC reminds us that inter-organizational relations are more than formal interactions between intergovernmental entities, it also shows the limits of such dynamics if they do not come with clear rules of engagement and hierarchical means of enforcement, as is so often the case in global governance (Hale and Held, 2018; Hale et al, 2013).

Conclusions and outlook

Due to their shared interest in institutional complexity and overlapping mandates, inter-organizational relations can help us to understand core dynamics of global governance. At the same time, IOR reminds us why this notion remains limited in terms of effectiveness and accountability. Relating IOR and global governance, there is potential, maybe even need, to study relations – formal and informal – between all kinds of different global governors. Taking the constitutive nature of relations seriously (Jackson and Nexon, 1999), we need to study IOR and its effects, specifically on MNEs, without prematurely taking their agency for granted. Given the size of the task, work towards this endeavour initially needs to develop ideal-type taxonomies of different relations and dynamics of the entities involved as they recognize each other relationally. Methodologically speaking, this is challenging since relations produce world order and the entities involved do not speak for themselves. Reconstructing documents and speech acts of those emerging from relations remains a proxy. That said, it still provides insights into how actors make sense of inter-organizational complexity stemming from overlapping initiatives, converging mandates, changing responsibilities and diverging stakeholder expectations. Being aware of these dynamics and framing them as contingent, I believe, helps us to maintain a critical distance and provide sharper assessments. Ultimately, it might also produce insights into how to better integrate MNEs through initiatives such as the UNGC. For example, we need to understand how and when the dynamics of loose inter-organizational relations indeed compel corporate actors to act more socially and sustainably, as envisioned by the creators of the Compact, and when they fail to do so. From a practical perspective, this raises the question of how to design and steer interaction in MSIs to make them more meaningful (that is, trigger change in corporate behaviour). While the UNGC so far does not live up to its own high hopes, we should not discard the potential of other initiatives and their relations to transcend the binary of binding versus non-binding in CSR.

For future theoretical work, I contend that IOR would benefit if it follows recent calls within IR and fully embraces a relational ontology to discuss world order(ing) effects (Jackson and Nexon, 1999; Kurki, 2021). Relationalism and its emphasis on process in this context reminds us that any notion of world order and the IOR it sustains remains a political and thus contested project (Zürn, 2018). Recognizing these contestations and shifting the focus away from formal rule output to world order more broadly (ideationally *and* materially), IOR can help us to consider how relational dynamics of governance transform entities and establish their agency in the first place (Avant et al, 2010). Against this background, as argued early on by Jackson and Nexon (1999), relations have to come first. Such an ontology can help IOR overcome the challenge of being interested in change that it otherwise cannot explain. It is this 'embarrassment of change' that haunts IR theory but ironically seems to reproduce itself within global governance and IOR as well. Thinking of world order as a consequence of relations, at least, allows us to begin to think through complexity and change in a system as intricate as global governance as the search for 'what makes the world hang together' continues (Ruggie, 1998).

Notes

1 Being both scholar and practitioner, George Kell was the founder and former Executive Director of the UNGC, while John Ruggie served as the UN Assistant Secretary-General for Strategic Planning (1997–2001) and later as the UN Secretary-General's Special

Representative for Business and Human Rights. Their contributions thus not only reflect inside knowledge but are also likely biased towards a positive reading of the UNGC.

2 An anecdotal, not systematically derived observation on the bibliometrics of UNGC publications shows that most recent articles are published in *Business & Society* and the *Journal of Business Ethics*.

3 Following Avant et al (2010: 2), 'global governors are authorities who exercise power across borders for purposes of affecting policy'. Who becomes a global governor and whether their exercise of power makes a difference remains subject to the specific dynamics to be unpacked through an IOR lens.

4 It is important to note that the original charge of the UNCTC was broad enough at least to entertain the idea of stronger MNE regulation. Ironically, after it decided not to pursue this route, it became rather meaningless and was quickly dismantled by then UN Secretary-General Boutros-Ghali in 1992 (Sagafi-nejad, 2008).

5 Data and classifications of membership taken from the UNGC's website. One striking trend is that larger companies, originally considered the primary target group, were outranked by small and medium-sized companies in 2016 and their 'share' has since dropped further. Additionally, local and global business associations represent corporate interests within the Compact. These include MNEs that also joined individually, creating further inter-organizational dynamics and strengthening corporate voices within. The UNGC also saw a significant number of participants leave the initiative. Thus, as has been discussed, in addition to the growth reflected here, there is also a large amount of fluidity, as new members come and others cease to participate (Rasche et al, 2020).

6 On that note, BP's commitment to the UNGC is often connected to its membership in the Voluntary Principles on Security and Human Rights, which represents a more focused MSI. As the name suggests, however, the voluntary principles are also based on a corporate-friendly approach focused on learning instead of regulation (Hofferberth, 2011).

7 It should be noted that this letter lists a more detailed report on how the enterprise picked up the ten UNGC principles.

References

Andrews, N. (2019) 'Normative spaces and the UN Global Compact for transnational corporations: the norm diffusion paradox', *Journal of International Relations and Development*, 22(1): 77–106.

Avant, D.D., Finnemore, M. and Sell, S.K. (2010) 'Who governs the globe?', in D.D. Avant, M. Finnemore and S.K. Sell (eds) *Who Governs the Globe?*, Cambridge: Cambridge University Press, pp 1–31.

Avery, C. (2000) *Business and Human Rights in a Time of Change* (2nd edn), London: Amnesty International UK.

Barrese, J., Phillips, C. and Shoaf, V. (2020) 'Why do U.S. public companies continue to join the UN Global Compact: ethics or economics?', *International Studies of Management & Organization*, 50(3): 209–31.

Berliner, D. and Prakash, A. (2015) '"Bluewashing the firm"? Voluntary regulations, program design, and member compliance with the United Nations Global Compact', *Policy Studies Journal*, 43(1): 115–38.

Biermann, R. (2011) 'Inter-organizational relations: an emerging research programme', in B. Reinalda (ed) *The Ashgate Research Companion to Non-State Actors*, Farnham: Ashgate.

BP (2022) 'Human rights', available from: bp.com/en/global/corporate/sustainability/improving-peoples-lives/human-rights.html [accessed 30 March 2023].

BP (2021) *Reimagining Energy for People and Our Planet: BP Sustainability Report 2021*, available from: bp.com/content/dam/bp/business-sites/en/global/corporate/pdfs/sustainability/group-reports/bp-sustainability-report-2021.pdf [sccessed 30 March 2023].

BP (2020) 'BP's continued commitment to the principles of the UN Global Compact', letter to the UN Secretary-General, available from: unglobalcompact.org/participation/report/cop/active/444496 [accessed 30 March 2023].

BP (2018) 'CEO commitment to the UN Global Compact', letter to the UN Secretary-General, available from: unglobalcompact.org/participation/report/cop/create-and-submit/active/417211 [accessed 30 March 2023].

BP (2011) *Building a Stronger, Safer BP: Sustainability Review 2011*, available from: bp.com/content/dam/bp/business-sites/en/global/corporate/pdfs/sustainability/archive/archived-reports-and-translations/2011/bp_sustainability_review_2011.pdf [accessed 30 March 2023].

BP (2008) *Sustainability Report 2007*, available from: bp.com/content/dam/bp/business-sites/en/global/corporate/pdfs/sustainability/archive/archived-reports-and-translations/2007/bp_sustainability_report_2007.pdf [accessed 30 March 2023].

BP (2006) *Sustainability Report 2005*, available from: bp.com/content/dam/bp/business-sites/en/global/corporate/pdfs/sustainability/archive/archived-reports-and-translations/2005/bp-sustainability-report-2005.pdf [accessed 30 March 2023].

BP (2004) *Sustainability Report 2003*, available from: bp.com/content/dam/bp/business-sites/en/global/corporate/pdfs/sustainability/archive/archived-reports-and-translations/2003-1998/bp-sustainability-report-2003.pdf [accessed 30 March 2023].

Brown, J.A., Clark, C. and Buono, A.F. (2018) 'The United Nations Global Compact: engaging implicit and explicit CSR for global governance', *Journal of Business Ethics*, 147(4): 721–34.

Butler, N. (2000) 'Companies in international relations', *Survival*, 42(1): 149–64.

Commission on Global Governance (1995) *Our Global Neighbourhood: The Report of the Commission on Global Governance*, Oxford: Oxford University Press.

Cropper, S., Ebers, M., Huxham, C. and Smith Ring, P. (2008) 'Introducing inter-organizational relations', in S. Cropper, M. Ebers, C. Huxham and P. Smith Ring (eds) *The Oxford Handbook of Inter-Organizational Relations*, Oxford: Oxford University Press, pp 3–21.

Dell, S. (1990) *The United Nations and International Business*, Durham: Duke University Press.

Deva, S. (2006) 'Global compact: a critique of the U.N.'s "public-private" partnership for promoting corporate citizenship', *Syracuse Journal of International Law and Commerce*, 34(1): 107–51.

Finnemore, M. (2014) 'Dynamics of global governance: building on what we know', *International Studies Quarterly*, 58(1): 221–4.

Franke, U. (2017) 'Inter-organizational relations: five theoretical approaches', in R. Marlin-Bennett (ed) *Oxford Research Encyclopedia of International Studies*, New York: International Studies Association and Oxford University Press, available from: oxfordre.com/internationalstudies/view/10.1093/acrefore/9780190846626.001.0001/acrefore-9780190846626-e-99 [accessed 30 March 2023].

Franke, U. and Hofferberth, M. (2022) 'Proclaiming a prophecy empty of substance? A pragmatist reconsideration of global governance', *Journal of International Political Theory*, 18(3): 312–35.

Franke, U. and Koch, M. (2013) 'Inter-organizational relations as structures of corporate practice', *Journal of International Organizations Studies*, 4(special issue): 85–103.

Hale, T. and Held, D. (2018) 'Breaking the cycle of gridlock', *Global Policy*, 9(1): 129–37.

Hale, T., Held, D. and Young, K. (2013) *Gridlock: Why Global Cooperation is Failing When We Need it Most*, Cambridge: Polity Press.

Held, D., and McGrew, A. (eds) (2002) *Governing Globalization. Power, Authority and Global Governance*, Cambridge: Polity Press.

Hirschmann, G. (2020) *Accountability in Global Governance*, Oxford: Oxford University Press.

Hofferberth, M. (2019a) 'Corporate actors in global governance', in M. Hofferberth (ed) *Corporate Actors in Global Governance: Business as Usual or New Deal ?*, Boulder: Lynne Rienner, pp 1–24.

Hofferberth, M. (2019b) 'Get your act(ors) together! Theorizing agency in global governance', *International Studies Review*, 21(1): 127–45.

Hofferberth, M. (2017) 'And of course our major contribution remains to run a decent business: making sense of Shell's sense-making in Nigeria during the 1990s', *Business and Politics*, 19(1): 135–65.

Hofferberth, M. (2011) 'The binding dynamics of non-binding governance arrangements: the voluntary principles on security and human rights and the cases of BP and Chevron', *Business and Politics*, 13(4): 1–32.

Hofferberth, M. and Lambach, D. (2022) 'Becoming global governors: self-agentification, recognition, and delegation in world politics', *Global Studies Quarterly*, 2(3): 1–12.

Jackson, P.T. and Nexon, D.H. (1999) 'Relations before states: substance, process and the study of world politics', *European Journal of International Relations*, 5(3): 291–332.

Kell, G. (2013) '12 years later: reflections on the growth of the UN Global Compact', *Business & Society*, 52(1): 31–52.

Kell, G. (2005) 'The Global Compact: selected experiences and reflections', *Journal of Business Ethics*, 59(1): 69–79.

Kell, G. and Levin, D. (2003) 'The Global Compact Network: an historic experiment in learning and action', *Business and Society Review*, 108(2): 151–81.

Kell, G. and Ruggie, J.G. (1999) 'Global markets and social legitimacy: the case for the "Global Compact"', *Transnational Corporations*, 8(3): 101–20.

Kinderman, D.P. (2012) '"Free us up so we can be responsible!" The co-evolution of corporate social responsibility and neo-liberalism in the UK, 1977–2010', *Socio-Economic Review*, 10(1): 29–57.

Kostova, T., Roth, K. and Dacin, M.T. (2008) 'Institutional theory in the study of multinational enterprises: a critique and new directions', *Academy of Management Review*, 33(4): 994–1006.

Krisch, N. (2017) 'Liquid authority in global governance', *International Theory*, 9(2): 237–60.

Kurki, M. (2021) 'Relational revolution and relationality in IR: New conversations', *Review of International Studies*, online first.

Orzesa, G., Morettob, A.M., Ebrahimpourc, M. et al (2018) 'United Nations Global Compact: literature review and theory-based research agenda', *Journal of Cleaner Production*, 177: 633–54.

Palazzo, G. and Scherer, A.G. (2010) 'The United Nations Global Compact as a learning approach', in A. Rasche and G. Kell (eds) *The United Nations Global Compact: Achievements, Trends and Challenges*, Cambridge: Cambridge University Press, pp 234–47.

Pingeot, L. (2016) 'In whose interest? The UN's strategic rapprochement with business in the sustainable development agenda', *Globalizations*, 13(2): 188–202.

Podrecca, M., Sartor, M. and Nassimbeni, G. (2021) 'United Nations Global Compact: Where are we going?', *Social Responsibility Journal*, online first.

Pouliot, V. and Thérien, J-P. (2018) 'Global governance in practice', *Global Policy*, 9(2): 163–72.

Rasche, A. (2009) 'A necessary supplement: what the United Nations Global Compact is and is not', *Business & Society*, 48(4): 511–37.

Rasche, A. and Gilbert, D.U. (2012) 'Institutionalizing global governance: the role of the United Nations Global Compact', *Business Ethics: A European Review*, 21(1): 100–13.

Rasche, A. and Kell, G. (2010) 'Introduction: The United Nations Global Compact – retrospect and prospect', in A. Rasche and G. Kell (eds) *The United Nations Global Compact: Achievement, Trends, and Challenges*, Cambridge: Cambridge University Press, pp 1–19.

Rasche, A. and Waddock, S. (2014) 'Global sustainability governance and the UN Global Compact: a rejoinder to critics', *Journal of Business Ethics*, 122(2): 209–16.

Rasche, A., Gwozdz, W., Lund Larsen, M. and Moon, J. (2020) 'Which firms leave multi-stakeholder initiatives? An analysis of delistings from the United Nations Global Compact', *Regulation & Governance*, online first.

Reinicke, W.H. and Deng, F. (2000) *Critical Choices: The United Nations, Networks, and the Future of Global Governance*, Ottawa: International Development Research Centre.

Ringmar, E. (2016) 'How the world stage makes its subjects: an embodied critique of Constructivist IR Theory', *Journal of International Relations and Development*, 19(1): 101–25.

Ruggie, J.G. (2001) 'global_governance.net: the Global Compact as learning network', *Global Governance*, 7(4): 371–8.

Ruggie, J.G. (2000) 'Globalization, the Global Compact, and corporate social responsibility', *Transnational Associations*, 52(6): 291–4.

Ruggie, J.G. (1998) 'What makes the world hang together? Neo-utilitarian and the social constructivist challenge', *International Organization*, 52(4): 855–85.

Sagafi-nejad, T. (2008) *The UN and Transnational Corporations: From Code of Conduct to Global Compact*, Bloomington: Indiana University Press.

Schwartz-Shea, P. and Yanow, D. (2012) *Interpretive Research Design: Concepts and Processes*, New York: Routledge.

Sethi, S.P. and Schepers, D.H. (2014) 'United Nations Global Compact: the promise-performance gap', *Journal of Business Ethics*, 122(2): 193–208.

Sinclair, T.J. (2012) *Global Governance*, Cambridge: Polity Press.

Tesner, S. and Kell, G. (2000) *The United Nations and Business: A Partnership Recovered*, Basingstoke: Macmillan.

Thérien, J.-P. and Pouliot, V. (2006) 'The Global Compact: shifting the politics of international development?', *Global Governance*, 12(1): 55–75.

Torfing, J. (2016) 'Metagovernance', in C. Ansell and T. Torfing (eds) *Handbook on Theories of Governance*, Cheltenham: Edward Elgar, pp 525–37.

UNCTC (United Nations Centre on Transnational Corporations) (1988) *Transnational Corporations in World Development: Trends and Prospects*, New York: United Nations Publications.

UNGA (United Nations General Assembly) (1992) Report of the President of the UN General Assembly, A/47/446, 15 September, available from: https://digitallibrary.un.org/record/150947 [accessed 30 March 2023].

UNGC (United Nations Global Compact) (2019) 'Basic guide: communication on progress', available from: https://d306pr3pise04h.cloudfront.net/docs/communication_on_progress%2FTools_and_Publications%2FCOP_Basic_Guide.pdf [accessed 30 March 2023].

UNGC (nd) 'The Ten Principles of the UN Global Compact', available from: unglobalcompact.org/what-is-gc/mission/principles [accessed 30 March 2023].

United Nations (2000) 'Executive summary and conclusion of high-level meeting on global compact', UN press release SG/2065/ECO/18, 27 July, available from: un.org/press/en/2000/20000727.sg2065.doc.html [accessed 30 March 2023].

United Nations (1999) 'Secretary-General proposes global compact on human rights, labour, environment', UN press release SG/SM/6881, 1 February, available from: un.org/press/en/1999/19990201.sgsm6881.html [accessed 30 March 2023].

United Nations (1998) 'Unite power of markets with authority of universal values, secretary-general urges at World Economic Forum', UN press release SG/SM/6448, 30 January, available from: un.org/press/en/1998/19980130.sgsm6448.html [accessed 30 March 2023].

United Nations (1997) 'Secretary-General, in address to World Economic Forum, stresses strengthened partnership between United Nations, private sector', UN press release SG/SM/6153, 31 January, available from: un.org/press/en/1997/19970131.sgsm6153.html [accessed 30 March 2023].

Weiss, T.G. and Wilkinson, R. (2014) 'Rethinking Global Governance? Complexity, authority, power, change', *International Studies Quarterly*, 58(1): 207–15.

Whelan, G. (2012) 'The political perspective of corporate social responsibility: a research agenda', *Business Ethics Quarterly*, 22(4): 709–37.

Williams, O.F. (2004) 'The UN Global Compact: the challenge and the promise', *Business Ethics Quarterly*, 14(4): 755–74.

Zürn, M. (2018) 'Contested global governance', *Global Policy*, 9(1): 138–45.

8

World Sports and Russia's War Against Ukraine

Ulrich Franke and Martin Koch

Introduction

Sports is a relevant subject for international relations (IR). Countless people around the world organize in sports clubs and associations or practice independently regardless of their specific circumstances. Cities bid for hosting sports events that many want to attend and watch. Companies place advertisements at these events and their broadcasts, politicians show up and pose with athletes. Supporters or athletes point out human rights violations or other grievances related to federations organizing or countries hosting an event, usually followed by officials of major sports federations claiming sports to be apolitical. These attempts, however, only increase the political character of sports and the necessity to study it.

Along these lines of the global relevance of sports and sports federations, the focus of this chapter is on how both the International Olympic Committee (IOC) and FIFA, the International Federation of Association Football (Fédération Internationale de Football Association), responded to Russia's invasion of Ukraine on 24 February 2022. Since 1896 and 1930 respectively, the IOC and FIFA have been holding tournaments that are now among the largest sports events in terms of participation and attention. Athletes representing countries from all continents take part in these events, while around 40 per cent of the world population are watching (Fett, 2020).

Interested in inter-organizational relations (IOR) and their contributions to world order, we study the IOC and FIFA through the lens of both an open system's perspective from organization studies (Scott, 1992 [1981]) and classical pragmatism (Peirce, 1998 [1903]; Dewey, 1991 [1927]). We ask how both organizations are embedded in their environments and what beliefs as rules for action they follow in the context of Russian aggression. We assume that the beliefs held by those who speak on behalf of the IOC and FIFA contribute to world order, understood as a specific constellation of beliefs on how human life is organized (Roos, 2015). These beliefs become manifest in practice, in what those who act in the name of states, intergovernmental organizations (IGOs) or non-governmental organizations (NGOs), such as the IOC, FIFA or other 'structures of corporate practice' do (Franke and Roos, 2010: 1065–9).

The following section deals with three strands of research on the IOC and FIFA. Subsequently, we introduce our theoretical framework consisting of concepts from organization studies and classical pragmatism as well as the reconstructive methods we used. Against this background, we present our analysis of the environmental embedding of the IOC and FIFA and illustrate the variety of organizations and events within. To get a closer look of this environmental embedding, we address a specific event, the Russian invasion of Ukraine. From the IOC's and FIFA's immediate responses we reconstruct their world-ordering beliefs as rules for action. In a final step, we answer the research question and provide some implications for the two organizations as well as related further research.

State of the art: the IOC and FIFA in world politics

The literature dealing with the IOC and FIFA mostly covers three major topics. These centre on *events* organized by the two sports federations and their relations to host countries; the IOC's and FIFA's *governing styles* and *positions in the global system*; as well as the issues of *finance, corruption* and *accountability*.

First, the IOC and FIFA are well-known for the sports events they organize. Steadily evolving 'in terms of value and costs' (Fett, 2020: 465) these events increase host countries' 'international visibility and familiarity' (an effect that is smaller the more visible the country already is), but do not necessarily improve their image (Kobierecki and Strożek, 2021). FIFA's 2018 World Cup, for instance, did not have 'an impact with regard to Russia's image building or nation branding attempts' (Meier et al, 2021: 804–5). The impact of the Olympic Games and the World Cup on host cities varies. Whereas enormous infrastructure investments often have detrimental effects on the environment or do not pay off (Geeraert and Gauthier, 2018), Summer Olympics see temporary increases in the host region's economic output (Firgo, 2021). Primed 'to oversee transnational sports rules and ultimately challenge, alter or supersede national laws' (Jerabek et al, 2017: 2–3), FIFA inconsistently interferes in host countries' domestic affairs and undermines its imperative of political neutrality (Eisenberg, 2006). Before the 2010 World Cup in South Africa, it promoted social development and health policies there (Cornelissen, 2011). Guided by monetary instead of humanitarian interests, 'FIFA intervened in the Brazilian law system for a sponsorship issue', but 'remained neutral for serious human rights violations in Qatar' (Pouliopoulos and Georgiadis, 2021: 786). In general, '[m]ore democratic, market-led hosts' are 'better able to mitigate negative impacts' of large sports events and to enhance the positive ones (Müller and Gaffney, 2018: 263).

Second, the classification of sports federations as 'genuine forms of global governance' (Bishop and Cooper, 2018: 36) points to the governing styles of the IOC and FIFA and their position in the global system. Adopting rational-legal bureaucratic forms taken for granted by states and intergovernmental organizations (Peacock, 2010), the IOC, for some time, ensured unchallenged authority and autonomy that made it a 'world government unto itself' (Wang and Rosenau, 2001: 26–7). FIFA had expanded internationally, secured its continuation by turning the World Cup into a financially attractive event and established 'a sporting, political, and economic balance of power' between its members (Dietschy, 2013: 280–1), before its 'leadership system' shifted from an era of 'volunteer idealists' to one of 'supreme leaders' in the mid-1970s (Pouliopoulos and Georgiadis, 2021: 781). As 'marketeers' replaced 'missionaries', FIFA's vulnerability to 'exploitation by individuals and well-placed agencies' increased (Tomlinson, 2014: 1160). In 1981, a similar transformation took place when the IOC cleared the way for professional athletes to compete at the Olympic Games (Krieger and Wassong, 2021). In the decades to come, criticism of their 'autocratic' leadership styles grew as the IOC and FIFA lacked ethical procedures or failed their own standards (Nelson and Cottrell, 2015; Tomlinson, 2014). Regarding the global position of sports federations, emphasis is put on FIFA membership as a symbol for the legitimacy of newly independent countries (Pouliopoulos and Georgiadis, 2021; Bucher and Eckl, 2022) and on the organization's capacity to both reinforce 'the "naturalness" of the sovereign territorial nation state' and reaffirm a mode of state competition 'that does not escalate into conflict' (Bucher and Eckl, 2022: 330).

Third, finance, corruption and accountability matter in academic writings on the IOC and FIFA. Among the effects of an unprecedented commercialization of international sports federations (Clausen et al, 2018) is a growing dependence of FIFA's management on the solvency of its business partners and of members on FIFA payments (Homburg, 2008). In this context, 'corruption and lack of transparency became the dominant institutional tenets' (Pouliopoulos and Georgiadis, 2021: 786) so that FIFA needs 'to find a consensus on the meaning of corrupt activities' and 'to minimise the risks of illicit payments' (Szymanski, 2016: 212). Given FIFA's 'culture of self-aggrandizement, unaccountability, and sometimes corruption' (Tomlinson, 2014: 1160), its lack of 'hierarchical, supervisory, peer or public reputational accountability' and its 'minimal fiscal accountability' (Pielke Jr,

2013: 265), possible solutions include government authorities responding to public blaming (Hock and Gomtsian, 2018), legislation on FIFA's marketing partners or indirect legal authority by (inter)national oversight bodies (Pielke Jr, 2013) – despite FIFA's capacity to manipulate these in its own favour (Geeraert and Drieskens, 2015). The market logic of 'supply and demand' is also trusted to solve the problem that both the IOC and FIFA have become the usual suspects for corruption in the bidding for hosting sports events since hosting major sports events has become less desired (Matheson et al, 2018).

In summary, research on the IOC and FIFA concentrates on the impact that both organizations have on host countries, cities and member associations. Both organizations are also studied according to their internal developments and governing attitudes, with a particular focus on commercialization and corruption. We add a new perspective to this research by examining the organizations' embeddedness in a larger environment and specifying the beliefs that guide their action and order the world.

Theoretical framework: organization studies and classical pragmatism

To deal with the IOC's and FIFA's environmental embedding and their rules for action requires a theoretical framework inspired by both an open system perspective and classical pragmatism. We start from the assumption that organizations are never self-sufficient or autarchic but embedded in a larger social environment. Studying an organization in world politics thus implies looking at its relationship to this environment. In doing so, we follow a general organization studies perspective of organizations as open systems. This implies that organizations can be separated analytically from their environment but 'are open to and dependent on flows of personnel, resources, and information from outside' (Scott, 1992 [1981]: 25).

From this perspective, an organization is shaped, supported and infiltrated by its environment, which is considered the basic source for the organization's survival because it consists of the necessary resources and elements an open system needs to exist (Scott, 2004). Organizations interact and observe their environment, which mainly consists of other organizations, to make sensible decisions or produce outputs demanded by the environment (DiMaggio and Powell, 1983). However, organizations are not conceived as monolithic entities but as composed of participants that have 'differing interests and value various inducements. They join and leave or engage in ongoing exchanges with the organization depending on the bargain they can strike' (Scott, 1992 [1981]: 25).

Accordingly, both the IOC and FIFA are embedded in an environment and interact with various entities within it. These entities can range from national and international sports federations to broadcasting companies, city councils, national governments and NGOs, just to name a few. The various manifestations of these relations include economic transactions when rights are sold to broadcasting networks, governmental relations in the bidding process for the hosting of upcoming events and political relations between both organizations and their member organizations (Matheson et al, 2018; Byun and Leopkey, 2021). In our analysis, we aim to study the environmental embeddedness of the IOC and FIFA in general and their specific references and relations to others in the wake of the Russian invasion of Ukraine.

In addition to the open system's perspective, assumptions from classical pragmatism serve to further specify our understanding of organizations, the relationship to their environment and their contributions to world order. Informed by both the agent-structure problem (Wendt, 1987; Dessler, 1989) and the state-personhood debate (Wendt, 2004; Wight, 2004), we grasp organizations, like all other collectives, as structures (of corporate practice), human beings as sole actors, and the interplay between actors and structures as process (Franke and Roos, 2010). Structures of corporate practice refer to states, all kinds of formal organizations and informal groups as well as sets of IOR embedding the fore-mentioned or other collectives (Franke and Koch, 2013). Following Dewey's (1991 [1927]) concept of the public, structures of corporate practice emerge whenever individuals cannot cope alone with problems of action (Roos, 2010).

From a pragmatist point of view, human actors solve problems of action, individually and collectively, with the help of beliefs. Peirce (1992 [1878]: 129), therefore, refers to a belief as 'a rule for action'. Beliefs take the form of imperatives and guide people as routines. When their beliefs no longer bear, actors get into a crisis in which they have to form new beliefs and new rules for action, by means of their potential for creative action (Oevermann, 1991; Joas, 1996). Beliefs are more far-reaching than norms or interests and precede them. Actors might ignore norms but they cannot avoid following the underlying rules for action (Oevermann, 2000). Beliefs can be about one's own actions or directed at others, can be general or specific, contradictory or consistent. What matters, for practitioners, is that beliefs guide concrete action. For scholars, it is just the reconstruction of beliefs in greatest detail that matters.

Not all beliefs are relevant to the composition of world order, but all components of world order can be considered beliefs. As a complex set of beliefs about how the various facets of life are organized in political, economic and cultural terms, world order is in a permanent process of reproduction and transformation. With every act, be it a decision or communication attributable to an organization or another structure of corporate practice, an actor turns away from or backs specific beliefs. This way, beliefs are permanently weakened or strengthened. Put differently, actors are loyal to their beliefs. Since this loyalty is shifting over time, increases and decreases in loyalty strengthen and weaken patterns of order (Roos, 2015).

Methodology

To address our two-part research question, we proceed in two steps. First, we examine the IOC's and FIFA's environmental embedding by means of external descriptions to illustrate the variety of relations and irritations both organizations face in their surroundings. In a second step, we conduct detailed sequential analyses of self-descriptions from the IOC and FIFA to take a closer look of their environmental embedding.

The reconstruction of the environmental embedding does not result in a complete map of both organizations' external relations, but does exhibit which of their relations are publicly observed in a German daily, the *Frankfurter Allgemeine Zeitung* (FAZ).[1] Regional issues linked to the situation of organized sports in Germany notwithstanding, we assume that the samples would have looked quite similar if we had been searching references to the IOC and FIFA in quality newspapers from other countries. Specifically, we scan how many references to both organizations are made in FAZ articles in one year (2021), before we filter and examine those articles that primarily deal with one of the two organizations.

The reconstruction of the IOC's and FIFA's rules for action sequentially deciphers the meaning of both organization's self-descriptions in immediate response to a crisis when beliefs are challenged. We assume the escalation of Russia's war against Ukraine on 24 February 2022 to present such an external event of concern for sports organizations, too. Like any text, the selected self-descriptions – two press releases (IOC, 2022; FIFA, 2022b) – refer to meaning. Thus they can be grasped as linked or concatenated sequences, that is, the smallest particles of meaning, and as manifestations of practice, that is, concatenated choices realized by actors. To wit, meaning is considered socially produced in a process based on rules that can be sequentially reconstructed by means of the researcher's socially acquired competence to act (Oevermann, 2000; Maiwald, 2005).

Inspired by these pragmatist assumptions, the deciphering of meaning proceeds as a close reading in three steps. First, we set forth the possibilities that could meaningfully follow in a given sequence. Second, we explicate the meaning of the sequence that actually follows. Third, we make sense of the choice manifest in that sequence in light of those possibilities that had not been realized (Oevermann, 2000). In this manner, the structure of the examined texts taken as cases of interest is reconstructed sequence by sequence. As openings and closings of scopes for action, each sequence is held to be particular and general at the same time. Consequently, the sequential reconstruction of meaning allows for a certain kind of generalization without relying on large numbers of cases (Oevermann, 1991, 2000). It draws on abduction that 'merely offers suggestions' but 'is the only logical operation which introduces any new idea' (Peirce, 1998 [1903]: 216–7).

The IOC, FIFA and Russia's invasion of Ukraine

After having introduced both our theoretical framework and the methods we used, this section summarizes our findings. Along the lines of our two-part research question, we present first the environmental embedding of the IOC and FIFA, followed by the (world-ordering) beliefs that became manifest in both organizations' responses to Russia's escalation of its war against Ukraine on 24 February 2022.

The IOC's and FIFA's environmental embedding

Regarding our reconstruction of the IOC's and FIFA's environment, we take one distinction for granted. Following Dewey (2019 [1919/20]), we separate societal activity into three realms: politics, economy and culture (including sports, thus opposing an elitist understanding of culture). We start with the IOC's and continue with FIFA's environment.

In 2021, the FAZ published more than 300 articles referencing the IOC, around 120 of them were primarily about it. In the sphere of *politics*, the IOC mostly relates to states and intergovernmental organizations. Beyond host countries of the Olympic Games, such as Japan and China, conflict-prone countries (Afghanistan) and countries with difficult relations to the IOC, like Russia, Belarus and North Korea, are mentioned. The IOC's counterparts are heads of states and governments as well as administrative bodies, among them cities of current or upcoming sports events, such as Tokyo, Beijing and Brisbane. Besides countries, international organizations (IOs) such as the United Nations and the Court of Arbitration for Sport are of importance.

In the *economic* sphere, the IOC is linked to a wide range of enterprises involved in organizing and carrying out the Olympic Games. The FAZ points to sponsors, such as the financial services provider Allianz, automotive manufacturer Toyota and other multinational enterprises (MNEs) and, concerning the right to broadcast the Games, to news agencies and commercial television companies. The IOC also maintains special relations to pharmaceutical companies offering the donation of Corona vaccines for all Olympic participants.

Regarding the sphere of *culture*, the FAZ emphasizes vulnerable groups of athletes, such as those with disabilities, child athletes and refugee athletes who are either insufficiently protected by their home country or cannot represent it for political reasons. The FAZ also mentions protesters who criticize that an Olympic Games during a pandemic puts athletes, coaches and other team members, as well as spectators on site, in jeopardy. Finally, the IOC relates to the non-governmental World Anti-Doping Agency (WADA), various National Olympic Committees (NOCs) and international sports federations, among them weightlifting, boxing, modern pentathlon, equestrian sport, tennis, biathlon and ice hockey.

FIFA was referenced in more than 200 FAZ articles in 2021, around 20 of them were primarily about it. In the sphere of *politics*, three sorts of body appear – states as well as supranational and non-state entities. As to countries, FIFA maintains relations with (heads of states and) governments and administrations, among them patent offices in Argentina and Brazil, public-service media, courts and investigators. The European Court of Justice (ECJ) figures prominently among the supranational entities referred to. Amnesty International and other human-rights organizations illustrate FIFA's relations with non-state agencies.

Regarding the *economy*, the FAZ addresses capital and labour issues. On the capital side, investors in football clubs, the hospitality industry in Qatar – host of the 2022 Men's World Cup – private media, news agencies and television rights managers find reference. Similar applies for FIFA's relations with independent auditors of World Football Remission Fund expenses, suing Brazilian and Argentine small businesspeople and a provider of sports-related business-to-business services. On the labour side, migrant workers on World Cup construction sites are mentioned, representatives of international trade unions and the International Federation of Professional Footballers.

As to the sphere of *culture*, the FAZ stresses the IOC, some of its bodies and representatives, NOCs, and the FIFA president as an IOC member. FIFA also relates to the independent FIFA ethics committee, FIFA federations like the Confederation of African Football (CAF) and the Union of European Football Associations (UEFA), their representatives such as the UEFA president or executive committee, FIFA member associations, and national World Cup organizing committees. Moreover, FIFA's environment consists of football clubs, national teams, coaches, players and various related interest groups, football fans and spectators, FIFA critics and other world sports federations such as tennis, cycling, golf, gymnastics, swimming, athletics and Formula 1 racing.

Based on just one year (2021), this overview illustrates the diversity of the IOC's and FIFA's environmental embedding. To fulfil their tasks, both organizations maintain manifold relations with other entities. These relations are by no means limited to the economic sphere. Politics and, as part of the cultural sphere, world sports, are of utmost importance, too. Next, we will examine the beliefs that guide IOC and FIFA officials in response to a critical event in their external surroundings.

The IOC, FIFA and their responses to Russia's invasion of Ukraine

For a closer look at the IOC's and FIFA's multifaceted environmental embedding, the focus of this subsection is on two press releases that the organizations issued in immediate response to Russia's escalation of its war against Ukraine on 24 February 2022 (IOC, 2022; FIFA, 2022b). Starting with the IOC, we give a brief introduction into the organization before we summarize the findings of our sequential analysis paragraph for paragraph. Each of these paragraphs is opened by the corresponding lines from the interpreted statement. Regarding FIFA, we then proceed in the same way. We conducted the sequential analyses following the three steps explicated in the methodology section. For the sake of clarity, however, this subsection does not present the sequential unfolding of the reconstructed meaning, but its summary. For the same reason, the brief introductions into both organizations are put separately, although they are integral parts of the sequential analyses, combining immanent reconstructions of the meaning of the terms 'IOC' and 'FIFA' with common knowledge and insights from foundational documents.[2]

The International Olympic Committee

The IOC is a non-profit NGO. Founded at the first Olympic Congress in Paris in 1894, it is the leading body of the Olympic Movement and acts as a catalyst for cooperation among the entire Olympic Community. According to its self-perception, the IOC is located at the centre of world sports, supporting all players in the Olympic Movement, which, in addition to the IOC, consists of international sports federations and NOCs. The IOC promotes Olympism worldwide and, as their self-appointed guardian, oversees the regular hosting of the Olympic Games. Furthermore, the IOC promotes sports in society, strengthens the integrity of sport and supports clean athletes as well as other sports organizations (Peacock, 2010). The IOC currently has 102 members, natural persons who represent the IOC in their countries. Taking an oath when elected, the members commit themselves to serve the Olympic Movement, to respect the IOC and the Olympic Charter, and to act independently of economic or political interests (IOC, 2021; Krieger and Wassong, 2021).

The IOC's press release on Russia's invasion of Ukraine (IOC, 2022) begins:

> The International Olympic Committee (IOC) strongly condemns the breach of the Olympic Truce by the Russian government. The respective UN resolution was adopted by the UN General Assembly on 2 December 2021 by consensus of all 193 UN Member States. The Olympic Truce began seven days before the start of the Olympic

> Games, on 4 February 2022, and ends seven days after the closing of the Paralympic Games.

The IOC condemns the Russian government's breach of the Olympic Truce.[3] The choice of verb indicates that the IOC is not in a position to pass judgment, which must be the responsibility of other entities not explicitly addressed. What legal and moral criteria motivate the condemnation? In this regard, the IOC refers to a UN General Assembly resolution. On 2 December 2021, all 193 UN member states had adopted this resolution and thus committed themselves to the Olympic Truce, which covers both the Olympic Games and the Paralympic Games. The IOC does not disapprove of Russia's war of aggression on Ukraine or war in general but the Russian government's breach of the Olympic Truce. What exactly the breach consists of does not become an issue. Underpinning the importance of the Olympic Truce, unanimously adopted through UN Resolution 76/13, the IOC is strictly guided by its duties to ensure that the Olympic Games are held and that all participants, be it athletes or spectators, can travel safely to the Games and back home.

The IOC avoids talking about war and does not condemn or name the Russian army's attack on Ukraine. Unspecified action by the Russian government must have violated the Olympic Truce and the related resolution to which its representative had agreed in the UN General Assembly. In this way, the Russian government only – and implicitly the Russian president – is held accountable for what has happened. The army, the Russian population and the Olympic Community in Russia are cleared from any responsibility for the war. The IOC thus tends to follow the narrative according to which the Russian president dragged his people into a war it did not want.

> Today, IOC President Thomas Bach reiterates his call for peace, which he expressed in his speeches at the Opening Ceremony and the Closing Ceremony of the Olympic Games. At the Opening Ceremony, he called on the political authorities: 'Observe your commitment to this Olympic Truce. Give peace a chance.' At the Closing Ceremony, he asked the political leaders 'to be inspired' by the 'example of solidarity and peace' set by the Olympic athletes. (IOC, 2022)

First of all, the subject changes in this paragraph. Emphasizing the most outstanding position within the IOC, the text is no longer about the organization as a whole but about its president and his speeches. In these speeches the IOC president paints a bleak picture of world politics, which – one must assume – is characterized by the permanency of wars. Only the Olympic Games grant a brief period of peace, whereas fighting resumes after the Olympic Truce. The IOC, and above all its president, is portrayed as a peace-making authority in a world dominated by war, in which political leaders must be called upon to give peace a chance. This implies that the addressed political authorities usually rely on military rather than diplomatic solutions in cases of conflict. At the same time, the president's call for peace discloses his low level of confidence in the work of IOs, and in particular the UN. From this perspective, the resolution of the UN General Assembly appears to be merely a non-binding declaration of interest that can be disregarded at any time as states might wish.

The IOC president denies the UN the ability to make a substantial contribution to keeping peace. However, he sees himself in a position to call on politicians for peace because they have been given a taste of lasting peace through the Olympic Truce institutionalized by the IOC. Moreover, the president can point to athletes who lead by example and stand as a blueprint for solidarity and peace in the world. His message is to do as the athletes do and settle your disputes in a fair competition without physically hurting your opponents. Backed by this implicit analogy, the IOC president uncovers his perception of world politics. For him, world politics is like a competition between athletes and the challenge is to establish fair rules for this competition.

> Following recent events, the IOC is deeply concerned about the safety of the Olympic Community in Ukraine. It has established a task force to closely monitor the situation and to coordinate humanitarian assistance to members of the Olympic Community in Ukraine where possible. (IOC, 2022)

The IOC reveals that it is only concerned about the people who belong to the Olympic Community in Ukraine, a group not specified. In a narrower sense, it includes all Olympic athletes, the Olympic delegation and the NOC. In a broader sense, all people in Ukraine who profess Olympism constitute the Olympic Community. The IOC also formulates how it intends to help those it is concerned about. To this end, a task force is being set up to monitor the situation in Ukraine. The IOC thus chooses a rather reserved response to the breach of the Olympic Truce and its deep concern for the Olympic Movement in Ukraine. No sanctions are envisaged for the Russian government, the NOC or Russian athletes. The task force is established only to monitor the situation and coordinate humanitarian assistance. Thus, the IOC does not *provide* humanitarian assistance; it only provides the *coordination* of assistance.

This coordination of assistance does not benefit all people in Ukraine. It is, again, limited to the Olympic Community only. Other people may also experience suffering and need help but are not taken into consideration. Even less, the IOC only wants to support the Olympic Community 'where possible'. In this way, the IOC reserves the right to stop support, if, for example, the situation is considered too dangerous or if any other circumstances arise that impede the task force. In a country at war, this is likely to be the case at any location. The IOC thus reduces its support for the Olympic Community in Ukraine to minimal services (monitoring and coordination of humanitarian assistance), without providing any resources or imposing sanctions beyond the condemnation of the Russian government. Even though the IOC does not limit itself to a proclamatory condemnation, it responds cautiously to the breach of the Olympic Truce.

FIFA

As a federation, FIFA refers to a formally equal relationship between the united associations. A federation expresses the idea of managing specific aspects of social life by rules it has to write down and enforce. These rules concern the kind of football that is organized by an association and thus recognized by the state in which this association is registered. This kind of football is thus strictly distinguished from football not organized by associations. FIFA obviously does not claim any regulatory competence for the latter. The vast majority of FIFA's 211 current member associations represent states that are broadly recognized as independent and thus have external sovereignty. However, football associations that do not represent sovereign states, such as those in England and Wales, can become members, too.

Founded in Paris in 1904, FIFA is 'an association registered in the Commercial Register of the Canton of Zurich' according to its current statutes (FIFA, 2022a: 10). Its main purpose is the worldwide dissemination and control of association football and the organization of international competitions.

FIFA's press release on Russia's invasion of Ukraine (FIFA, 2022b) opens as follows:

> FIFA condemns the use of force by Russia in Ukraine and any type of violence to resolve conflicts.

The act of condemnation raises the question of the legal and moral standards on which it is based. Those who condemn rather than judge are unlikely to be in a position to pass legal judgment. Because it is up to other units of action to evaluate in legal terms what has been condemned, FIFA is obviously limited to making a moral evaluation. In its condemnation, FIFA refers to the use of coercive means by an authority that is in principle entitled to do so, such as the police or the military of a particular state or group of states. FIFA's criticism therefore relates more to the proportionality of the intervention than to its carrying out per se. What is condemned is not the fact that organs of the Russian state are in Ukraine, but that they use coercive means there. If Russian (armed) forces have been in Ukraine for a long time, it no longer matters to FIFA why they are there at all or whether this is in accordance with international law. The presence of Russian forces in Ukraine is not central from FIFA's point of view.

The use of coercive means is morally condemned because, for FIFA, conflicts should not be solved by means of violence as a matter of principle. No distinction is made between legitimate and illegitimate, legal and illegal violence. FIFA's position tends to be a radical pacifist one. It even claims the moral superiority of this position over Article 51 of the UN Charter, which guarantees an inherent right to individual and collective self-defence. However, FIFA's concept of violence is highly unspecific. Its condemnation of Russia is undermined by the condemnation of any violence to resolve conflicts. The Russian use of force loses its specific character and becomes something that FIFA always condemns anyway, regardless of specific occasions. For, whoever defends oneself against an attack is, from FIFA's point of view, behaving as wrongly as the aggressor. Accordingly, FIFA refrains from taking sides. This raises the question of why Russia has been called by its name at all and why violence alone has not been condemned as a means of resolving conflicts. What exactly the Russian forces in Ukraine are doing is of no further interest to FIFA. Nor will the condemnation of Russia have any consequences for the time being.

> Violence is never a solution and FIFA calls on all parties to restore peace through constructive dialogue. (FIFA, 2022b)

FIFA's condemnation of Russia is followed by a call for the restoration of peace and dialogue, another rather reserved form of action. Condemnations and appeals are the means of those who, unlike the Russian state, have no more effective methods of achieving what they seek or believe to be right and proper. How effective is such an appeal on the part of a football federation likely to be? Does FIFA have a sufficient level of integrity, standing or legitimacy for its appeal to be heard and heeded? By calling for constructive dialogue rather than negotiation, FIFA is depoliticizing and trivializing the conflict. Its message is: settle it among yourselves, there is no need for a third party, a mediating authority. Since 'all' warring parties are called upon to restore peace, this means that Ukraine, which was attacked by Russia, now bears the same responsibility for conflict resolution as Russia. Here, FIFA is equalizing, not asking about attacker and attacked; the question of guilt does not play a role.

> FIFA also continues to express its solidarity to the people affected by this conflict. Regarding football matters in both Ukraine and Russia,

> FIFA will continue to monitor the situation and updates in relation to the upcoming FIFA World Cup Qatar 2022™ qualifiers will be communicated in due course. (FIFA, 2022b)

FIFA states that its solidarity with those affected by what it calls 'this conflict' continues. Thus, the condemned Russian use of force in Ukraine is not seen to have started the conflict. In what FIFA's solidarity is manifest is not specified. To whom exactly FIFA's solidarity is directed is not specified either. This way, the eminent speech act of expressing solidarity decays into an empty phrase. It becomes clearer that the concrete occasion of its statement makes no difference to FIFA. FIFA's solidarity with the people who have been affected before the Russian use of force also stands afterwards. FIFA relies on continuity, on its routines. FIFA responds neither specifically nor distinctively, it homogenizes a highly heterogeneous group (those affected by the conflict) and thus undermines its expression of solidarity.

Fatalities of the Russian use of coercive means in Ukraine are not mentioned. With the trivializing non-differentiation between those directly, strongly or less strongly affected, FIFA with its (prefabricated, routinely used) rhetoric of solidarity fails to clearly side with those who have fallen victim to Russia's use of coercive means. FIFA's response to belligerent force seems rather to be a disinterest in concrete information about the constellation in which the use of such coercive means occurs. Like someone who is dealing with small children, FIFA's position is: I don't care who started it. On this basis, the same routines of action always take effect: condemnation of violence, call for peace and dialogue, expression of solidarity. No matter which violent conflict is involved, FIFA always rejects violence as a means of resolving conflict. Violence is always wrong; circumstances do not matter. Details of the specific situation are not necessary to know; the usual (standard) formulations suffice.

By emphasizing the continuity of its actions, FIFA indicates that it has everything under control and does not need to change anything. FIFA has a routine of action that does not need to be questioned because it has proven itself. At least from its own perspective, FIFA has always done well with this routine so far. By proclaiming that it will stick to its routines and continue to do what it has done before, FIFA is downplaying the occasion of its own condemning statement. FIFA places itself in a passive observer role. This way, the current situation is further de-dramatized; it does not require any decisions. FIFA is in control of everything that concerns it.

FIFA refers to the Men's Football World Cup it is organizing in Qatar at the end of 2022 as a registered trademark ('™') in this context. So, one reason why no one at FIFA may deviate from routines at the moment may be that they do not want to jeopardize monetary interests in staging this event. However, a final reference to possible updates regarding the qualifiers for the upcoming tournament makes it clear that the last word has not yet been spoken. The passive construction used here underscores that, contrary to the previous rhetoric of perennial routines, things could get tricky. The use of the passive undermines the clear accountability of a decision to the unit of action that made and is responsible for it.

The summaries of our sequential analyses of two press releases issued by the IOC and FIFA reveal world-ordering beliefs that officials from both sports organizations are following. As rules for action, these beliefs are not limited to rather idiosyncratic condemnations of Russia's invasion of Ukraine; they also refer to the IOC's and FIFA's self-perception and general outreach to their environment. In this regard, both organizations focus on ensuring that sports events can take place and are considered an example of peaceful and fair competition worldwide.

Answering the research question

The first part of our enquiry exhibits that the IOC and FIFA are embedded in a social environment consisting of a variety of organizations, and they maintain multifaceted forms of relations with other entities in the spheres of politics, economy and culture. For a closer look at a detailed excerpt of their inter-organizational environment, we studied the responses of both organizations to a specific event in their surroundings. Based on our sequential analyses of their press releases issued on 24 February 2022 when Russia escalated the war against Ukraine it had initiated in 2014, the second part of our enquiry identifies beliefs that guide IOC and FIFA officials as rules for action. We concentrate on those beliefs that contribute to world order (considered to be in a permanent process of reproduction and transformation) and present them in the form of imperatives covering three topics: self-organization and purpose; relations to the external environment; and positioning on Russia's invasion of Ukraine.

The IOC's beliefs on its self-organization and purpose are:

- Establish an international non-profit non-governmental body to organize the Olympic Games; ensure that the Games are held regularly and supervise them.
- Focus and limit yourself to your core mission, that is, the promotion of the Olympic Movement and regular hosting of the Olympic Games; accept no political directives and tolerate no other organization making similar claims in this regard.
- Characterize the Olympics as an example of peace and solidarity among athletes rivalling in fair competition.
- Protect the Olympic Community by taking action in case of crisis.

The IOC's beliefs on the regulation of relations to its external environment are:

- Exhort all political authorities, especially heads of state and government, to the traditional observance of the Olympic Truce (*ekecheiria*), an ancient tradition, and thus underline your relevance in world politics; remind heads of state and government of the unanimously adopted resolution of the UN General Assembly on the Olympic Truce; advocate that weapons remain silent during the Olympic Games (including seven days before and after) in a world marked by war.
- Do not condemn war per se, but only those wars that could jeopardize the smooth running of the Olympic Games.
- Point to the Olympic Games, where athletes face each other in fair competition, as an example for world politics with regard to its transformation into an equally fair contest with countries behaving like athletes and respecting the common rules of competition.
- Do not expect IOs in general and the UN in particular to maintain peace and prevent future wars.

Regarding Russia's invasion of Ukraine, the IOC is guided by the following beliefs:

- Condemn the Russian government's breach of the Olympic Truce, but do not threaten any consequences for the Russian government, the Olympic Community or Russian athletes – refer to the Olympic Truce and its observance only.
- Express your deep concern for the Olympic Community in Ukraine and establish a task force to both monitor the situation and coordinate humanitarian assistance to it; set the task force to act only where clearly possible and be careful that it does not put itself in unnecessary danger and, thereby, damages itself and the IOC.

FIFA is guided by the following beliefs concerning its self-organization and purpose:

- Organize as an association, submit to state jurisdiction, and link member associations in a formally equal relationship with each other.
- Establish and enforce uniform rules for organized, state-recognized football.
- Spread and control organized football worldwide and arrange international competitions; organize the Men's World Cup (in Qatar) as a registered trademark with which you are pursuing monetary interests.
- Announce updates regarding the qualifying matches for an upcoming tournament in case of warlike conflicts, but do so without attributing any decisions due in this context.

FIFA's beliefs as to regulating relations to its external environment are:

- Accept federations from sovereign and not (yet) sovereign states as members.
- Postulate that no conflict can be resolved by force and do not distinguish between legitimate and illegitimate or legal and illegal violence; claim moral superiority over Article 51 of the UN Charter that guarantees an inherent right to individual and collective self-defence.
- Rely on continuity and stick to your routines in the case of armed conflict (condemn violence, call for dialogue, express solidarity); observe, indicate that you have everything under control, and de-dramatize the situation by not making a decision.

Finally, FIFA's positioning on Russia's invasion of Ukraine is guided by the following beliefs:

- Condemn Russia's use of force in Ukraine, but not the presence of Russian armed forces there, undermine your condemnation of Russia by condemning *any* use of force to resolve conflicts.
- Abstain from taking sides in the conflict between Russia and Ukraine; assign Russia and the attacked Ukraine the same responsibility for conflict resolution; avoid the question of guilt and ignore the difference between attackers and attacked; homogenize the highly heterogeneous group of those affected by conflict.
- Call for the restoration of peace and thereby suggest that you have the level of integrity, prestige or legitimacy necessary to do so.
- Depoliticize and trivialize the conflict (by calling for constructive dialogue rather than negotiation and suggesting that the parties to the conflict work out their problems among themselves, without a mediating authority).
- Degrade the expression of solidarity to an empty phrase (by declaring your solidarity with all those affected by the conflict without making clear what your solidarity is expressed in and to whom exactly it applies).

For now, our reconstruction of both the environmental embedding and three clusters of world-ordering beliefs that guide the IOC and FIFA leaves open three tasks: to consolidate the findings, (re)connect them to the state of research and formulate follow-up questions for further research. We address these tasks in the next and final section.

Conclusion and outlook

Starting from the assumption that sports organizations matter in world politics, this chapter has methodologically taken two steps. The first step illustrated that the IOC and FIFA maintain manifold external relations. Their environment, reconstructed using articles from a German newspaper in 2021, does not only consist of entities from the economic sphere, such as television networks or advertising partners. The two organizations under study also hold a variety of relations to world sports as part of the cultural sphere and to political entities, among them representatives of national governments and cities as well as IGOs and NGOs.

The second step enquired into this multifaceted environmental embeddedness in greater detail, focusing on two press releases, of 24 February 2022, issued by the IOC and FIFA in immediate response to Russia's escalation of its war against Ukraine. The sequential reconstruction of these documents yielded three clusters of world-ordering beliefs that guide the officials of both organizations. A first cluster includes beliefs about self-organization and purpose. For both the IOC and FIFA it is of utmost importance to ensure that the sports events they are responsible for can take place without interference. A second cluster of beliefs comprises relations to the external environment. While the IOC promotes the Olympic Games as an example of peaceful and fair competition worldwide, FIFA stresses and sticks to its (pacifist) routines in times of war. A third cluster of beliefs addresses Russia's invasion of Ukraine, which is, rather idiosyncratically and somewhat implicitly, condemned by both organizations.

Our findings connect strongly with two of the three strands of the presented state of research on the IOC and FIFA and rather weakly with its third strand. First, our analysis helps to understand why sports events hosted by both organizations and their effects are extensively covered in the literature (Kobierecki and Strożek, 2021; Müller and Gaffney, 2018). The IOC and FIFA define themselves very strongly through these events and try to ensure their execution, even against adverse circumstances such as war. Second, with regard to the position of sports organizations in the global system, the IOC's claim to be located at the centre of world sports is striking. From this central position, it promotes peaceful competition as an example for the world to follow – as FIFA does (Bucher and Eckl, 2022). In addition, FIFA uses its global position for the promotion of its maxims – radical pacifism including dialogue with aggressors in the case at hand. Third, our findings connect with the topic of finance, corruption and accountability rather weakly (Matheson et al, 2018; Szymanski, 2016). Financial issues are visible only in the labelling of the FIFA World Cup as a registered trademark. However, it would be prejudiced to portray the great interest of the IOC and FIFA in executing their events as commercially driven, since this reading follows as little from our analysis as its opposite. Finally, our findings go beyond the presented state of research through their focus on the issue of war and peace as well as more explicit efforts to address aspects of world order.

As the authority for the Olympic Movement and the hosting of the Olympic Games, issues of war and peace do not challenge the IOC as long as the Olympic Truce is observed. The president of the IOC only encourages the political authorities to be inspired by the example of the athletes who subject their competition to rules and abide by these rules. Speaking of political authorities instead of heads of state and government in this context, the IOC refers to the transience of states and expresses its disinterest in the concrete quality of the political world. The IOC relies on an internal differentiation of world order in which it has the responsibility for questions of (Olympic) sports, while other organizations, first and foremost the UN, account for questions of war and peace. Precisely because of overlapping responsibilities in this field, the IOC seeks cooperation with the UN and, prior to the Games, solicits the adoption of a resolution affirming the Olympic Truce. In general, however, the IOC does not interfere in matters of war and peace.

FIFA, on the other hand, takes a radical pacifist position and firmly rejects any form of violence. In its view, peace can only be (re)established through constructive dialogue. However, FIFA does not mention who exactly should enter into such a dialogue. It leaves open who is responsible for war and denies an attacked state such as Ukraine the right to defend itself in line with Article 51 of the UN Charter. In a world ordered by FIFA, there would be no need for national defence and thus no need for an army, let alone UN intervention. Consequently, instead of commenting on the war in its press release, FIFA simply could have stated that it will continue to monitor the situation and examine possible consequences for the upcoming World Cup. Nonetheless, FIFA's rejection of any form of violence is a political statement. It does not take sides on the Russian invasion of Ukraine and abandons the distinction between attackers and attacked or between legitimate and illegitimate violence. Engaging in shallow expressions of solidarity, FIFA's core belief is: during external crises, follow your routines.

To further substantiate our very preliminary findings, additional research could address further IOC and FIFA communications in the course of the war in Ukraine. How have their responses changed since February 2022? To which of their beliefs are both organizations loyal? What additional rules for action can be derived from subsequent responses? How do their responses differ from those of other organizations, such as the UN? Beyond Russia's war against Ukraine, further research could focus on immediate responses of both organizations to the initiation or escalation of other wars. Do the IOC and FIFA always respond to wars in the same manner? Do they respond to any other conflicts at all? If so, to which do they respond? Moreover, studying direct communication between the IOC and FIFA would also be a promising point of departure. The same holds for the organizations' responses to similar challenges, such as human-rights issues or corruption charges.

Finally, the current focus on the IOC's and FIFA's self-descriptions could be complemented by spotting external descriptions from their environment, be it other sports federations or athletes, heads of states and governments or IOs. What are their takes on the beliefs that guide the IOC and FIFA? So much remains for students of world order interested in sports organizations.

Acknowledgements

The authors would like to thank Bernd Bucher and Julian Eckl for valuable suggestions on an earlier version of this chapter.

Notes

1 Published since 1949, the FAZ is centre-right in its political orientation and can (probably for this reason) be regarded as the most important daily newspaper in Germany, with its rather structurally conservative population.

2 The sequential analyses of the two press releases involved both authors and were conducted in German. The two resulting documents of, taken together, some 21,500 words can be shared through the authors. For a longer illustration of sequential analysis in IR, see also Franke (2010).

3 With the Olympic Truce, the IOC takes up the ancient Greek tradition of *ekecheiria*. It demands the laying down of arms to enable Olympic Games (since 776 BCE) as competition in peace. In the wake of the war in Yugoslavia, this tradition was revived. In a call for the restoration of the Olympic Truce, the IOC negotiated with the UN to allow athletes from the dissolved Republic of Yugoslavia to participate in the 1992 Summer Games in Barcelona under the Olympic flag. Since then, the Olympic Truce has been proclaimed at all Olympic Games and adopted by resolutions of the UN General Assembly.

References

Bishop, M.L. and Cooper, A.F. (2018) 'The FIFA scandal and the distorted influence of small states', *Global Governance*, 24(1): 21–40.

Bucher, B. and Eckl, J. (2022) 'Football's contribution to international order: the ludic and festive reproduction of international society by world societal actors', *International Theory*, 14(2): 311–37.

Byun, J. and Leopkey, B. (2021) 'The relationship between the IOC and international sport federations', in D. Chatziefstathiou, B. García and B. Séguin (eds) *Routledge Handbook of the Olympic and Paralympic Games,* London: Routledge, pp 294–308.

Clausen, J., Bayle, E., Giauque, D. et al (2018) 'International sport federations' commercialisation: a qualitative comparative analysis', *European Sport Management Quarterly*, 18(3): 373–92.

Cornelissen, S. (2011) 'More than a sporting chance? Appraising the sport for development legacy of the 2010 FIFA World Cup', *Third World Quarterly*, 32(3): 503–29.

Dessler, D. (1989) 'What's at stake in the agent-structure debate?', *International Organization*, 43(3): 441–73.

Dewey, J. (2019 [1919/20]) *Sozialphilosophie: Vorlesungen in China 1919/ 20*, Berlin: Suhrkamp.

Dewey, J. (1991 [1927]) *The Public and Its Problems*, Athens, Ohio: Swallow Press and Ohio University Press.

Dietschy, P. (2013) 'Making football global? FIFA, Europe, and the non-European football world, 1912–74', *Journal of Global History*, 8(2): 279–98.

DiMaggio, P.J. and Powell, W.W. (1983) 'The iron cage revisited: institutional isomorphism and collective rationality in organizational fields', *American Sociological Review,* 48(2): 147–60.

Eisenberg, C. (2006) 'Der Weltfußballverband FIFA im 20. Jahrhundert: Metamorphosen eines "Prinzipienreiters"', *Vierteljahrshefte für Zeitgeschichte*, 54(2): 209–30.

Fett, M. (2020) 'The game has changed – a systematic approach to classify FIFA World Cups', *International Journal of Sport Policy and Politics*, 12(3): 455–70.

FIFA (International Federation of Association Football) (2022a) *FIFA Statutes, May 2022 edition*, available from: digitalhub.fifa.com/m/3815fa68bd9f4ad8/original/FIFA_Statutes_2022-EN.pdf [accessed 30 March 2023].

FIFA (2022b) 'FIFA expresses hope for rapid cessation of hostilities and peace in Ukraine', available from: fifa.com/about-fifa/organisation/fifa-council/media-releases/fifa-expresses-hope-for-rapid-cessation-of-hostilities-and-peace-in-ukraine [accessed 30 March 2023].

Firgo, M. (2021) 'The causal economic effects of Olympic Games on host regions', *Regional Science and Urban Economics,* 88(3): 103673.

Franke, U. (2010) *Die Nato nach 1989: Das Rätsel ihres Fortbestandes*, Wiesbaden: Springer VS.

Franke, U. and Koch, M. (2013) 'Inter-organizational relations as structures of corporate practice', *Journal of International Organizations Studies*, 4(special issue): 85–103.

Franke, U. and Roos, U. (2010) 'Actor, structure, process: transcending the state personhood debate by means of a pragmatist ontological model for international relations theory', *Review of International Studies*, 36(4): 1057–77.

Geeraert, A. and Drieskens, E. (2015) 'The EU controls FIFA and UEFA: a principal–agent perspective', *Journal of European Public Policy*, 22(10): 1448–66.

Geeraert, A. and Gauthier, R. (2018) 'Out-of-control Olympics: why the IOC is unable to ensure an environmentally sustainable Olympic Games', *Journal of Environmental Policy & Planning,* 20(1): 16–30.

Hock, B. and Gomtsian, S. (2018) 'Private order building: the state in the role of the civil society and the case of FIFA', *International Sports Law Journal*, 17(3): 186–204.

Homburg, H. (2008) 'Financing world football: a business history of the Fédération Internationale de Football Association (FIFA)', *Zeitschrift für Unternehmensgeschichte*, 53(1): 33–69.

IOC (International Olympic Committee) (2022) 'IOC strongly condemns the breach of the Olympic Truce', available from: olympics.com/ioc/news/ioc-strongly-condemns-the-breach-of-the-olympic-truce [accessed 30 March 2023].

IOC (2021) *Olympic Charter, in force as from 8 August 2021*, available from: rstillmed.olympics.com/media/Document%20Library/OlympicOrg/General/EN-Olympic-Charter.pdf [accessed 30 March 2023].

Jerabek, M.M., Maxwell Ferreira de Andrade, A. and Figueroa, A.M. (2017) 'FIFA's hegemony: examples from World Cup hosting countries', *Global Society*, 31(3): 417–40.

Joas, H. (1996) *The Creativity of Action*, Chicago: University of Chicago Press.

Kobierecki, M.M. and Strożek, P. (2021) 'Sports mega-events and shaping the international image of states: how hosting the Olympic Games and FIFA World Cups affects interest in host nations', *International Politics*, 58(1): 49–70.

Krieger, J. and Wassong, S. (2021) 'The composition of the IOC. Origins and key turning points in the governance of the Olympic movement', in D. Chatziefstathiou, B. García and B. Séguin (eds) *Routledge Handbook of the Olympic and Paralympic Games,* London: Routledge, pp 293–216.

Maiwald, K.-O. (2005) 'Competence and praxis: sequential analysis in German sociology', *Forum: Qualitative Social Research*, 6(3).

Matheson V.A., Schwab, D. and Koval, P. (2018) 'Corruption in the bidding, construction and organisation of mega-events: an analysis of the Olympics and World Cup', in M. Breuer and D. Forrest (eds) *The Palgrave Handbook on the Economics of Manipulation in Sport*, Cham: Palgrave Macmillan, pp 257–78.

Meier, H.E., Mutz, M., Glathe, J. et al (2021) 'Politicization of a contested mega event: the 2018 FIFA World Cup on Twitter', *Communication & Sport*, 9(5): 785–810.

Meyer, J.W., Boli, J., Thomas, G.M. and Ramirez, F.O. (1997) 'World society and the nation-state', *American Journal of Sociology*, 103(1): 144–81.

Müller, M. and Gaffney, C. (2018) 'Comparing the urban impacts of the FIFA World Cup and Olympic Games from 2010 to 2016', *Journal of Sport and Social Issues*, 42(4): 247–69.

Nelson, T. and Cottrell, M.P. (2015) 'Sport without referees? The power of the International Olympic Committee and the social politics of accountability', *European Journal of International Relations,* 22(2): 437–58.

Oevermann, U. (2000) 'Die Methode der Fallrekonstruktion in der Grundlagenforschung sowie der klinischen und pädagogischen Praxis', in K. Kraimer (ed) *Die Fallrekonstruktion. Sinnverstehen in der sozialwissenschaftlichen Forschung*, Frankfurt: Suhrkamp, pp 58–156.

Oevermann, U. (1991) 'Genetischer Strukturalismus und das sozialwissenschaftliche Problem der Erklärung der Entstehung des Neuen', in S. Müller-Doohm (ed) *Jenseits der Utopie*, Frankfurt: Suhrkamp, pp 267–336.

Peacock, B. (2010) '"A virtual world government unto itself": uncovering the rational-legal authority of the IOC in world politics', *Olympika,* 19: 41–58.

Peirce, C.S. (1998 [1903]) 'The nature of meaning', in The Peirce Edition Project (ed) *The Essential Peirce: Selected Philosophical Writings, Vol. 2 (1893–1913),* Bloomington and Indianapolis: Indiana University Press, pp 208–25.

Peirce, C.S. (1992 [1878]) 'How to make our ideas clear', in N. Houser and C. Kloesel (eds) *The Essential Peirce: Selected Philosophical Writings, Vol. 1 (1867–1893),* Bloomington and Indianapolis: Indiana University Press, pp 124–41.

Pielke Jr, R. (2013) 'How can FIFA be held accountable?', *Sport Management Review,* 16(3): 255–67.

Pouliopoulos, T. and Georgiadis, K. (2021) 'FIFA and UEFA, a critical review of the two organizations through the lens of institutional theory and MacIntyre's philosophical schema', *Soccer & Society*, 22(7): 778–90.

Roos, U. (2015) Beliefs and loyalties in world politics: a pragmatist framework for analysis, in G. Hellmann and K.E. Jørgensen (eds) *Theorizing Foreign Policy in a Globalized World*, Basingstoke: Palgrave Macmillan, pp 176–98.

Roos, U. (2010) *Deutsche Außenpolitik: eine Rekonstruktion der grundlegenden Handlungsregeln*, Wiesbaden: VS Verlag.

Scott, W.R. (2004) 'Reflections on a half-century of organizational sociology', *Annual Review of Sociology*, 30: 1–21.

Scott, W.R. (1992 [1981]) *Organizations: Rational, Natural, and Open Systems*, Englewood Cliffs: Prentice Hall.

Szymanski, S. (2016) 'Compromise or compromised? The bidding process for the award of the Olympic Games and the FIFA World Cup', in Transparency International (ed) *Global Corruption Report: Sport*, available from: transparency.org/files/content/feature/3.5_CompromiseOrCompromised_Szymanski_GCRSport.pdf [accessed 30 March 2023].

Tomlinson, A. (2014) 'The supreme leader sails on: leadership, ethics and governance in FIFA', *Sport in Society*, 17(9): 1155–69.

Wang, H. and Rosenau, J.N. (2001) 'Transparency International and corruption as an issue of global governance', *Global Governance,* 7(1): 25–49.

Wendt, A. (2004) 'The state as person in international theory', *Review of International Studies*, 30(2): 289–316.

Wendt, A.E. (1987) 'The agent-structure problem in international relations theory', *International Organization*, 41(3): 335–70.

Wight. C. (2004) 'State agency: social action without human activity?', *Review of International Studies*, 30(2): 269–80.

9

Conclusion: A Pragmatist View of Inter-Organizational Relations and World Order

Ulrich Franke

Inter-organizational relations research revisited

Committed to the idea of re-pluralizing the discussion and exploration of inter-organizational relations (IOR) within international relations (IR), this volume began from the assumption that a broader understanding was required of what exactly is to be examined and of how this research could take place. To achieve such a broadening, three levels offer room for innovation. These relate to subject matter or research object (organization type and policy field/societal sphere), theory and methodology.

First, at the level of the *research object*, innovation seems to be easiest to achieve. The narrow focus of the study of IOR on intergovernmental organizations (IGOs) can be countered by broadening the research agenda to non-governmental organizations (NGOs) and multinational enterprises (MNEs). This is done in Chapters 5, 6, 7 and 8, while Chapter 2 addresses the relations of a hybrid form of governance. Besides IOR in the dominant policy fields of security (Chapters 3, 4 and 6) and economy (Chapter 7), topics linked to the rule of law (Chapters 2 and 3) and sports (Chapter 8) are also covered. The same holds for a topic from security studies that is not directly associated with it (Chapter 5). However, more could have been achieved here with regard to pressing issues such as health or climate/environmental policy (but see, for instance, Eckl and Hanrieder, 2023; Holzscheiter, 2015; or Smith et al, 2021).

Second, on *theoretical* innovation, this volume contains only one contribution based on a rationalist approach. Rationalist accounts have come to dominate the discussion of IOR in IR so far. This discursive power is not only reflected in numbers of publications; it is also wielded through the capacity to create and disseminate key terms, such as 'inter-organizationalism' (Koops, 2008; also Biermann, 2009), or to define the field (Koops and Biermann, 2017). Regardless of the reasons for their dominance, this volume enlarges the space for alternatives to rationalist accounts. In addition to sociological neo-institutionalism (Chapters 3 and 5) and classical pragmatism (Chapter 8), which have already been proposed in the introduction, options include post-structuralist discourse theory (Chapter 3) and relational sociology (Chapter 7), along with combinations of rationalist regime complexity with constructivist considerations from (critical) norms research (Chapter 4) and public administration with organization studies (Chapter 6).[1] The diversity of these approaches refutes an objection that this volume, by means of the accounts presented in the introduction, aims at replacing the diagnosed dominance of rationalism with a canonization of alternative approaches. On the contrary, the high variance of approaches used here serves the goal of re-pluralizing the debate on IOR in IR.

In terms of content-related concerns, the problem with rationalist accounts is that they cannot adequately cope with a social constellation which, empirically, is constitutive for human life: a crisis or, as the pragmatist philosopher John Dewey (1938: 107–8) coins it, a 'problematic situation'. Despite the inflationary and often imprecise use of the term, a crisis is characterized by the fact that our routines fail and we do not know what to do. Since we cannot *not* act, we do go on. In this moment of crisis, however, we do not know whether what we do will turn out to be helpful or not. It is only with hindsight that we will be able to qualify our action as either rational or irrational. As this holds for the everyday person as it does for representatives of all types of organization, rationality – so broadly discussed in the social sciences following Weber (2006 [1920]) – is indeed surprisingly ill-suited a concept to establish an all-encompassing paradigm (Oevermann, 1991, 2016).

Despite the strong role of rationalist approaches in the study of IOR, their challengers should avoid re-enacting the debate between rationalists and constructivists known from the theory debate in IR (for a prominent critique of it, see Fearon and Wendt, 2002). As overused as the metaphor of building bridges may appear, attempts to overcome dualisms are welcome. The blendings of regime complexity with critical norms constructivism, public administration with organization studies, or global governance with relational sociology, are, as stated, some of the bridge-building efforts in this volume (Chapters 4, 6 and 7). In a discipline that, like larger society, is in a permanent process of differentiation, the pragmatist concept of beliefs as rules for action provides another tool for this task (Chapter 8; see also Peirce, 1992 [1878]; Franke and Roos, 2010). It opens the possibility to translate the implications of theoretical and practical knowledge into *beliefs as rules for action* portrayed in the form of imperatives and, thus, facilitates making differences transparent and understandable or finding a common meta-language. The further course of this conclusion will provide initial clues for the viability of this idea when world-order contributions of IOR, often implicitly contained in these chapters, are made explicit.

The handling of the concepts of cooperation, competition and conflict in this volume also points to a slight theoretical broadening of the state of research on IOR in IR. Although the distinction between direct conflicts and indirect competitions as two forms of social struggle (Werron, 2010) is not made use of, the contributions to this volume refrain from seeing relationships in a binary way as either cooperative or conflictive/competitive. The relevance of this step is not to be underestimated, as the multifaceted coexistence of cooperative and competitive relations (Chapter 5) and the complex path to transform competitive into cooperative relations between organizations illustrate (Chapter 6). Moreover in this context, some of the chapters refer to the 'dark side' of cooperation (Chapters 2, 3 and 7). The importance of this aspect is not so much theoretical or conceptual, but empirical and normative, not least regarding inter-organizational contributions to world order. It demonstrates that this volume is not based on a one-sided or naïve understanding of cooperation as a kind of superordinate telos that, per se, could be expected to improve the state of the world.

Third and finally, *methodological* innovation has to be explored. At stake is the volume's claim to overcome, through approaches more reflective, more refined and thus more open to criticism, the narrow focus on content-analytical methods to study IOR. On the surface, this level may have seen the least achievements. A closer look, however, reveals that the contributors have spent quite some energy on considerations of case selection and data gathering. That is a good start, but research does not have to and will not stop there. Given that generalizations are explicitly shied away from, with reference to the one processed case as 'only' one case, pragmatist philosophy may point a way forward. A reconstruction of the chapters' findings concerning inter-organizational contributions to world order can be achieved by turning to the Aristotelian concept of abduction, which the pragmatist philosopher Charles S. Peirce had reintroduced in the philosophy of science discourse in the late 19th century (Franke and Weber, 2012).

Peirce does not reduce the logic of research to an opposition between deduction and induction. Following Aristotle, he distinguishes three modes of reasoning: deduction, induction and abduction. In the research process, these follow each other cyclically again and again. 'Deduction proves that something *must* be, Induction shows that something *actually is* operative, Abduction merely suggests that something *may be*' (Peirce, 1998 [1903]: 216, italic in original). Abduction thus is the weakest of the three but 'the only logical operation which introduces any new idea' (Peirce, 1998 [1903]: 216). As argued earlier, we depend on the introduction of a new idea when our routines fail and no longer take us forward. As capacity to solve problems of action, abduction is therefore not only suitable for everyday people and representatives of organizations, but also for researchers. Pragmatism as an approach of theory and practice is coming full circle here.

The promise of abduction is that it enables the researcher to draw far-reaching conclusions from few materials or data. A dialectical understanding is needed: of any expression of life, any particle of meaning; as both general and particular at the same time; as simultaneous opening and closing of various scopes for action and as generated by universal rules, while realizing possibilities among many others that have not been realized (Oevermann, 1991, 2000). Think, for instance, of the formalization of cooperation between organizations by means of 'linking pins' and their various roles (Chapter 6). Why should the rules for action that guide them not also be valid for or at least of interest to all those who aim at establishing cooperation between other 'structures of corporate practice' (Franke and Roos, 2010: 1058), be it governments, ministries, clubs or associations? In light of the pragmatist belief that all conclusions are provisional and fallible, well-considered generalizations do not harm. Nor are they unscientific. What they do instead is advance research and 'keep the conversation going' (Rorty, 1979) among the scientific community or even humanity.

In a next step, research on IOR is lifted up or, in Hegelian terms, 'sublated' to world order research, which already includes the *classical* study of international politics as relations among national governments. Certainly, the turn from studying IOR to world order is not new (see for instance Lipscy, 2017). It helps to secure the theoretical innovations described here and to push forward the agenda of world order research, which, especially in terms of its normative implications – on what kind of world we (want to) live in – can hardly be valued highly enough. Furthermore, a turn to world order research can prevent the study of IOR from being absorbed with rather unproductive problems linked to defining both its field and organizations.

What exactly belongs to the field of inter-organizational research, what does not and where are its borders? Definite answers to these questions tend to get lost in a politics of theory or disciplinary politics. Instead of stating, '*This* is research on IOR', the position underlying this volume, in line with a suggestion by Matthias Hofferberth, is, 'This *also* is research on IOR.' Instead of establishing IOR as a separate field of research, the independence of which needs to be defended, it is more promising to understand the dynamics examined from their end, from how they stabilize or destabilize a current world order. From this perspective, the study of inter-organizational relations and their contributions to world order functions as a kind of global governance plus (social) theory.

A second aspect of the definitional problem that could be escaped from through lifting IOR up to world order research is IR's peculiar use of the terms *organization* and *institution*. First, international organizations (IOs) are often equated with international institutions. Organizations are formal institutions, while sets of (repeated) practices, such as friends shaking hands whenever they meet, are informal institutions. Formal organizations can evolve from informal institutions. Second, governments and administrations are organizations too. In IR, however, hardly anyone would expect relations among governments or among administrations to be addressed by research on IOR. Sociologists, on the other hand, would rather be surprised to see these relations *excluded* from IOR.

Similar to the decades of dispute about whether or not IR is exclusively about states (acting through governments), such issues of classification are exhausting and fruitless. A resolute turn to world order research would definitely bring about new conceptual struggles but would also provide the opportunity to leave the ones just mentioned behind. Whether or not contributions to world order have been produced in a type of field defined in a certain way, by a type of organization defined in a certain way, or in a type of relation defined in a certain way is of secondary importance. Both more relevant and innovative are questions like these: What are the political, economic, and cultural ideas that contributions to world order involve? Are these ideas consistent? Is their popularity increasing or decreasing on a global scale? What do world order contributions and the ideas they are based on imply for whom?

Inter-organizational contributions to world order

In this volume, world order is grasped as a complex set of beliefs about how the various facets of life are organized in political, economic and cultural terms. It is considered to be in a permanent process of reproduction and transformation because an actor turns away from or backs specific beliefs with every act, be it a decision or communication attributable to an organization or another 'structure of corporate practice' (Franke and Roos, 2010: 1065–8; see also Dewey, 1991 [1927]). Beliefs are thus permanently weakened or strengthened. Actors are loyal to their beliefs, but this loyalty shifts over time. Increases and decreases in loyalty strengthen and weaken patterns of order (Roos, 2015). Not all beliefs are relevant to the composition of world order, but every component of world order is representable as belief, that is, in the form of an imperative.

Against this background, the remainder of this conclusion consists in addressing the various inter-organizational contributions to world order that, implicitly and explicitly, have been formulated in the seven main chapters of this volume. Five of them provide world-ordering beliefs as rules for action on behalf of the United Nations (UN) or its organs; two of these chapters do so for the European Union (EU) and one of these for NATO (the North Atlantic Treaty Organization). Next to these intergovernmental or supranational organizations, three chapters contain inter-organizational contributions to world order made by NGOs – the Stockholm International Peace Research Institute (SIPRI), the International Institute for Strategic Studies (IISS), the European Interagency Security Forum (EISF), known as the Global Interagency Security Forum (GISF) since 2020, as well as the International Olympic Committee (IOC) and the International Federation of Association Football (FIFA). One chapter each allows for the explication of world order contributions of an MNE, BP, and a hybrid between international and domestic forms of governance, the Comisión Internacional Contra la Impunidad en Guatemala (CICIG).

Translating the world-order contributions in this volume into beliefs as rules for action

CICIG, the anti-impunity hybrid active in Guatemala, is addressed by Theresa Reinold in Chapter 2. Formulated as imperatives, the following beliefs as rules for action that guide those in charge of the commission could be read from her text:

- Reject the idea of impunity and consolidate a culture of lawfulness in a hostile environment.
- Defend the rule of law together with those selected state institutions that are supportive.
- Serve and strengthen the independence of the judicial power from the state.
- Establish and maintain good relations with state institutions, civil society and external donor states to fulfil your mandate.
- Try to fulfil your mandate even if the UN, which enabled your existence, or host state institutions, do not support you unconditionally.
- Weaken and strengthen state sovereignty at the same time, by limiting the country's independence from outside actors (external sovereignty) and effectively providing core public goods such as the rule of law (internal sovereignty).

Regarding the UN, the following world-order contributions become apparent:

- Strengthen judicial independence and enable novel forms of governance such as hybrid anti-impunity commissions, but qualify your support for them when they take their mandate seriously.

- Stick to a diplomatic approach and turn away from an anti-impunity commission you enabled if it tries to fulfil its full mandate by going after high-ranking incumbents or removing obstructionist officials from power.

The UN is also, in line with the EU, the topic of Chapter 3 by Eva Herschinger and Martin Koch, who focus on the governance practice of listing suspected terrorists. Both organizations contribute to world order by means of the following beliefs as rules for action, in imperative form:

- Declare individuals 'specially designated global terrorists'; create watch lists with individuals and organizations suspected of having terrorist links; freeze their funds; and continuously update and expand the list.
- Exchange information with the EU/UN and act in symbiosis with it when it comes to policies of listing and delisting.
- Govern through the closure of discursive fields and produce fragmented and diffuse judicial inter-organizational connections to reduce uncertainty.

In addition, the UN, exclusively, is guided by these imperatives:

- Do not provide any substantive criteria for including individuals and organizations on the terrorist watch list; do not hear their cases; do not inform them about discussions or decisions regarding their inclusion; and ignore non-governmental and intergovernmental organizations' strong opposition against your committee in charge meeting behind closed doors.
- Respond to human-rights concerns; show your respect for human rights and civil liberties; meet human-rights standards and create an office of the ombudsperson as a possibility for filing a request to be removed from the terrorist watch list; set out a general criterion for the listing of individuals and organizations and adopt a delisting procedure.
- Act in partnership with the EU.

The EU contributes to world order by means of the following beliefs as rules for action:

- Enter the organizational field of countering international terrorism by applying the institutionalized practice of listing suspected terrorists and be a partner of the UN in the global fight against terrorism instead of a mere part of its institutional environment.
- Comply with the UN's terrorist watch list although you are not required to do so; underpin the UN's authority and its capacity of listing.
- Refer to the UN's overall role as a provider of global legitimacy and thus increase this legitimacy.

- Make the general idea of listing as a means in fighting terrorism your own instead of part of your environment only – and thus preserve your identity.
- Review the terrorist watch list at least once every six months and outline the judicial basis for the listings more forcefully than the UN does.
- Distinguish between external and internal terrorists.
- Provide no information on how many persons and groups have been delisted but do on how to achieve a delisting process.
- Stick to the rule of law and comply with the European Court of Justice, which makes you provide the UN's justification for placing individuals on a terrorist watch list.

Written by Anna Geis and Louise Wiuff Moe, Chapter 4 on international military interventions in Mali also offers insights on how the UN and the EU contribute to world order. Regarding the UN, the corresponding beliefs as rules for action are:

- Follow the US and other countries in reviving the 'stabilization' doctrine and in expanding the counterterrorism regime, but discursively maintain your distinction from this regime; strengthen the idea of counterterrorism-inspired stabilization and contribute to a subtle 'militarization' of the protection of civilians (PoC).
- Remain a 'relevant' actor within the field of counterterrorism-inspired stabilization, which is defined by increasing institutional density and gravitation towards military responses.
- Reshape the conditions for implementing PoC in peacekeeping missions – do not focus on dialogue and engagement, physical protection and a protective environment alone but also support states' stabilization efforts.
- Strengthen the host governments' capacity to protect civilians and to improve the rule of law but also act in consent and collaborate with host governments and side with their armed forces to defeat a designated 'enemy'.
- Compromise/undermine impartiality as a peacekeeping key norm; increasingly align with governments' security forces and extend coercive state power or contribute to it.
- Reframe operational rules and accept them countering established peacekeeping norms and in doing so accept one of your peacekeeping missions to become a 'soft target' for retaliations against the counterterrorism coalition, its reputation harmed, and your activities to protect civilians more difficult.
- Reset the parameters for interventions and invert the relationship between intervention and sovereignty.
- Regionalize security policy and re-prioritize state security.

Further world-ordering beliefs as rules for action that hold for both the UN and the EU can be formulated as these imperatives:

- 'Defer' enforcement tasks to regional (African) units of action in international stabilization and peace operations; support or fund them and transfer to them risks that emerge from contentious use of force tasks.
- Minimize autonomy costs and benefit from resource pooling.

From Chapter 5, Thomas Müller's look at the production of military statistics since the Cold War, the following world-order contributions can be drawn on behalf of the UN:

- Try to agree on a method for measuring military expenditures, and task groups of experts to develop a calculation method based on purchasing power.
- Develop a definition of military expenditures that includes pensions (as NATO does), civil defence (as the IMF does) and the expenses for the personnel working in armed forces; the research, procurement and maintenance of weapon systems, as well as the costs for military operations (as both NATO and the IMF do).
- Do not offset the limits of your military expenditure reporting instrument through open-source analysis as the League of Nations had done; do not wade into the contentious debate between West and East about whether or not the numbers disclosed by the East were reliable.

NATO is guided by the rule to:

- Develop a definition of military expenditures that includes contributions to military alliances and UN peacekeeping (as the IMF does) and the stockpiling of strategic goods.

Moreover, SIPRI and the IISS, ACDA and the US State Department (DoS), order the world by means of the following imperatives:

- Draw on classified US intelligence estimates (ACDA).
- Engage in open-source analysis and emulate the reporting instruments of the UN, NATO and the IMF by sending questionnaires to states, although a considerable number of which generally do not respond (IISS and SIPRI).
- Rely on NATO's definition of military expenditures and depict the patterns of military expenditures not only in absolute numbers but also in the percentage of their GDP (IISS, DoS).

Finally, world-order contributions made by all structures of corporate practice mentioned in Müller's chapter, be it NATO, the IMF or the UN, SIPRI or the IISS, ACDA or the DoS, are:

- Govern the world through statistics.
- Cooperate and compete with each other at the same time.

World-order contributions manifest in Jutta Joachim's and Andrea Schneiker's study of the formalization of security-related cooperation among humanitarian NGOs (Chapter 6) exclusively refer to the (then) European Interagency Security Forum, or, rather, the 'linking pins' working for its member organizations. As imperatives, these contributions read:

- Instigate and direct interaction between IOs; get a critical mass of organizations together; monitor the environment; draw on your personal networks; organize informal meetings; and create awareness for cooperation (boundary spanners in the initial phase).
- Motivate and convince others to participate in cooperative arrangements; seize opportunities and mobilize resources/obtain funding; move the network from informal to formal cooperation (by convincing organizations to do so); overcome organizational barriers; organize the group, its structure, goals and mandate; secure adequate financing (entrepreneurs in initial phase).
- Relay information from one organization to the other; be familiar with the practices of your organization and speak the language of the organization(s) you are reaching out to; make concessions and convince sceptics; manage differences among organizations' interests and expectations; frame and translate information and forge consensus; standardize processes, products and services; continue cooperation despite staff turnover; subordinate personal ideas and preferences to a broader objective and a common goal (purposive practitioners in the expansion phase).
- Be empathic and find out participants' expectations; deal with an endangered existing consensus among members; build mutual trust and a common identity (caretakers in the expansion phase).
- Control the flow of and select information coming into and out of the network; limit the information exchanged with governmental authorities; attract new members and expand the network but ensure its effectiveness; coordinate and control membership and monitor who obtains access to the network; protect the mandate of the cooperation mechanism (gatekeepers in the consolidation phase).

The UN's attempt to make economic globalization more socially and ecologically sustainable along with companies in the form of the UN Global

Compact (UNGC) is addressed by Matthias Hofferberth in Chapter 7. As to world-order contributions made by the UN, these beliefs as rules for action, formulated as imperatives, can be found:

- Be the centrepiece of global governance and establish a broad range of different entities as legitimate global governors; bring together different stakeholders to collectively manage problems; confirm global governance and its commitment to 'multi-stakeholderism'.
- Bring about and sustain corporate agency in global governance and increasingly view corporate actors as partners of regulation; prefer voluntariness over binding rules when it comes to dealing with enterprises; create non-binding and loose commitments.
- Embrace a logic of IOR that not only treats MNEs as global governors but also proactively accommodates their interests; facilitate an environment in which MNEs can 'lead the way'; sustain the notion that MNEs legitimately and meaningfully contribute to global governance but do not necessarily change anything on the ground; create an illusion of impactful action instead of immediate change in corporate behaviour.

BP plc, one of the earliest corporate parties or members to the UNGC, contributes to world order like this:

- Present yourself as having already integrated the principles of the Global Compact in corporate decision-making.
- Declare to strongly support and follow guidance from the UNGC, but be unspecific about what it means to be guided by it or its shared principles, and do not be influenced by the loose, fluid nature of UNGC relations.
- Make sure that 'industry practice', your own experience, as well as national and international law are equally important as the Compact.

Moreover, all companies that joined the UNGC follow these world-ordering beliefs:

- Come together to govern collectively and further your own agenda.
- Keep interactions within the UNGC open-ended and indeterminate.

Finally, world order contributions made by the IOC and FIFA in the context of the Russian invasion of Ukraine in 2022 have been the topic of Chapter 8 by Martin Koch and the author.

The IOC, to begin with, makes these contributions of relevance:

- Establish an international non-profit non-governmental body to organize the Olympic Games; ensure that the Games are held regularly and supervise them.

- Focus and limit yourself to your core mission, that is, the promotion of the Olympic Movement and regular hosting of the Olympic Games; accept no political directives and tolerate no other organization making similar claims in this regard.
- Characterize the Olympics as an example of peace and solidarity among athletes rivalling in fair competition.
- Protect the Olympic Community by taking action in case of crisis.
- Exhort all political authorities, especially heads of state and government, to the traditional observance of the Olympic Truce (*ekecheiria*), an ancient tradition, and thus underline your relevance in world politics; remind heads of state and government of the unanimously adopted resolution of the UN General Assembly on the Olympic Truce; advocate that weapons remain silent during the Olympic Games (including seven days before and after) in a world marked by war.
- Do not condemn war per se, but only those wars that could jeopardize the smooth running of the Olympic Games.
- Point to the Olympic Games, where athletes face each other in fair competition, as an example for world politics with regard to its transformation into an equally fair contest with countries behaving like athletes and respecting the common rules of competition.
- Do not expect IOs in general and the UN in particular to maintain peace and prevent future wars.
- Condemn the Russian government's breach of the Olympic Truce, but do not threaten any consequences for the Russian government, the Olympic Community or Russian athletes – refer to the Olympic Truce and its observance only.
- Express your deep concern for the Olympic Community in Ukraine and establish a task force to both monitor the situation and coordinate humanitarian assistance to it; set the task force to act only where clearly possible and be careful that it does not put itself in unnecessary danger and, thereby, damages itself and the IOC.

FIFA's world-ordering imperatives are:

- Organize as an association, submit to state jurisdiction, and link member associations in a formally equal relationship with each other.
- Establish and enforce uniform rules for organized, state-recognized football.
- Spread and control organized football worldwide and arrange international competitions; organize the Men's World Cup (in Qatar) as a registered trademark with which you are pursuing monetary interests.
- Announce updates regarding the qualifying matches for an upcoming tournament in case of warlike conflicts, but do so without attributing any decisions due in this context.

- Accept federations from sovereign and not (yet) sovereign states as members.
- Postulate that no conflict can be resolved by force and do not distinguish between legitimate and illegitimate or legal and illegal violence; claim moral superiority over Article 51 of the UN Charter that guarantees an inherent right to individual and collective self-defence.
- Rely on continuity and stick to your routines in the case of armed conflict (condemn violence, call for dialogue, express solidarity); observe, indicate that you have everything under control, and de-dramatize the situation by not making a decision.
- Condemn Russia's use of force in Ukraine but not the presence of Russian armed forces there; undermine your condemnation of Russia by condemning any use of force to resolve conflicts.
- Abstain from taking sides in the conflict between Russia and Ukraine; assign Russia and the attacked Ukraine the same responsibility for conflict resolution; avoid the question of guilt and ignore the difference between attackers and attacked; homogenize the highly heterogeneous group of those affected by conflict.
- Call for the restoration of peace and thereby suggest that you have the level of integrity, prestige or legitimacy necessary to do so.
- Depoliticize and trivialize the conflict (by calling for constructive dialogue rather than negotiation and suggesting that the parties to the conflict work out their problems among themselves, without a mediating authority).
- Degrade the expression of solidarity to an empty phrase (by declaring your solidarity with all those affected by the conflict without making clear what your solidarity is expressed in and to whom exactly it applies).

Some dynamics of the current world order and an agenda for its future exploration

What do all these beliefs as rules for action in the form of imperatives teach us about the contemporary order of the world? In terms of *anti-impunity* and a culture of lawfulness, we see that anti-impunity commissions such as CICIG strengthen these concepts, while the UN does not support them unconditionally but turns away from them and sticks to diplomacy if sitting presidents are charged. This does not only point to a well-known clash between *diplomacy* and the *rule of law* but illustrates where the UN is located when it comes down to the wire. We also see that IGOs such as the UN and the EU, in their fight against terrorism, are willing to damage *human rights* for the sake of *security considerations* and to respond to corresponding public concerns only slightly. As to *state sovereignty*, we see hybrid anti-impunity commissions, such as CICIG, both strengthening and weakening this concept by effectively providing core public goods such as the rule of law and limiting a country's independence from external entities. We see FIFA weakening the concept of sovereignty by allowing membership of federations that do not represent independent states. At the same time, the UN, strengthening the concept of counterterrorism-inspired stabilization to preserve its relevance, reprioritizes state security and sovereignty when it sides with host governments' armed forces to defeat designated 'enemies' – at the price of undermining the traditional peacekeeping principle of impartiality.

The IOC and FIFA strengthen the idea of *equality* when linking member associations in a formally equal relationship with each other but tend to undermine the UN Charter when its *prohibition of the use of force* is put into perspective or its *inherent right to self-defence* is ignored. To underline its own relevance in world politics, the IOC even downplays the UN's capacity to maintain peace and prevent future wars. The EU, on the other hand, underpins UN authority. Both the UN and the EU follow an *economic logic of action* when they transfer enforcement tasks to African units of action to minimize their autonomy costs and to benefit from resource pooling. Further down that road, the UN, with its Global Compact, not only establishes a broad range of different entities as legitimate global governors but also creates non-binding and loose commitments that facilitate an environment in which MNEs can set the agenda. Accordingly, BP and other enterprises interact within the Compact in an open-ended and indeterminate way, while they avoid being influenced by it and defend their leeway.

While organizations such as the UN, IMF, NATO, SIPRI or the IISS, in line with the US State Department, stick to the idea of *governing the world through statistics*, they also cooperate and compete with each other at the same time over epistemic authority in the field of military statistics. The UN and the EU strengthen the idea of *cooperation through the exchange of information* in the context of their counterterrorist policies, and members of the EISF show that controlling the flow of information and mobilizing resources are essential for actively transforming a competitive setting into a cooperative one. Cooperation needs to be organized, they teach us.

Taking seriously Peirce's account of abduction as a weak but effective mode of reasoning, the only one leading to novel insights, an endless research agenda on the composition of world order throughout human history unfolds at the end of this volume. This composition is changing whenever actors' 'loyalty' towards their beliefs shifts (Roos, 2015). Cherished ideas are weakened and disappear, others are strengthened and spread rapidly: appreciated, less appreciated or feared ones. Some may conclude by mapping the dynamics between the world-ordering beliefs not only relatively but absolutely, and devising some form of quantification. Others will turn their attention to the normative implications of the dynamics revealed and ask what strategies are required to advance the real-world strengthening of these beliefs or the weakening of them. A third group will patiently reconstruct on and on, piecing together their snapshots of the state of world order at different points in time into a moving sequence. What all these approaches have in common is that their interest is in world order and the inter-organizational relations that contribute to it.

Note

1 Where to locate accounts referring to the global governance paradigm (Chapters 2 and 7) on the spectrum of rationalist approaches and its challengers is not trivial. In terms of the history of IR theory, global governance accounts can be understood as descendants of regime theory (Young, 1982), which clearly places them among rationalism. On the other hand, global governance accounts are often characterized by a lack of (social) theory, which makes it possible, as in Chapter 7 of this volume, to blend them with theoretically more sophisticated approaches rooted in relational sociology (Emirbayer, 1997), for instance.

References

Biermann, R. (2009) 'Inter-organizationalism in theory and practice', *Studia Diplomatica*, 62(3): 7–12.

Dewey, J. (1991 [1927]) *The Public and Its Problems*, Athens, Ohio: Swallow Press and Ohio University Press.

Dewey, J. (1938) *Logic: The Theory of Inquiry*, New York: Holt.

Eckl, J. and Hanrieder, T. (2023) 'The political economy of consulting firms in reform processes: the case of the World Health Organization', *Review of International Political Economy*, online first.

Emirbayer, M. (1997) 'Manifesto for a relational sociology', *American Journal of Sociology* 103(2): 281–317.

Fearon, J. and Wendt, A. (2002) 'Rationalism v. constructivism: a skeptical view', in W. Carlsnaes, T. Risse and B.A. Simmons (eds) *Handbook of International Relations*, London, Thousand Oaks and New Delhi: Sage, pp 52–72.

Franke, U. and Roos, U. (2010) 'Actor, structure, process: transcending the state personhood debate by means of a pragmatist ontological model for international relations theory', *Review of International Studies*, 36(4): 1057–77.

Franke, U. and Weber, R. (2012) 'At the Papini Hotel: on pragmatism in the study of international relations', *European Journal of International Relations*, 18(4): 669–91.

Holzscheiter, A. (2015) 'Interorganisationale Harmonisierung als sine qua non für die Effektivität von Global Governance? Eine soziologisch-institutionalistische Analyse interorganisationaler Strukturen in der globalen Gesundheitspolitik', *Politische Vierteljahresschrift*, special issue 49: 322–48.

Koops, J. (2008) 'Towards effective and integrative inter-organizationalism: from conflict to regional stability: linking security and development', in K. Brockmann, H.B. Hauck and S. Reigeluth (eds) *From Conflict to Regional Stability: Linking Security and Development* (DGAP-Bericht, 9), Berlin: Forschungsinstitut der Deutschen Gesellschaft für Auswärtige Politik, pp 23–31.

Koops, J.A. and Biermann, R. (eds) (2017) *The Palgrave Handbook of Inter-organizational Relations in World Politics*, London: Palgrave Macmillan.

Lipscy, P.Y. (2017) *Renegotiating the World Order: Institutional Change in International Relations*, Cambridge and New York: Cambridge University Press.

Oevermann, U. (2016) '"Krise und Routine" als analytisches Paradigma in den Sozialwissenschaften', in R. Becker-Lenz, A. Franzmann, A. Jansen and M. Jung (eds) *Die Methodenschule der Objektiven Hermeneutik: eine Bestandsaufnahme*, Wiesbaden: Springer VS, pp 43–114.

Oevermann, U. (2000) 'Die Methode der Fallrekonstruktion in der Grundlagenforschung sowie der klinischen und pädagogischen Praxis', in Klaus Kraimer (ed) *Die Fallrekonstruktion. Sinnverstehen in der sozialwissenschaftlichen Forschung*, Frankfurt: Suhrkamp, pp 58–156.

Oevermann, U. (1991) 'Genetischer Strukturalismus und das sozialwissenschaftliche Problem der Erklärung der Entstehung des Neuen', in S. Müller-Doohm (ed) *Jenseits der Utopie*, Frankfurt: Suhrkamp, pp 267–336.

Peirce, C.S. (1998 [1903]) 'The nature of meaning', in The Peirce Edition Project (ed) *The Essential Peirce: Selected Philosophical Writings, Vol. 2 (1893–1913)*, Bloomington and Indianapolis: Indiana University Press, pp 208–25.

Peirce, C.S. (1992 [1878]) 'How to make our ideas clear', in N. Houser and C. Kloesel (eds) *The Essential Peirce: Selected Philosophical Writings, Vol. 1 (1867–1893)*, Bloomington and Indianapolis: Indiana University Press, pp 124–41.

Roos, U. (2015) 'Beliefs and loyalties in world politics: a pragmatist framework for analysis', in G. Hellmann and K.E. Jørgensen (eds) *Theorizing Foreign Policy in a Globalized World*, Basingstoke: Palgrave Macmillan, pp 176–98.

Rorty, R. (1979) *Philosophy and the Mirror of Nature*, New Jersey: Princeton University Press.

Smith, J., Hughes, M.M., Plummer, S. and Duncan, B. (2021) 'Inter-organizational relations in transnational environmental and women's activism: multilateralists, pragmatists, and rejectionists', *Globalizations*, 18(2): 300–20.

Weber, M. (2006 [1920]) 'Prefatory remarks to the Collected Essays in the Sociology of Religion', in S. Whimster (ed) *The Essential Weber: A Reader*, Abingdon and New York: Routledge, pp 101–12.

Werron, T. (2010) 'Direkte Konflikte, indirekte Konkurrenzen: Unterscheidung und Vergleich zweier Formen des Kampfes', *Zeitschrift für Soziologie* 39(4): 302–318.

Young, O.R. (1982) 'Regime dynamics: the rise and fall of international regimes', *International Organization*, 36(2): 277–97.

Index

References to figures appear in *italic* type; those in **bold** type refer to tables.
References to endnotes show both the page number and the note number (231n3).